THE BOOK THAT REVEALS EVERYTHING THERE IS TO RE-
VEAL ABOUT HARVARD: HARVARD FOOTBALL, HARVARD
EATING, HARVARD RIOTS, HARVARD CLUBS, HARVARD
ROOSEVELTS, HARVARD KENNEDYS AND HARVARD
ACCENTS.

YOU CAN ALWAYS TELL A HARVARD MAN

"HARVARD-MAN BISSELL MISSES VERY LITTLE
IN HIS EXCEEDINGLY ENTERTAINING DISQUISITION ON
HARVARD, ITS HISTORY, ITS CUSTOMS, ITS
CONCEITS AND ITS MYSTIQUE."

New York Herald Tribune

"A BOOK OF SUCH WIT, JOY AND UNEXPECTED FUN,
THAT EVEN THE MOST NON-PARTISAN READER
WILL FIND IT AMUSING."

Charleston News and Courier

"RICHARD BISSELL IS THE FUNNIEST WRITER
TO COME OFF THE MISSISSIPPI SINCE MARK TWAIN."

Chicago News

Books by Richard Bissell

A STRETCH ON THE RIVER
THE MONONGAHELA
7½ CENTS
HIGH WATER
❦ SAY, DARLING
❦ GOOD BYE, AVA
❦ YOU CAN ALWAYS TELL A HARVARD MAN
❦ STILL CIRCLING MOOSE JAW

❦ Published by Bantam Books

RICHARD BISSELL

YOU CAN ALWAYS TELL A HARVARD MAN

BANTAM BOOKS
TORONTO · NEW YORK · LONDON

*This low-priced Bantam Book
has been completely reset in a type face
designed for easy reading, and was printed
from new plates. It contains the complete
text of the original hard-cover edition.*
NOT ONE WORD HAS BEEN OMITTED.

YOU CAN ALWAYS TELL A HARVARD MAN

*A Bantam Book / published by arrangement with
McGraw-Hill Book Company, Inc.*

PRINTING HISTORY
*McGraw-Hill edition published March 1965
Bantam edition published February 1966*

*Bantam Books are published by Bantam Books, nc., a subsidiary
of Grosset & Dunlap, Inc. Its trade-mark, consisting of the words
"Bantam Books" and the portrayal of a bantam, is registered in the
United States Patent Office and in other countries. Marca Registrada.
Bantam Books, Inc., 271 Madison Avenue, New York, N. Y. 10016.*

To my brother, Frederick Ezekiel ("Mycroft") Bissell, Jr., Harvard '31, M.A. '33, Phi Beta Kappa, without whose constant suggestions this book would have been finished much sooner.

CONTENTS

W A R N I N G !

Cable Crossing!
Do Not Drag Anchors.

All the facts in this book are incorrect.

The author lives on a small island off the coast
of New Zealand with no postal service.

CHAPTER I

Yes, Virginia,
There Really Is
a Harvard

THERE ARE several ways of approaching a big subject like Harvard. One is to take the subway cars from Park Street or South Station, getting a fine view of the Carter's Ink sign as you cross over the Charles River bridge. A fluvial attack on this tantalizing topic is also possible via rental canoe from Watertown on the Charles River. (Each canoe is equipped with a pamphlet of instructions giving advice on laundry and all the college cheers, plus a complete set of the Harvard Classics.)

Harvard is the oldest college in the country; founded in 1636, it is 65 years older than its rival, Yale, and 289 years older than Jack Lemmon, Harvard '47. Yale is a nice school located at New Haven, Conn., near the football stadium, but visiting potentates from foreign shores usually ask for the conducted tour of Harvard.

"Did you go to Harvard?" is the first question your average royalty asks on meeting an American and if the reply is in the negative his chagrin is often quite comical to witness.

This attitude is a source of irritation to Yale men and

causes them to recite in loud voices many very naughty jokes at Harvard's expense. But Harvard is not so slow at repartee even if it is located only twenty-five miles from New Hampshire, and comes right back at Yale with some funny ones of her own. Like "When a Yale man is sick, the authorities immediately assume that he is drunk. When a Harvard man is drunk, the authorities assume that he is sick." [1]

From far-off Scotland, source of a nourishing beverage much in favor with the Harvard undergraduate and graduate, comes a typical comment of a sort to make the Yale man blanch, stamp his foot, and crush a defenseless grape:

We have no equivalent in Britain to the Harvard man. He is part of the American mystique. He keeps on cropping up in novels and plays. When you say of someone, "He's a Harvard man," the expression is full of status undertones. To be a Harvard man is something much more significant than to be a Yale or a Princeton man, or even an Oxford man or a Cambridge man or a Neanderthal man. Exposure to life in Harvard apparently has a mysterious influence on your metabolism and social prestige. Although Oxford and Cambridge, not to mention our Scottish universities, and many public schools are much older than Harvard they do not invest their products with the same universal significance. If you say that a man is an Etonian, a Wykehamist, or a Balliol man, it means something, according to what you think of these foundations, but the indication is a low pressure rather than a high pressure yardstick which it has when applied to men who studied where, among others, William James and George Santayana taught.[2]

But Yale should not pout, feel neglected, or write a rude letter home. Yale actually has many advantages over Harvard. Such as:

1. The Yale student does not have to bear the brunt of criticisms leveled at "another crazy Yale man in the White

[1] Note to reader: Cheer up, this is the last Harvard-Yale joke in the book. I think.
[2] *The Scotsman,* Edinburgh.

House and all those Yale eggheads around him," because instead of being in the White House all the Yale men are down on Wall Street, although the President of the New York Stock Exchange is G. Keith Funston, Harvard M.B.A. '34. This constant parade of Harvard Presidents is getting to be embarrassing, even though Harry Truman, Field Artillery School, Fort Sill, Oklahoma, Class of '18, says "Eggheads can be very useful in Government. In fact we need them." No egghead he. Dwight D. Eisenhower, B.S. U.S. Military Academy, '15, LL.D. Harvard, '46, when President of the United States filled a number of top positions with such Harvard graduates as Winthrop W. Aldrich, '07, Clarence B. Randall, '12, James B. Conant, '14, Marion B. Folsom, M.B.A., '14, Sinclair Weeks, '14, Robert Cutler, '16, Amory Houghton, '21, Henry Cabot Lodge, '24, Charles H. Haskins, '36, and C. Douglas Dillon, '31.

Warren G. Harding attended Ohio Central College.

2. The Yale student does not have the idyllic Charles River with its well-tended grassy banks covered with lovely Radcliffe girls and cute waitresses laying around in abandoned attitudes; but he doesn't have to try to cross Massachusetts Avenue several times a day either. This hazard to life and limb has existed since the earliest times and the careful reader will find several references to intolerable traffic conditions in Cotton Mather's *Magnalia Christi Americana* (1702). It was undoubtedly a contributing factor in his resignation as a Fellow of Harvard in 1703. He had taken his A.B. in 1678 and twenty-five years of dodging taxis and Lewandos laundry trucks just wore him down. Nathaniel Bowditch also got the traffic treatment, being crunched in a howling mob trying to get a look at the Marquis de Lafayette, who had arrived to get an honorary Harvard degree in 1784. Bowditch himself, a seaman with no schooling, subsequently also received an honorary degree for his *Practical Navigator* (1802) and apropos of the ceremonies is said to have remarked, "What does all that Latin mean?" And only recently Professor

Howard Mumford Jones referred to "the nightly dangers of going home from work through the rush hour in Harvard Square," and also mentions the seasoned Harvard professor's "skill in dodging motorcycles, Radcliffe girls on bikes, and M.T.A. buses charging at us from three or four directions at one time," and he adds, "Dorothy Parker once remarked that the automobile has divided the human race into two unequal parts, the quick and the dead. She must have been studying life in Harvard Square."

3. If you live in Bridgeport you can save a lot of carfare by going to Yale instead of Harvard. This does not apply if you live in Gloucester, Mass.

4. Yale has good taste. When Sinclair Lewis was an undergraduate there, nobody could stand him. Later on, when he gained world fame, it became unanimous.

5. The Shubert Theatre, where the Broadway-bound shows try out, is only half a block from the campus. For a lark the Yale student can don rubber-soled shoes, tiptoe into the Taft Hotel next door to the theatre, watch the greats of Show Biz eating breakfast in the grand dining room, and listen to them praising the coffee.

6. The Yale lads are very fond of outdoor sports and usually have a better football team than Harvard. The Harvard chaps like sports but bruise easily.

So there you are. At least six good reasons why Yale has got the edge over Harvard. I hope the word gets to Scotland.

But what is Harvard? Is it a large group of academic buildings surrounding Mike's Club, or is it America's most distinguished University? Are the malteds and hamburgers at Mike's only an offshoot, so to speak? [3] Let's try to put it in its proper perspective and decide which has advanced the glory of the Bay State and the United States the more, Mayor Curley, Governor Curley, and Senator Curley, or Eliot, Lowell, Conant, Pusey, and Co. To some Harvard graduates, memories cluster around rainy afternoons, cue

[3] See *Crimson* editorial, Oct. 19, 1961, "The Great Hamburger Blight."

in hand, at Leavitt and Pierce's pleasant pool hall, with the gaily colored pool balls kissing each other coyly, and white-haired Billy ever ready to "Rack them up again"; to others it's sticky kisses and wet feet, promises of all sizes and shapes, six million books and twenty million footnotes, and to others it's a girl who lived in a room on Pinckney Street off Louisburg Square, Gypsy Rose Lee peeling off her long gloves at the Old Howard, and Ann Corio's mincing gait, or the forty-yard pass that beat Yale with seconds left in The Game. (The times the forty-yard pass hit the receiver on the head and bounced into the end zone we try to forget.)

Harvard has no drum-majorettes with cute pink knees. It is swarming with adorable Radcliffe girls, all equipped with knees but dreadfully preoccupied with the pursuit of knowledge. Harvard is being hotly pursued in the national race for scholastic supremacy, but she is 326 years old and operates on a budget of $85,000,000 a year and that adds up to just about as much culture as one town can stand. Whether the competition likes it or not, Harvard is Harvard. There is only one Ringling Bros., no matter how many elephants the other shows add to their rosters. There is only one Mount Everest, and you can't knock it down with a tack hammer.

Scholastically Harvard stands in majesty unchallenged (do I hear shouts of "No! No!" from New Haven and New York, from Chicago and the sun-kissed shores of California?) and in its relentless search for the truth of things falls to with the broadsword. No drum-majorettes have we, but even the dullest Harvard student (and we have some dandies) knows that Widener Library is the greatest college library in the world and that it belongs to him; it's his, he owns it. Even if he's a dope he can go right in and say, "Let me see the boxoffice receipts for *Hamlet* written in Shakespeare's own hand. And while you're at it, I'd like to hear that original tape of Charlemagne talking to Lady Guinevere."

However, having a Harvard degree does not always

strike Mr. Average Bystander as a real keen biographical note. Certainly not to be compared, for example, with having shaken hands with Gregory Peck or owning outright a home-run baseball autographed by Roger Maris, who stated, when asked how come he was seen in the Art Institute in Chicago: "There was no game that day and our wives were in town. So they wanted to go to this museum. It was all filled with old pictures." In fact non-Harvard people have even been known to take what might be interpreted as an unfriendly attitude toward America's Greatest University. (NOTE: This book is slanted.)

Or, in the words of a captain of Marines, who addressed John Marquand quaintly thus:

"You really wouldn't be a son-of-a-bitch at all if you weren't a Harvard man."

The meaning behind this forthright statement is clear to me because I've been on the receiving end of similar compliments and it can be briefly summed up thuswise: "You are a pretty good guy and I like you OK but us tough guys we gotta save face. I hear this Harvard is all full of bigdomes and sissies. Even if it ain't, Harvard is funny, see? It's a good joke."

Another more ambiguous version was served up to me piping hot during my adventurous years when I was pilot of a greasy old tugboat on the Monongahela River (versatility is our middle name, us Harvards). The mate on watch came up to the pilot house, set my coffee down, and stated:

"Cap, did you really go to that there Harvard? Jee-sus!"

That's the way it goes and we get used to it.

Apropos of the Marine captain, Marquand goes on to say:

"It did not appear to occur to him that I might still have been what I was if I had gone to Dartmouth or Cornell. I like to think he meant that I speak with a broad *a*, and obviously many people feel that all Harvard graduates should. But a few experiences such as this have taught me one great truth. If you have ever been to Harvard, you will never be allowed to forget it. . . .

"Actually I have found that I can get on very well with most people until they discover this error in my past. Then there is a slight pause in the conversation, a lifting of the eyebrows, an exchange of meaning glances, and someone always says, 'You never told us you were a Harvard man. . . .' A mental picture has arisen and an iron curtain has descended."

That's very true, John, and the trouble is there is no use to try and conceal the facts; it is just like having done time at Sing Sing for falsifying poultry receipts—your record will always catch up with you and it will follow you to the tomb. There is no use when applying for work to cheat on your application and put down "North Dakota State Teachers College" under *Colleges Attended*. Everything will go along smooth as silk for a while and you meet this nice girl in the accounting department and buy a little cottage by a waterfall and baby makes three and you have a good fallout shelter about half built when one day you receive a message to report to the Personnel Manager.

"Close the door, Freebey," says the Manager, looking plenty somber.

"Freebey," he says, "is there something in your past that you'd like to tell me about?"

That night you are stowed away in the chain locker of a tramp steamer bound for Yokohama and Molly has to meet the mortgage payments and the bill from the lumber yard for the bomb shelter by going onto the streets and it is all the time raining and getting her hat damp and her feather boa wet and mud on her kid boots.

Five years later you have risen to mate on a sampan in the China Sea and the captain (played by Warner Oland) calls you into his cabin and says:

"Please to shut honorable door, Mister Mate . . ."

And while Mr. Marquand is talking about mental pictures I am trying to fix one in my mind of Marquand at

Dartmouth, as he mentions in his little piece. I just couldn't see him in a parka leaning against an ice statue and talking over the latest developments in ski wax with his date, a cute trick in stretch pants up from Goucher for Carnival Week. Neither could I see him at Cornell, in the stadium up by the waters of Lake Cayuga, yelling "Come on you BIG RED TEAM!" and planning a hot week end in Rochester. He was just kidding around when he said he would have been the same person if he had not gone to Harvard. Anybody else—OK. But taking Marquand that far away from Back Bay and Wickford Point and the Ritz Hotel—why, that would be worse than sending like Miss Natalie Wood to work in the Wilson Bros.' shirt factory in South Bend, Ind. It would have bent and warped his character until he looked like a pretzel and where would that leave George Apley and Bo-Jo Brown at? Definitely up the Charles River adrift somewhere in the neighborhood of Watertown, without a paddle.

No, it wouldn't have done at all. Boston would deny it because he came from Newburyport, which is a long trip for a Bostonian, but actually John Marquand was about the most Bostonian boy I have ever met except perhaps for Charles Morton of the *Atlantic*, who hails from Omaha. But, unlike the traditional Bostonian Harvard graduate, Marquand was able to look at both Boston and Harvard with the detached eye of an observer from Lower Slobbovia, and moreover, praise God, with a sense of humor. He was terribly involved with a disintegrating Boston, with a falling-apart-at-the-seams Newburyport, with the swan boats in the Boston Public Garden, with the old bricks and the Parker House, with Atlantic Avenue and the North Shore and Topsfield and Ipswich and the Somerset Club and snow falling on Charles Street and young people who arose, knocking over the teacups, when he entered the room. He was a gentleman and he had that accent.

Well, here we are at "the accent."

Although there are a lot more Bill Kings at Harvard

than there are Harry Pulhams, the fiction about the broad *a* persists. George Ade said that his Alma Mater, Purdue,[4] to which he was fiercely loyal and a generous benefactor, "gives you everything that Harvard does except the pronunciation of *a* as in *father*." Walter Prichard Eaton, a classmate of my father's in '00, at Harvard, says, "George did not intend this remark to be complimentary to the university on the Charles, but as a matter of fact it is, for it points out one of the chief reasons for Harvard's greatness," and he adds: ". . . the fact remains that for the best speakers of the language as a whole, on both sides of the Atlantic, it is standard; it is the pronunciation which has brought the music of Shakespeare most magically to our ears, whether spoken by Edwin Booth or Ellen Terry or John Gielgud or Walter Hampden. It is the pronunciation which has trumpeted the noblest prose in our language from the loftiest pulpits, and without which even Isaiah loses some of his rolling majesty. It is a kind of hallmark of oral dignity and of English style; it is a syllabic sound around which cluster the associative ideas of richest·dignity and least provincial scope. . . ."

It is hard to get Mr. Eaton stopped once he gets going.

Come come, Mr. Eaton, and also tut-tut. This may all be true enough, but why call it a *Harvard* accent? Who at Harvard has this accent except the Bostonian boys who were born with it and who are stuck with it? My intimate friends at Harvard spoke (*a*) New York English, (*b*) Down-East Maine English, (*c*) Winnetka, Ill., English, (*d*) South Boston English, (*e*) Nebraska English, (*f*) Texas English (if we stretch a point and call that English at all), and I myself speak Iowa English. My accent has been compared to scraping a broken beer bottle over a

[4] (1) Lafayette, Ind. (AP) November 1, 1961. "Do hogs, like human beings, worry themselves into having stomach ulcers? Purdue University has been given $45,000 to find out."

(2) "During these college years [at Purdue] I continued attending church, thinking it was expected of a campus Big Wheel, and it was a nice place to take a date."—*I Met Christ on the Campus*, by Nate Krupp.

poorly laid cement sidewalk. It's true that a fellow in my class in English 28, representative of one of New England's noblest ancient families, spoke with the rolling majestic accents of Walter Hampden and Edwin Booth. But as he suffered from very poor projection and had almost nothing to say about Shakespeare or anything else, his influence had little if any effect on the rest of us, who continued to speak with the oral dignity of Mickey Rooney. Sonny Tufts, incidentally (yes, Sonny Tufts), for whom I coxed on the crew at Exeter, had one of the finest "Harvard" accents I've ever heard. He was also the funniest guy I ever knew and I followed him around like a dog. I weighed eighty-three pounds. With his "Harvard" accent he went on to Yale.

But what of the professors? Surely they gave Isaiah his due in the rich and thundering accents of the Cabots and the Lowells? (Come to think of it, didn't Isaiah write his stuff in Hebrew? Is Mr. Eaton suggesting that Isaiah was raised in Louisburg Square and talked Hebrew like Ellen Terry?)

Well, Kirtley Mather, the eminent Harvard geologist (now emeritus), was born in Chicago, got his B.S. from Denison University in Granville, Ohio, and spoke with an *r* so hard and an *a* so flat that he could break a pane of plate glass merely by repeating *cherty nodule* or *molten magma* three times at a distance of fifteen feet.

The great Harvard scholar Arthur Darby Nock was born in Portsmouth, England, attended Trinity College at Cambridge, and speaks like forty Englishmen rolled into one.

I don't know how Professor Kenneth Galbraith speaks, but he was born in Iona Station, Ontario, and got his B.S. at the University of Toronto, so I think it quite unlikely that his tones resemble those of Abbott Lawrence Lowell. Perhaps by now he has acquired a Washington, D.C., accent or a Calcutta accent.

My Spanish teacher spoke Spanish with a Castilian accent and English with a Barcelona accent.

Professor Vsevolod Setschkareff, Professor of Slavic Languages and Literatures, speaks with a Russian accent more opaque than that of Gregory Ratoff.

Professor Roger Bigelow Merriman addressed the hordes in his famous History One in a voice that alternately roared, rumbled, and squeaked like a windup phonograph with a busted governor.

Anyway, this whole bit about accents is pretty tedious, especially the "Harvard" accent, and I think Mr. Eaton (God rest his soul) was full of Boston scrod when he wrote that stirring eulogy of the "nonprovincial" and hence most highly desirable form of American speech. The fact is that nowadays everybody else in the U.S.A.— including New Jersey—thinks of *Boston* as the epitome of the provincial. Witness The Hub's attitude toward New York. You can knock N.Y. all you want to; it is undoubtedly a frightening mess, as dirty as Edna Ferber says it is, unattractive, smelly, probably corrupt, the mating place of devils in every form, and the crossroads of nutdom with no apparent change in sight—but who can doubt that it is the center, pivot, and general forum of American "culture"? Chicago publishes *Playboy*, at least; in Boston they still sit around fingering their watchchains wondering what happened to Charlie Ross.

To explore further this soporific topic of correct, incorrect, and medium-rare accents, or of illegal and unsportsmanlike accents which will cost you a fifteen-yard penalty, there is a rumor going around that the purest English being huzzed around the country today is that spoken by some tribe in the backwoods of Kentucky or some such place, but if they talk anything like the deckhands from Kentucky we used to get on the Central Barge Line over on the Ohio River it is no advertisement for Ben Jonson and William Shakespeare.

Now you go down the line of American artists, poets, patriots, statesmen, and famous flagpole-sitters, Mr. Eaton, and how many rare old Boston type accents do you run into? Jimmy Foxx with two *x*'s used to pole them over the left-field fence regularly for the Red Sox; there were no complaints about how he talked. Does Carl Sandburg have a Boston accent? How about Sinclair Lewis, Cordell Hull, and Red Grange? Man, it's just silly. Take a great statesman like Warren G. Harding: When he used to say "I'll raise you ten dollars," it was in a good Ohio accent with no apologies. Who's the greatest man in America today? Bob Hope, of course, and just listen to him! From a guy born in Eltham, Kent, England, we could expect a lot more in the diction department—especially somebody whose original tag was Leslie.[5]

Just glance through the *Celebrity Register*, U.S. edition, 1959, edited by Cleveland Amory, Earl Blackwell, and Sydney Wolfe Cohen. On page one we have Hank Aaron, a ball-player from the sandlots of Mobile, Alabama; Bud Abbott, the straight man who was born in Asbury Park, N.J., so he could be with his mother and who was a bareback rider for Ringling Brothers Circus; and George Abbott, born in Forrestville, N.Y. None of these boys owes his celebrity to pronouncing *a* as in *father*.

Eight hundred sixty-four fun-filled pages later we end up with Maurice Zolotow, the Boswell of Broadway. He went to Brooklyn High School. I have no idea how he pronounces his *a*'s and I am not going to call him up and find out; he lives in Hastings-on-Hudson and it would cost thirty-five cents.

Cleveland Amory on the other hand *does* have a "Harvard" accent, which I presume means a Boston accent, since he was born in Nahant, a minuscule "resort" north of Boston (Some resort! It hasn't even got a fun house or a single salt-water-taffy machine), "one which," he says, "if you were not born there you are mispronouncing."

There are, in short, about as many Harvard accents at

[5] (1) "Hope sings 'True Blue Love' for laughs and 'Pagan Love Song' straight—both very good."—*Variety*, "New Acts, 1929," review of Hope debut in New York at Proctor's 86th.

(2) "Love is like hash. You have to have confidence in it to enjoy it."—Leslie Townes (Bob) Hope.

Harvard as there are Sioux Indian accents at the University of Kansas. Hunting for a Harvard accent in Cambridge is about as rewarding as trying to find the Ivy League football scores in the Sunday Dubuque *Telegraph-Herald*. They are there, if you've got patience and a powerful miscroscope.

I hope I have scotched (which means "to inflict such hurt upon as to render harmless for the time," as in *Macbeth*, iii, 2, 13) the legend about the Harvard accent but I am sure I have not killed it. Americans like simple jokes and simple ideas such as that husbands are all helpless, all Negroes are terribly musical, and red-headed girls are all volcanoes of passion. The Harvard accent falls into this category and I am sure that when I am breathing my last the doctor will say with a chuckle, "Oh, so you went to *Hah-vud*, did you?" and his nurse will giggle appreciatively as I am in the process of being welcomed to the celestial shores by Ralph Waldo Emerson, Class of 1821, Bob Benchley, '12, and Percy Haughton, '99.

Having disposed of the accent, we will now explore another catch phrase, popular in the classified ads where it generally appears as "Harvard indifference." Now some of you in the back row will have to stop drawing pictures and curlicues in the margins of your notebooks and give me some quotes. Harvard indifference was very popular in the past, and so were Murad cigarettes—which one always lit in a crisis to demonstrate nonchalance, *savoir-faire*, and the ability to light a cigarette.

First let us call on Norman Hapgood, who wrote *The Changing Years* (1930). Stop looking out the window at the squirrels frolicking in the elm trees, Norman, and give us your impressions of indifference at Harvard.

"The phrase most used in our time to describe the college was 'Harvard indifference,' and it was most inaccurate. To Harvard's glory, be it conceded, the effective part of her was more indifferent than some colleges to mob interests, to victories on the field, to classmates merely as such, to social elections that were badges of popularity en masse. To intellectual interests she was the opposite of indifferent, though it is true she questioned all things. . . . In our college, as in the first University we seem to know, which was led by Socrates in the market place, the purpose of the students was inquiry into life."

If the *Crimson*, the Harvard student daily paper, reflects the mood of the college there is certainly no lack of interest in the larger issues of our times. I pick up an issue at random (which I am using to enclose a cheese sandwich with two pickle slices for my lunch) and find on the front page such spicy campus headlines as:

LATTIMORE ASKS FOR END OF U.S. AID TO DICTATORS

ADENAUER COMPROMISES FOR SUPPORT;
FELLOW CHRISTIAN DEMOCRATS OBJECT

HUGHES CALLS SOBLEN TRIAL "SCANDALOUS"

M.I.T. SCIENTISTS FAIL TO OBSERVE WIRES SHOT INTO SPACE

Inside, the editorial, a full column, is headed THE CITY ELECTION and is all about electing a new Cambridge City Council—an election in which few of the *Crimson*'s readers can vote—and contains such grand collegiate phrases as "proportional representation," "partisan civic group," "triple orientation," "significant testimony," and "tangible progress."

This is indifference? This is a college paper? What about that chafing-dish party held up at Radcliffe last night when the Welsh rarebit caught fire and they had to throw it out the window? What about the paper bag full of dilute Moxie dropped on kindly old absent-minded Professor Smoot's head from the third floor of Holworthy Hall? What happened to the Rampant Age? Not to mention The Plastic Age and Our Dancing Daughters? Listen fellows, get on your coonskin coats and Whoopee hats and I'll pick you up in my Velie roadster and we'll get up a good Pep Rally. I've got two Mason jars of good moonshine and later on we'll go over and put a chamber pot on the statue of John Harvard. On his head.

You can't go? Why not? Oh . . . you're going down to Central Square and picket Woolworth's on account of Negroes can't get no banana splits down in Birmingham at the dime store of their choice? I don't dig this. Come on, you guys, how about we drop in on Maureen de Vere, the College Widow, and then we'll go in town and have an oyster supper at Locke's and after that we'll go out on Boston Common and stage a snake dance and lead some cheers for Head Coach John Yovicsin? Say, boys, the trolleys run until 1 A.M. Come on, men, let's have a little indifference here. Forget about Adenauer and those M.I.T. scientists.

Say, I've got half a notion to call up Betty Coed,[6] but she's probably at a Ban-the-Bomb conclave.

Way back in 1894 an Englishman wrote:

Harvard has not been quite free from a certain kind of affectation which is only too common in the English Universities, but which is known in America as "Harvard indifference." . . . It is the contempt for all that eagerness of heart and thought and life which inspires "the young enthusiast" when first "he quits his ease for fame." "I do not love a man," said Goldsmith, "who is zealous for nothing."

More than sixty years ago Channing [7] rebuked it. When the Revolution of 1830 broke out in France, he was "astonished that the freemen of America, especially the young, should be so moderate in their expressions of joy." He went back in memory to his boyish days, when the Cambridge collegians had processions, speeches, and bonfires. Now all was still. One evening a graduate called upon him. "Well, Mr. ———," said Dr. Channing, "are you too so old and so wise, like the

[6] Not to be confused with Bettws-Y-Coed, an urban district on the Llugwy River in Caernarvonshire, Wales.
[7] Edward Tyrrel ("Potty") Channing, Boylston Professor of Rhetoric and Oratory from 1819 to 1851.

young men at Harvard, as to have no foolish enthusiasm to throw away upon the heroes of the Polytechnic School?" "Sir," answered ———, "you seem to me to be the only young man I know." "Always young for liberty, I trust," replied Dr. Channing with a bright smile and a ringing tone, as he pressed him warmly by the hand. Thirty years had to pass, and then this Harvard indifference was swept away by the Southern revolt. In the presence of that dreadful strife, indifference would no longer have been ridiculous, it would have become hateful.[8]

Just to show you how far Harvard indifference to the really important things of life can get, here's a bit of dialogue that took place on a sparkling October afternoon recently in the parlor of my luxurious fish house on the shores of quaint Long Island Sound:

[*Dear Old Dad, '36, is listening to the radio as Harvard fullback Bill Grana plunges across from the one-yard line to make it Harvard 20, Dartmouth 0.*]

DEAR OLD DAD, '36
Yahoo! Oh you Harvard! Go team go! Yipee!! [*He hops up and down rather absurdly, losing his glasses.*]

[*Son Tom, '63 home from Cambridge for the week end, looks up from an article in Collision, an advanced monthly printed on the same paper of which paper towels are made, in which he is immersed in an article entitled "Zane Grey, Rimbaud, and Salinger: A Critical Evaluation."*]

SON TOM, '63
Gee, Pop, what are you getting so excited about?

DEAR OLD DAD, '36
Damn it, Son, we just scored again! It's twenty to nothing! *Yahoo!*

SON TOM, '63
Gee, that's swell, Pop. Who are we playing?

[8] George Birbeck Hill, D.C.L., in *Harvard College by an Oxonian,* Macmillan & Co., 1895.

Now here is a case of reasoned nonconformity, extreme perhaps which at most colleges would not be labeled so much indifference as amnesia. What about that, Will Oursler, '37? Will you please put down that pea-shooter and comment briefly?

"In sports and other extracurricular activities the doctrinaire disdain of Harvard [That's a fancy variation on "indifference"—*Ed.*] shuns organized rah-rah-ism. The old school spirit exists in a measure. Harvard likes to beat Yale, but doesn't go in for cutting its collective throat if it loses—which it often does.[9] One contingent showed up at a game they were supposed to lose badly with a big sign reading, '*So?*' "

Unbelievable as it may seem to some, I personally never saw the football team play a game until my sophomore year, but it wasn't "doctrinaire disdain" for organized sports or a lack of the rah-rah spirit. I barely just squeaked into Harvard and I figured it would be very easy to squeak right out. So I spent the fall, including Saturdays, in the library. Harvard already had me in its grip, and Harvard means books. Reading them, that is. The pursuit of *Veritas* and all that jolly old cole slaw. Or as Anthony Trollope, an itinerant Englishman who found America in 1861 "tedious and confused," said of Harvard: "Study is more absolutely the business of the place than it is at our Universities." And the immortal Robert Benchley echoes these words in describing "Things I Learned Freshman Year" when he says, "By placing one paper bag inside another paper bag you can carry home a milk shake in it."

Cotton Mather, Class of 1678, who suffered periodic troubles with boll weevils, couldn't have expressed it better.

Lastly, Harvard has a reputation for being filled with eggheads. Eggheads, it seems, are intellectuals. Unfortunately, in the popular thinking of our country, intel-

[9] "By reputation, Harvard men are supposed to behave with 'studied indifference,' and the chronic ineptness of their team has given them an excellent chance to exhibit this trait."—*The Gilded Age of Sport*, Herbert Warren Wind, 1961.

lectuals are visualized as dopey dreamers, as absent-minded professors who bump into telephone poles, wear socks that don't match, and are long on theory and short on practice. In Europe intellectuals are looked up to. (It hasn't helped them with their problems much, one must admit.) But here, while the sales of books, records, tickets to concerts, and works of art are soaring, we still hear sneers about "eggheads." Eggheads are the people who write the books, compose the music, paint the pictures. The country is on the biggest egghead binge in history, so why pin it on Harvard? Elevator boys are reading Thomas Wolfe as they sail past your floor, waitresses spill soup down your neck with one hand while they manipulate a paperback edition of *The Charterhouse of Parma* in the other, and greenhouse attendants knock off early to go to lectures on The Middle East. Frankly, I've had it on universal eggheadism, and if Harvard started it I'm going up to New Haven and enroll at Yale in a course on electric welding.

THE PENNY ARCADE

Fun for All

"Brown of Harvard"

A movie review by Robert E. Sherwood in *Life* magazine, May 24, 1926.

I have seen many college movies in my time and have been constrained to smile tolerantly at the views of rollicking undergraduate life as reflected on the screen. "This, of course, seems utterly absurd," I told myself, "but it is probably a true picture of those hick universities in the Far West where such nonsensical antics are really carried on."

Then I saw "Brown of Harvard"—and for the first time the thing hit home. From this production I gathered that Harvard is not different from the rest: that Harvard students wear "shiek belts," that they have dates with professors' daughters under the pepper trees of Cambridge, that they are led in triumph through the streets by the members of the Dickey (the "Honor Society"), that they rush in as substitutes and win football games in the last minute of play, that they are all at least thirty-five years of age—in short, that they are exactly like the other phony college boys who are represented in the movies.

It is a crushing blow, and I don't know what I shall do about it.

In spite of the terrible embarrassment occasioned by certain elements in "Brown of Harvard," I am compelled to confess that it isn't such a bad picture; in fact, it should prove extremely entertaining to those who are not so particular about accuracy. It is certainly far, far less obnoxious than the play on which it was based.

NEW
ENGLANDS
FIRST FRUITS:
2. In respect of the Colledge, and the
proceedings of *Learning* therein.

2. **A**Fter God had carried us safe to *New England*, and wee had builded our houses, provided necessaries for our liveli-hood, rear'd convenient places for Gods worship, and setled the Civill Government: One of the next things we longed for, and looked after was to advance *Learning* and perpetuate it to Posterity; dreading to leave an illiterate Ministery to the Churches, when our present Ministers shall lie in the Dust. And as wee were thinking and consulting how to effect this great Work; it pleased God to stir up the heart of one Mr. *Harvard* (a godly Gentleman, and a lover of Learning, there living amongst us) to give the one halfe of his Estate (it being in all about 1700. l.) towards the erecting of a Colledge: and all his Library: after him another gave 300. l. others after them cast in more, and the publique hand of the State added the rest: the Colledge was, by common consent, appointed to be at *Cambridge*, (a place very pleasant and accommodate) and is called (according to the name of the first founder) *Harvard Colledge*.

New England's First Fruits, *published in London in 1643, was the first booklet to give "Information about Harvard College"*

William Haines, as that romping fellow, *Tom Brown*, gives a marvelous performance, and so does Jack Pickford in a thoroughly uncharacteristic role. Between the two of them, they manage to convey a semblance of reality in scenes and situations that are ridiculously unreal.

"Brown of Harvard" was adapted to the screen by Donald Ogden Stewart (a prominent Yale "grad"), who must have derived a considerable amount of fiendish glee from his work. In retaliation, I only hope that some one will produce "Stover at Yale" on the screen, and that the adaptation will be made by Robert Benchley.

CHAPTER II

Brief Appearance
of One
Reverend John Harvard

Greek education included music and dancing and what we call the arts. It was supposed to fit people to live. Mediaeval education was supposed to fit people to die. Any schoolboy of today can still feel the effect of it.

—STEPHEN LEACOCK

NEW ENGLAND did not get its name by mistake. It was English and proudly English, especially in its cultural aspects. The Puritans wanted the same comfort and decency, such as it was in the seventeenth century, that they had had at home and, being adrift in a terrible remote colony, were very much concerned lest standards fall under the rude frontier conditions and their children and children's children revert by stages to an un-English condition of ignorance and frontier barbarism. They demanded learned ministers, not Jesus-shouters, men who could "expound the Sacred Scriptures from the original Hebrew and Greek, and be cognizant of what the Church Fathers, the Scholastic Fathers, the Scholastic Philosophers, and the Reformers had written, in Greek and Latin." They needed and for 150 years would need the brightest, brainiest, cleverest, and most educated men they could produce to deal with the mysteries of English colonial policy, to establish trade, keep the domestic peace, cope with the wily red man, establish industry, collect the taxes, quell disturbances, uplift the fainthearted, provide for the poor, control transportation, lay out the law, discourage excess, command the uncouth, and be pillars of intelligence and honor for all to behold and admire. Where could they find such men; how could they be sure of a supply of educated and high-toned Englishmen? A great number of their best people were still in England and would remain in England—no ocean voyage for them, no dismal rocky shores with an M.G.M. Indian behind each rock.

With the obvious necessity for schooling at higher levels preying on their minds, they took action at a very early date. They founded a "colledge," and John Harvard wasn't even in town. He was still in London.

In 1636, only sixteen years after Plymouth and before the Puritans had made any progress at all in even scratching the surface of one of the most inhospitable and wearisome hunks of real estate on the continent, The Great and General Court of Massachusetts assembled under the governorship of Henry Vane (an Oxford man) and on October twenty-eighth passed the following vote, which shows that even Oxford's spelling was not so hot and a college badly needed:

"The Court agreed to give 400 £ towards a schoale or colledge, whearof 200 £ to bee paid the next yeare, and 200 £ when the worke is finished, and the next Court to appoint wheare and what building."

This four hundred pounds is estimated to have been equal to a year's income of the colonial government at the time, which shows that the Forefathers were not fooling in their thirst for the better things. Also, the overseers of the project were the most important men of the colony, including Governor Winthrop.

Then, as is customary when votes have been taken, speeches made, and resounding clichés have filled the air, nothing happened.

Nothing except a war with the Pequot Indians, that is.

Finally, in November 1637, the redskins having been put in their place temporarily, a committee of one Oxonian and six Cantabrigians was appointed by the Court to "take order for a colledge at Newetowne." The lone Oxonian didn't have a chance and "Newetowne," which was nothing but a big cow pasture with three houses adjoining, was changed to "Cambridge" by those six loyal sons.[1]

Harvard College may now be said to have come into being—not the first in the New World, but the fourth. The others were at Mexico City, Lima, and Córdoba, Argentina. San Marcos at Lima is perhaps the most interesting in some ways, as the student body numbers one undergraduate who, in the interests of World Peace, bounced a rock off the head of a Vice-President of the United States, Richard M. Nixon. Its proximity to the Lima Country Club and the cocktail lounge of the Hotel Bolívar also make it ideal for an exploratory trip by a committee of six Congressmen and an eighteen months' resident study of Peruvian educational methods by a staff of U.S. government experts none of whom speak Spanish.

Now things nudged ahead a bit, a farmhouse was refurbished to house the new "colledge," and Nathaniel Eaton (a prominent Puritan and a Cambridge graduate) was selected as Master and promptly made a hash of it. He was a "rare scholar," Cotton Mather tells us, but entirely too fond of that old and popular traditional English academic pastime known as flogging, or beating up the students. His wife contributed to the homey atmosphere

[1] In all, there were about a hundred alumni of Oxford and Cambridge in the colony at this period, seventeen years after Plymouth Rock.

by feeding the lads, so they complained, a substandard diet including such delicacies as "ungutted mackerel" and hasty pudding with goats' dung in it.

While things were not going so well with the nine students at the as-yet unnamed college in Cambridge, Mass., a Master of Arts of Emmanuel College, Cambridge, England, named John Harvard was in residence in Charlestown. He had a young, pretty, and childless wife and was a candidate for the position of assistant minister to the church in Charlestown. Whether he had ever crossed over on the ferry and gone out to Cambridge to see what was going on there we do not know, but when he died in September 1638, within a year of his arrival, he bequeathed half his property and his entire library to the new college. As a result of this benefaction from the Reverend Harvard, by far the largest donation to date, the General Court on the thirteenth of March 1639 "ordered, that the colledge agreed upon formerly to bee built at Cambridg shal bee called Harvard Colledge." Thus, while he did not actually "found" the college—as is commonly supposed—he certainly is entitled to the credit, for the College half of his estate came to £779 17s 2d, nearly double the amount of the original grant of the General Court, and his library numbered four hundred volumes, rather an astonishing quantity of books for a part-time preacher and son of a London butcher in the teeming bawdy slum of Southwark. John Harvard was thirty years old when he died in the wretched (it must have been wretched, how could it have been otherwise?) and gloomy surroundings of cold old Puritan New England. He might have been cheered on that dreary September afternoon if he had known that the farmhouse across the river would grow into one of the world's greatest universities and that it would bear his name. And he no doubt glows with satisfaction as he looks down from the Puritan heaven on some of his other namesakes: Harvard Shoe Shine, Harvard Invisible Mending, Harvard Brand Genuine Jewish Rye Bread, Harvard the Athletic Support of the Champs, Harvard Brand Peppermint Schnapps, Harvard the Truly Unbreakable Shoe Lace, the Harvard Bar and Grill, and the Harvard Package Store We Deliver Day and Night.

In addition to the money and the books, John Harvard also donated to the college another of his holdings, the Queens Head Tavern in Southwark, near his old home on the south (and vicious) side of London. How did he come to own this interesting piece of property? Presumably he came to it through his father, who must have prospered in the meat-market line. John's father and four of his brothers and sisters died of the plague in 1625. There is no American survivor of the Harvard name.

Following announcement of John Harvard's legacy, a general subscription for the college took place. There were contributions not only of books and small sums of money, but also other gifts: several sheep, some yardage of cotton cloth worth nine shillings, a "silver-tipped jug," a fruit dish, one large and one small "trencher-salt," and —just what every fledgling college needs—"a sugar spoon."

Meanwhile, back at the college, our first prexy Mr. Eaton was not only juggling the funds at his disposal, but had committed another slight indiscretion in beating his assistant "with a walnut cudgel for the space of two hours, while servants held him down." The assistant, Nathaniel Briscoe, protested audibly during this seminar, and Thomas Shepard appeared from the parsonage next door and broke up the exercises. The head of Harvard College was hauled into court where he confessed his error and promised not to lay on the birch (or the walnut) any more. In the course of the trial Mrs. Eaton was cross-examined on the subject of the college cuisine provided by her to the hungry scholars. When she confessed that she had never set beef in front of the students, the judges grew pale. The horror of the magistrates, valiant English trenchermen all, increased when the good madame also confessed that she often served bread fabricated of "heated, sour meal" and that there had occurred periods of drought when the collegians went without beer "betwixt brewings, a week or half a week together."

The judges had themselves been flogged during their schooldays or happy college years since being whipped, beaten, punched, pinched, hurled about, cuffed, tweaked, and bastinadoed was an accepted ingredient of a Christian education in those times, but they had not been subjected to short rations and took a severe attitude on the food-and-drink question. Eaton was dismissed, and though Harvard students have been complaining about the food for three centuries, no President has been fired since on account of shortages in the dining halls and inadequately prepared mackerel.

With the departure of Eaton, who eventually died in debtors' prison in Southwark, England, near John Harvard's old home, Harvard became for a year a ghost college. The students returned to their homes and colonial woodpeckers hammered on the rooftop of the college building. Things could not possibly have got off to a worse start. There is no hall, dormitory, pavilion, or any college building bearing the name of our first Master. Harvard men would just as soon forget Mr. Eaton, great scholar though he may in truth have been.

The first President of Harvard to act like a president and not like a scholarly Captain Bligh was Henry Dunster, a farmer's son from Lancashire, who had worked his way through Magdalene College, Cambridge. He was thirty when the Overseers made the appointment in August 1640, the youngest of all Harvard presidents and one of the most courageous, certainly one of the most memorable. Such numbers of Eaton's starvation group as wished to risk the chain gang again returned, and four new freshmen showed up smoking bulldog pipes, ready to learn the college yells.

Dunster was not only a fine scholar and inspiring teacher (he taught all the courses—Greek, Latin, and Hebrew, Liberal Arts, and the Three Philosophies) but what was more important (and still is), he was a money-raiser, an organizer, a pusher of projects, a promoter of expansion and improvement in all departments. He completed a new college building, increased the enrollment, and set the standards, which were those of old England. Until the completion of the new building, known as "Old College," students had been "dispersed in the town and miserably distracted in their times of concourse," but now they were housed together, a solid unit under one roof, where they could hang up NO PARKING signs in their rooms, pie each other's beds and drop paper bags of water on passing Pilgrims. Cotton Mather himself, not really a rah-rah boy, said "the Government of *New England,* was for having their students brought up in a more *Collegiate* Way of Living." Of course he was not referring to Whoopee hats and bell-bottom trousers, but to the organization of the college along the traditional lines of Oxford and Cambridge. For one thing, Harvard was definitely not a divinity school, although naturally in the seventeenth century theological studies loomed large in the curriculum. For another thing, President Dunster was a driver. The hours were long; he used no walnut clubs but drove learning into his charges' heads by force of his personality and qualities as a teacher. That was a "*Collegiate* Way of Living."

No one knows how Dunster raised the money for the new college building. Built in 1644, this imposing edifice was a sort of a gabled monstrosity, apparently, and very poorly erected, for within seven years the sills were going bad and the building had begun to sag. It continued to sag, eventually taking on the appearance of some of those swayback, gray, cheerless buildings one sees from the club car of the New Haven Railroad that herald one's approach to Boston's romantic old Back Bay. In 1678 it was finally declared unfit for human habitation or even for the storage of last year's examination papers and unclaimed galoshes and was abandoned, only thirty-four years after it had been built, perhaps the earliest known example of the builder's art as practiced by Massachusetts contractors through the centuries, which has been enlivened by falling bridges, defective plumbing, leaky cellars, and scandalous paving contracts.

The building cost a thousand pounds to build. All of the original grant of the General Court disappeared into the contractors' pockets, as did John Harvard's legacy, a few sums from England, and possibly a fund raised from the sale of that sugar spoon. At any rate, finances were a continuous headache to President Dunster. In 1654 an audit of the accounts revealed that Dunster had operated the college for twelve years on the magnificent sum of £175 per annum, of which £55 was deducted annually for the President's salary.

Financial arrangements at the time were pretty weird. The tuition was £1 6s 8d per annum, and the commencement fee was £3. (I do not understand these figures, but maybe I am not trying very hard.) Students paid their term bills and their "commons and sizings"—bread and beer—not in cash but in assorted merchandise and livestock. Sheep, cattle, turkeys, chickens, and bantam hens were presented on their feet at the Bursar's office, as well as flour, meal, eggs, malt, corn, wheat, oats, rye, shoes, butter, lard, cheese, piece goods, turnips, doorknobs, horseshoes, mittens, hinges, old iron, hides, and ashtrays labeled *Souvenir of Kennebunkport, Maine*.

Actual money came from other sources. Lady Mowlson (Anne Radcliffe) sent a scholarship fund of £100 from England (and that's how Radcliffe Girls were born). In 1644, every family in the New England Confederation, which consisted of Massachusetts Bay, Connecticut, New Haven, and the Plymouth Colonies, agreed to give either a peck of wheat or a shilling in cash to Harvard College for "the advance of learning" (and the improvement of spelling). These donations were called "College Corn," which would make a good title for a song by Frank Loesser. So much College Corn rolled in that it paid the salaries of the whole teaching staff. Today the only college corn we have is medleys of college songs played by Lawrence Welk.

One curious source of revenue was the tolls of the Boston-Charlestown ferry, which had been granted *in toto* to the college at the time of President Dunster's appointment. These tolls amounted to thirty or forty pounds a year but there was a catch: they were mostly paid in wampum, or wampum-peague, and as Dunster stated, "badde and unfinished peague" at that. We are accustomed to associate wampum with the annual Indian Pageant presented by the fifth and sixth grades under the direction of Miss Melish of the Art Department, but in old New England it was actually used as money. In fact, it persisted as a means of exchange and was still circulating in some parts of New England as late as the beginning of the eighteenth century. Wampum consisted of shell beads, ground as smooth as glass and strung together. There were two kinds, purple and white, the purple being the more valuable. Dark or purple wampum was made from the hard shell of the quahog clam (*Venus mercenaria* or gold-digger); white wampum was made from whelks. Massachusetts was still on the wampum standard in 1640, the exchange being set at four to a penny and five shillings a fathom, which consisted of 240 beads. President Dunster grew discouraged over the junk wampum coming into the treasury and said that the college was getting stuck with practically all the substandard and counterfeit wampum being turned out in gloomy cellars from the Kennebec River to Harwich Port.

Yet money did keep dribbling in from here and there. Ten merchants in Portsmouth, New Hampshire, sent the college £60 a year for seven years.

One John Cogan of Boston presented a salt meadow near Revere which produced revenue of up to £25 a year.

In 1670 a Londoner named Pennoyer turned over the rents of a farm in Norfolk, which were still being paid in

1903, when the farm was sold and the proceeds converted to stock in a gold mine.

Some Puritans in the Bahamas sent the college a cargo of "ten Tuns of Brasiletto wood as a stock for your Colledges use. . . ." The proceeds of the sale were used to purchase a cowyard and house adjoining the college.

Two graduates of the Class of 1642 purchased and presented to the college a cowyard to the east and planted it with apple trees for presidential pies.

Finally, late in the century, the financial pressure was relieved greatly by the £1000 bequest of Harvard's second big-scale benefactor, Sir Matthew Holworthy, a dissenter and an enthusiast for the cowyard college across the seas.

But that was long after Dunster's time. In his first year money was scarce and as the result of an economic slump it grew scarcer. Henry's budget was cut drastically by the Court. His own personal fortune could not have been in very great shape. But at this point, when all seemed dark and dreary and the wampum very scarce, what ho! the Widow Glover appears over the horizon under full sail! Luck, as it must to all clean-living and high-thinking Harvard men, came to Henry Dunster all in a rush, and before he knew it he was nestled in matrimony on Elizabeth Glover's ample bosom (I put that last in there just in case this turns into a movie) in her house on Holyoke Street, "as well stocked with fine plate and furnishings as an English lord's."

Mrs. Glover had come over from England with a printing press and a husband. The printing press survived the ocean voyage but Mr. Glover did not, and she arrived in Boston a widow. Feeling that the deceased would have wanted Harvard College to have the use of the press, she had it set up nearby, in what is now Holyoke Street. The rest we know. Henry Dunster, farmer's son, acquired a classy wife with lots of purple wampum and Harvard acquired a printing press.

The first commencement of Harvard College took place in September 1642. Nine students were graduated. Here are the names of six of them and their accomplishments after leaving Cambridge:

1. Benjamin Woodbridge. Chaplain to King Charles II ("Old Rowley"); minister in Newbury; commissioner to the Savoy Conference in 1661; the first Harvard graduate to get in print.

2. Sir George Downing. Member of Parliament; chaplain in Army of the Commonwealth; knighted in 1660, became a baronet in 1663; Ambassador to the Netherlands from both Cromwell and Charles II; designated a "perfidious rogue" by Samuel Pepys; tighter than a Pullman window, Sir George donated the sum of five pounds to the building fund at Harvard.

3. Samuel Bellingham. Society doctor in London; of great renown.

4. William Hubbard. Minister in Ipswich and one of the first historians of New England.

5. Henry Saltonstall.[2] Earned an M.D. at Padua and became an Oxford Fellow.

6. John Bulkley. Minister and physician in England; first Harvard graduate to donate land to the college.

The first commencement was a proud day for New England and an occasion for jollifications and overeating, a "kind of New World Holiday, another feast of St. Giles." In subsequent years the carousing took on bacchanalian aspects, with immoderate drinking and boisterous conduct, and the authorities considered excluding the public from the not-so-solemn rites to limit the rowdyism, horseplay, and discharge of firearms. All the ministers and all the magistrates in the Colonies were invited to these festivities; in addition to the merrymaking, the expenses of which were paid by the graduating class, there were orations in learned tongues, disputations, pronouncements, resolutions, and finally the presentation of

[2] The Saltonstalls are the only family in America to have had ten successive generations graduate from the same college: Harvard.

degrees. If all the Latin and Greek unreeled at these functions were laid end to end it would put one to sleep immediately. No wonder everybody needed a drink.[3]

The life of the student of those days is hard for us to comprehend now. There were no Lambrettas or MGs, no discussions about Italian movies, no Joan Baez records to buy, no plumbing, not even any lights. The students arose at 5 A.M. and in between prayer and contemplation of the Scriptures, study, and eating, were kept busy until eight o'clock at night, when they had a one-hour "recreation period" until lights out. The students were expected to "honor as their parents, magistrates, elders, tutors, and aged persons by being silent in their presence." This rule has since gone by the board. Although I qualify as an "aged person," the massed beer drinkers do not rise and observe ten minutes of silence when I enter the Wursthaus. And I wish President Dunster would come back and reprimand the young man at the Princeton game who offered me a drink out of a pint bottle, referred to me as *Pop*, and bashed in my hat when Humenuk scored from the one-yard line. (Harvard 9, Princeton 7.) Doesn't he know that scholars are supposed to show "laudable expressions of honor and reverence" in the presence of us old fossils from '36?

"No scholar shall buy, sell, or exchange anything, to the value of sixpence, without the allowance of his parents, guardians, or tutors."

That's all very well, but let me ask you how is a fellow supposed to get to Northampton or Mt. Holyoke for the week end unless he sells those pearl studs the old man gave him when he graduated from Choate, or his roommate's J. Press overcoat?

"The scholars shall never use their mother tongue except that in public exercises of oratory, or such like, they be called to make them in English."

[3] Speaking of the capture of Louisburg in 1745, a Dr. William Douglass observed: "The siege was carried on in a tumultuary random manner, and resembled a Cambridge Commencement."

This is one rule still in effect at Harvard and in fact has spread its influence beyond the Yard and through the town. Cambridge is the only town in the U.S. in which the cab drivers habitually converse in Latin, the counter-men at Hayes-Bickford's cafeteria shout the orders in Homeric Greek, and the quarterback on the football team conducts the game in Church Slavonic. After four years at Harvard I personally forgot my English completely and had to carry on via sign language when home on vacation. After graduation I went to Berlitz and got my English back.

And next week at this same theatre, we present the new two-reel laff-riot from the Selig studios entitled *The Congregational Cutups*, starring Increase Mather, Cotton Mather, John Bunny, Edna Purviance, and Bronco Billy Anderson. Always a Clean Show for the Family at the Bijou. Ladies Please Remove Your Hats.

CHAPTER III

Incidents in the LIFE
of a Terribly SOPHISTICATED HARVARD FRESHMAN
in the Year 1932,
Transcribed from the ORIGINAL DIARIES of Same,
Now in the *British Museum*
and Here Printed for the *First Time*

Fri. Sept. 23, 1932
Stoughton Hall
Harvard Yard

WHEN I got over here to Cambridge I asked some guy where was Stoughton Hall and he said "I'm from Framingham how would I know?" I finally found it and I have a pretty nice room. I wasn't in there more than 10 minutes before some fello came and tried to sell me a subscription to the Crimson. I did not buy it as Fred told me not buy anything from those guys that will come to your door and try to sell you different stuff.

I bought some egyptian cigarettes.

So then I went in to Boston and saw a movie, Harold Lloyd in "Movie Crazy."

Fri. Sept. 30, 1932

The Yankees won again.

Tues. Oct. 4

Had my physical exam and the doc said my inlays are terrific and called another doc or dentist in to look at them. So I told them they were all installed in Iowa and they were surprised. I suppose they figure we have indian dentists out there.

Clarey showed up and we went to Sears Roebuck and I bought some nifty curtains for my room and two Cab Calloway records. I bought a rug from Clarey for $4.

Oct. 22

Some guy pinched my hat at the Union while I was reading *Life of Charlemagne* so I picked up a good one for myself (Finchley) down in the coat room so I came out on top.

Fri. Oct. 28, 1932

Went to the Old Howard burlesque with Howie and it was pretty good. Chickie Wells was there tonight—she is the first girl I ever saw in Burlesque. She always sings a song about "Just like Adam and Eve," and she holds an apple. I like her better than any of the others in fact I love her madly. Got home about 3 A.M. Good night, Chickie you darling.

Sun. Oct. 30

I am not very fond of Sunday here. It is not like Exeter. A lot of the Boston guys go home for Sunday dinner.

Nov. 16, 1932

Went in to Boston and bought a dandy new squash raquet for $5.50. At Geology lab I was the first one finished. Bill Peterson beat me at squash.

Fri. Nov. 18, 1932

I went to Sears Roebuck to price auto curtains for the Ford (Fred's) and they have a radio for $30.00, $5 down and $5 a month that I might get. But you have to get your parents to sign the contract.

Dec. 9 '32

I went to Central Square and bought myself a pair of pearl grey suede shoes for $3.

Dec. 10 '32 Saturday

Drove to Exeter with Fred and we had two flat tires and had to buy two new tires $15.00!!!

Fri. Dec. 16, 1932

Tonight I went to the Old Howard because Chickie Wells was there again. I went with Lew Perry. We watched a guy getting tattooed on Scollay Square. It got so late the subways closed so we had to return in a taxi to Cambridge. Chickie was great.

Dec. 31, 1932 Exeter, N.H.

Did my Geology work this afternoon on the dining room table and Margie did her History map and I helped her with her map of Italy. She goes to the Robinson Female Seminary. We drove to Hampton and walked by the sea.

Jan. 3, 1933

I went up to Sears Roebuck and looked at that radio again. I bought two german magazines, a pound of cheese, a loaf of rye bread, and two bottles of root beer.

Wed. Jan. 11, 1933

Went into Boston with my squash raquet to have it restrung and then to Jake Wirths for some kraut and knackwurst and beer and ice cream and came home and read for English 28.

Feb. 9, 1933

Massachusetts is the land of the dried-up overcooked hamburger.

Feb. 15, 1933

I went to a basketball game at M.I.T. with Dan, Dick,

and Jim. They are all from New York and went to "Horace Mann" which they talk about as though it was something great although nobody in New England has ever heard of it. They feel sorry for everybody that doesn't come from New York. Naturally none of them has ever seen the Mississippi River, the Rocky Mountains, or even Pittsburgh. They talk about basketball all the time.

Feb. 16, 1933

Dan and Dick cooked some steaks in the fireplace in Dan's room. Lew came in from Coolidges. Dick has a meerschaum pipe.

Studying deposition of coal beds in late Paleozoic.

March 7, 1933 Stoughton Hall

Roosevelt closed all the banks.

I wish I was married.

Movies .35

Lemon drops .05

Saddle shoes 3.95

Plaid shirt 1.95

March 16, 1933

Thought of the Day: Boston guys don't know too much what's going on.

May 17, 1933

Geology Field trip to Squantum. Lay in the grass and sun while the fellows went around trying to find the contacts.

May 22, 1933

Guzzled some 3.2 beer at the Wursthaus. Pretty devilish.

May 29, 1933

I was over in Holworthy with some guys and they called up a bootlegger and he brought around a bottle of gin which we mixed with ginger ale. It was awful. I chipped in $1.20.

June 6, 1933

History One Final. Passed it OK. Passed everything OK. Well nobody thought I would last at Harvard until Christmas but here it is June. So phooey to everybody.

Wrote Margie.

Went rowing.

Went to Wursthaus with the guys and drank 3.2 beer.

Went to movies.

Went back to Wursthaus.

Went to bed.

Now what in hell am I going to do in Iowa all summer?

Further INCIDENTS in the Life

of the SAME TERRIBLY SOPHISTICATED HARVARD MAN,

Now a JUNIOR, in the Year 1935,

Transcribed from the ORIGINAL

As Before, etc. etc.

Sat. Oct. 5, 1934

Margie came out on subway and Fred and I took her to the football game with Springfield which Harvard won 20—0. Dick and Sewall ate dinner with us and we drove to Fenway to the movies which were lousy with Warren William. Sewall bought some peanut brittle for Margie but we got separated from Dick and Margie in the movies and so didn't get in on it until the second show. Then they came back into the 8th row and sat with us and Margie gave me the peanut brittle and the box collapsed.

The Cubs lost.

Dec. 5th, 1934

Dick, Byron, Jim, Sewall, and Nate came up to my room and we played black jack all afternoon. Nate went down $6.40 on one hand and was very sad. Went to movies and saw Shirley Temple and resumed game at 9:30 until 1:00 A.M. I came out $1.85 ahead on the day's hard work.

Thurs., Jan. 10, 1935

Went to the Uni matinee and saw a swell bill, George Raft in "Limehouse Blues." Played billiards at Leavitt & Peirce with Blatch. Went to Wolff's tutoring school about Philosophy B. Frank Roosevelt was there. My new fountain pen came from Sears Roebuck $1.88.

Sunday, Jan. 20, 1935

Owe Sewall 60c for poker. Dick owes me 50c for movie. Reading about the dopy Incas for exam tomorrow. Boy are they boring.

Jan. 12, 1935

Met Margie in town and I had to go to Locke-Obers to arrange about a banquet for Scott Fitz. We went to San Remos spaghetti joint on Park Square.

Feb. 10, 1935

Dick and I went to Leavitt and Peirces and played some pool and we weren't very good so went home and read Philosophy B until Nate came in with Jim from Dartmouth Winter Carnival. They wanted to eat so went up to Square and had "Managers Suggestion" at Hayes-Bickfords—a steak sandwich and french fries 35c not bad. Played pool in Eliot House basement pool room and beat Nate. A radio downstairs is playing "P. S. I Love You," boy does that ever carry me back to the Hampton Beach Casino.

Sunday, April 28, 1935

No dough, so played catch around Eliot House and spent evening reading.

May 25

Went to court in Newton. Fined $5.00.

May 26

Drank beer and played cards. Schlitz is the best.

Wed., May 29, 1935

Went to the ball game at Fenway Park and saw the St. Louis Browns beat the Red Sox. Lefty Grove pitched but got shelled and Welch finished. Werber and Bejma hit homers.

Sat., June 8, 1935

Double-header at Fenway Park. Gomez pitched 2nd and lost. Lefty Fritz Ostermueller was hot for Sox. Lou Gehrig hit a homer. Studied Classical Archaeology.

June 13, 1935

Went in to Scollay Square and got tattooed on my right arm at Mr. Liberty's tattoo emporium. It doesn't look too good yet. Went in to the "Tent" tonight with Nate, Sewall, Jim, Joe, Stanley and a guy from Dartmouth. We picked up a bunch of girls and went to the "Ten Friends Club" which is a speakeasy (after hours) also someplace near Scollay Square and is a dump. Back to Cambridge at 5:15 A.M. after delivering the girls to Chelsea. My tattoo itches. I have got adhesive tape over it.

CHAPTER IV

Wuxtry!

Woman (*to tramp*): *Now if you don't go away at once I'll call my husband—and he's an old Harvard football player.*

   Weary Willie: *Lady, if yer love him, don't call him out, I used ter play wid Yale.*

THE *Crimson* was the first college paper in the country, only it was called the *Magenta*, which was Harvard's color at the time, and it was a weekly, first appearing in 1873. Magenta is a purplish-red color the dye for which was discovered in 1859, and is named for Magenta, Italy. Crimson is a deep-red color with a purplish tinge, from the Middle English *cremesyn*.

In 1875 the *Magenta*, changed to *Crimson*, became a daily paper, and has been flourishing ever since, usually to the accompaniment of hoaxes, cracked pates, and cries of pain from its adversaries. It has scored world-news beats, seesawed from the bitterest reaction to far-flung liberalism, campaigned, opposed, deplored, upheld, withstood, taken a firm stand on, rejected, viewed with alarm, found detestable, put the stamp of approval on, frowned upon, endorsed, found wanting, backed, stood firmly against, implemented, sallied forth, defended the right of, detached itself from, joined forces with, denied participation in, climbed on the bandwagon of, extended the hand of friendship toward, affirmed emphatically its interest in, washed its hands of, stood behind, walked in the vanguard of, noted with dismay, urged on, withdrawn its support from, been astonished to discover that, delved into, looked at both sides of, and withheld further comment on. Its editorials have at times caused Full Professors to swallow excessive doses of aspirin and lovely Radcliffe girls with stunning figures and beautiful auburn hair to burst into tears. Again and again, it has fallen on its chin policywise, and risen to demand better laundry service for fallen women in the suburbs of Cartagena.

Its editors have included such men as Lloyd McKim Garrison, '88, Henry James, '99, Frederick E. Bissell, '00, Franklin D. Roosevelt, '04, and James B. Conant, '14. But Heywood Broun tried three times for the *Crimson* and was always turned away into the empty streets, from which he promptly hied himself to the Red Sox park to watch that sterling outfield: Tris Speaker, Duffy Lewis, and Harry Hooper.

The *Crimson* owns its own building, plant, press, delivery service, inkwells, and spittoons, and is managed like an iron foundry and operated at a profit. (So I hear.) The University has "no control" over the *Crimson* in that there are no faculty advisors or other kibitzers in positions of academic authority on the premises.

In its early days, the *Crimson* was largely a record of college events with much space devoted to athletics, debating contests, and the prowess of the mandolin club. Gradually it began to gather momentum in the field of larger issues; today it devotes space to politics of local, national, and international scope to such an extent that it is now at times sort of a four-page undernourished *New York Times*. Like they run several big long dreary editorials on *"The Common Market"* on successive days. In all seriousness, what student who has a date in Wellesley that night, a Fine Arts paper to write, and a flat tire on his MG is going to read a piece by one of his fellow students sounding off about the Common Market and such topics? As the *Daily Princetonian*, which gives front-page space to the week end's dances (which are not even mentioned in the *Crimson* want ads) says:

". . . the *Crimson* incorporates national and international news into its columns, while the *Princetonian*, feeling that this job is competently handled by the New York and Philadelphia papers, devotes its news space to events of campus significance."

Then there is the Crusade. One of the first members of the *Crimson* to use it as an organ of complaint and pressure was a young man from Groton named Franklin D. Roosevelt who later on became famous on the Pantages time for his unicycle act. Not satisfied with digging up dope on the Glee Club and reporting which member of the crew had a blister on his thumb, young Roosevelt began to hunt up *news*, which became somewhat of a source of irritation to various members of the editorial board. (Irritationwise, he was just practicing up for later on.) He succeeded, however, in rousing a lethargic staff and creating a "fighting paper," waging campaigns which resulted in improvements in such diverse fields as a patty-cake football team and fire escapes for the Yard buildings. The Boxer Rebellion and the Boer War also came in for editorial space and the pattern was set.

Years later, the *Crimson* embarked on one of its most famous crusades in its open warfare on President Lowell's regime,[1] which culminated in all-out opposition couched in Peglerian vituperation against the $10,000,000 House Plan, the gift of Edward S. Harkness of Standard Oil. Sneers and sarcasm leveled at High Tables, House emblems, colors, and other aristocratic and fearsome tendencies, filled the columns. But Lowell, whose epidermis was of boiler plate and who was as fond of the press as he was of red ants (in twenty-five years as President of Harvard

---

[1] In the spring of 1962 the *Crimson* exploded an attack on President Pusey's management of the University, so bitter that *Time* magazine rose up in his defense.

he never gave a press interview), endorsed Mr. Harkness' check and the bricklayers and hod carriers arrived in Cambridge unopposed and on time.

With nothing else to raise hell about for the moment, in 1932 the editors of the *Crimson* began to insult each other. This resulted in the withdrawal of eleven top editors, who formed a new paper, the *Journal*. The rest of the year was devoted to skirmishes, bayonet practice, artillery fire, and street fighting between the two papers. The *Crimson* won, at the famous battle of Cold Harbor, and the *Journal* withdrew from the field to bury its dead and seek cover from its creditors behind the subway yards and under bushes in Jamaica Plain and Newton Upper Falls.

Following the defeat of the *Journal* and the signing of the treaty, the *Crimson* launched a campaign against the several commercial tutoring schools which operated around the Square and which it termed "intellectual brothels." I don't know whether the boys had ever been in very many brothels, but the tutoring schools bore slight resemblance to the one in *Tenderloin*, for example. They were small untidy rooms with soiled walls, filled with chalk dust, cigarette smoke, and unhappy students trying to cram the contents of the entire reading list for Philosophy B, History 1, Geology 4, or French 6 into their sluggish heads in two hours. The only resemblance I ever noted to the "House of All Nations" was the snobbish clientele. My closest contact at Harvard with a member of the Porcellian Club was sitting next to one and feverishly taking notes in Wolff's Tutoring School. The personnel of these establishments, far from exciting gay and licentious ideas, were a sorry lot of unfrocked section men in baggy pants, some of whom needed a shave, and all of whom needed a haircut. Although the *Crimson* took a moral stance on these dreary nonbrothels, my objection to them—and it was shared by most victims—was that the force-feeding rarely did any good. After one near-disaster I decided by far the best policy was to either go to the lectures or do the reading, preferably both, unless the lecturer created such a pall of boredom that one could justify one's absence. I took one course of this kind from a professor of considerable fame whose dronings were so dreadful that after the first lecture I never went back. (You do not have to go to classes at Harvard if you don't want to. I had a friend who used to go skiing in Switzerland for three weeks every year in the winter term. Nobody noted his absence.) By borrowing the notes of a classmate with a higher boredom threshold, I got a B in the course, which is the same mark I would have received had I submitted three times a week to The Drone.

College papers like to go in for the wild surmise, the sensational leadoff sentence, and the Big Positive Statement. On October 7, the day of the 1961 Cornell game, the Managing Editor led off a front-page story: "Boy, is the varsity football team ever going to get murdered this afternoon." (Out in the Big Ten this kind of funny talk would probably precipitate an editor-lynching bee, but at Harvard it was greeted with yawns.) Well anyway, this piece goes on to give plenty of advice to coach Yovicsin on how to "stay in the shooting match." ("He would do well, it seems, to revise his outlook on passing," says the editor, adjusting his spectacles.) The rest of the article is a buildup in breathless tones of the Cornell team. ("Gogolak is the best place kicker in football, period," "a legend before his second varsity game," "dangerous halfbacks," "the great Big Red backfield," etc.)

Apparently coach John Yovicsin did not read the *Crimson* that day, because he did not revise his outlook on passing and the pathetic Harvards creamed Gogolak and the great Big Red Cornell backfield 14–0.

Unabashed, the Managing Editor also wrote the story of the game and, quickly shifting gears, led off with a three-paragraph sneer at Gogolak the Legend. No mention is made of the author's twenty-four-hour-previous pontifications on What's to be Done with the Team.

This is a really professional approach to journalism worthy of some great metropolitan sheet, and I predict that this Harvard journalist will soon be Managing Editor of the New York *Journal-American* or the Boston *Herald* or be having stories about Castro (facts gleaned from a disgruntled Cuban busboy at the Lamb's Club) in a box across the front of the *Herald Tribune* above the daily story about the New Haven Railroad and its troubles.

Even more typical of the average college paper is the fact that in the same issue, the same editor (everybody gets a byline in the *Crimson* except the linotype man), having revealed his expertise in the sports field, also has a fancy critique of the movie version of *West Side Story*. In other words, one minute he's in the locker room chewing on a cigar with his hat shoved back like Lee Tracy and an hour later he is puffing a Melachrino in the lobby of the Colonial Theatre and making like Walter Kerr.

Just to linger on the sports scene a moment or two longer, here is what the *Crimson* had to say about the Cincinnati Reds, probably the worst team ever to find itself dazed and adrift without a paddle in a World Series. Just before the series, in which the Yankees tied the Cincinnati lads' clothes in knots, soaked the knots, and pounded them with rocks, the *Crimson* advanced this bit of inside dope:

But everybody had better realize now that the Reds are indeed the N.L. champs, and a real blood and guts ball team at that. The New York Yankees especially should take Cincinnati seriously—although it will do them little good. For the Yankees are about to get bumped off in six games in the World Series by one of the most unobtrusive pennant winners of all time.

A week later Red Smith was saying of the dreariest World Series in many a moon: "The Reds didn't even look good throwing the ball back to the pitcher."

Come on, fellows, ease off, will you? [2]

Movie reviews are inclined to be complex and lithic. (I use *monolithic* on Mondays, Wednesdays, and Fridays and *lithic* on Tuesdays, Thursdays, and Saturdays at eleven.) Especially since the motion picture is no longer looked upon in fashionable circles as entertainment but as an art form. With the exception of Peter Sellers' movies, nobody in Cambridge ever cares to admit he is having fun at the movies, and even in the case of funny-man Sellers we hear sincere youths exclaim that his "timing is as good as Keaton" and "his pantomime is in a class with Chaplin." (I daresay they have never heard of Larry Semon or the immortal Charlie Chase.) This vocabulary—which is extensive and includes "neorealism," "brilliant camera work," and "totally inadequate musical underscoring"—can be acquired very easily, in case you want to amaze your friends without becoming a master of the five-string banjo by mail, by reading the film-program notes of the Museum of Modern Art.

Under no circumstances nowadays are you supposed to settle down at the movies with a box of popcorn and allow yourself to be wafted away from the cares and routine of daily life into other wondrous shimmering worlds through the magic of the silver screen. No, it is strictly an intellectual exercise and requires that you make constant mental notes as to how badly the part of the sister-in-law was cast, how poor the dubbing is in the rape scene, the "really solid acting" of the one-eyed soldier in his bit part ("He should have had the lead"), plus manifold suggestions as to how it should have been cut ("One episode,

---

[2] They are not about to ease off. For some reason prognosticating football seems to set their pulses racing madly:

CRIMSON SEEK IVY VICTORY AGAINST DANGEROUS QUAKER SQUAD

On paper, the Penn-Harvard game this afternoon in Philadelphia looks like a deceptively tame pushover for the Crimson. It won't be. (*Crimson*, 11/4/61)

The score was Harvard 37, Penn 6. Penn was about as dangerous as Major Hoople in a vacant lot showing Alvin how to drop-kick.

in which Bardone accepts money from a girl he had deserted, is irrelevant and should have been cut completely," says the *Crimson* of *General della Rovere*. All right Rossellini, you've got your orders, don't just stand there).

The consumption of popcorn by the "new" movie fan is taboo, since the sound effects are likely to interfere with the inadequate underscoring on the inadequate sound track. As for Jujuy Fruits, Charleston Chews, Baby Ruth, Oh Henry, Coconut Mounds, Bit-O-Honey, Clark Bar, Butterfinger, Mars, Three Musketeers, Milky Way, and Peanut Jumbo Block—all of which were formerly an integral part of the enjoyment of film viewing—I gather they are out of the picture, as I have not seen a one of them even mentioned in a single review in the *Crimson*. Despite this I imagine there would even today be no objection in the case of frivolous film fare such as *Where the Boys Are, The Moon Pilot,* or *Breakfast at Tiffany's* to smuggling a Hershey Bar (no nuts) into your favorite film palace. Wait a minute, kill that *Breakfast at Tiffany's,* as it probably is "social comment" and requires respect and no chocolate.

Hollywood takes it in the neck with deadening regularity from the *Crimson* and there is almost never a kind word for guys like old Jerry Wald who used to try so hard for Class by announcing every week that he had acquired the film rights to *Finnegan's Wake,* the entire works of Gertrude Stein, and "Sartor Resartus" and already had Frank Sinatra, Debbie Reynolds, Elizabeth Taylor, Rosalind Russell, Hank Fonda, Jack Lemmon, Shirley MacLaine, Paul Newman, Stan Laurel, Alfred Lunt, Barbara Nichols, and Chill Wills out in his front yard trampling on his hollyhocks, banging on his door, and demanding parts in the new productions. All these excitable pronouncements don't cut no ice in Harvard Square. As soon as Hollywood sets them up, the boys knock them right on their cans.

Recently a freshman, who was obviously not With It and who probably not only eats Deluxe buttered popcorn, but also Crackerjack and Black Crows at the movies, rose up in mighty indignation and gave the *Crimson* a vicious stab with his Paper-Mate pen:

The Mail

A FRIEND OF HOLLYWOOD

To the Editors of the *Crimson:*

Most often, of course, the *Crimson* is considered as holding and exercising unorthodox viewpoints. In my opinion this is good, and the *Crimson* is highly enjoyable because of it. But I find it not to the credit of the *Crimson* to exhibit a policy which is not far short of ridiculous.

Since the *Crimson* and *Crimson Review* resumed publication, virtually every foreign film in the Boston area has been reviewed, characteristically with words like "magnificent," "brilliant," and "incomparable."

In regard to American films, however, the *Crimson* has panned or disregarded every film—with one notable exception.

Exodus, Cold Wind in August, The Guns of Navarone, Fanny, Romanoff and Juliet, and Scream of Fear have been vivisected by the *Crimson's* knife; and this often flagrantly in opposition to both the opinions of major critics and of public opinion, as expressed through box-office receipts. . . .

The exception to prove the rule is Mr. Lottman's review of *West Side Story*, in which he, having personally enjoyed the film, attempts to APOLOGIZE to his readers for NOT finding bad performances by Natalie Wood and Russ Tamblyn, or NOT finding poor direction, or NOT finding bad photography, and hence NOT being able to confirm what Mr. Lottman considers his readers' preconceived "shudders" over Hollywood's version of the play.

Indeed, I think I can accuse the *Crimson* correctly of exhibiting an over-whelming bias—which is surely not far short of ridiculous. It seems to me a ridiculous "policy" for the major guide of many Harvard students to Boston's entertainment to categorically WANT to find fault with EVERY American film.

Fortunately, I have found some of the *Crimson's* victims enjoyable despite its vivisection. I ask for a little more reality in outlook.

James A. Mecklenburger, '65.

Go right ahead and ask, Mr. Mecklenburger, and I wish you luck.

All kidding aside, the boys put out a good paper and they do not follow the standard pattern of the big and little American dailies by filling their sheet with drivel, corset ads, ten-pound supplements containing stories on Gary Moore's home life, magazine sections filled with hot dope on East Berlin (photo of dejected crowd by a fence), South Africa (photo of dejected crowd having bricks thrown at them), Cuba (photo of dejected crowd in an airport), Detroit (dejected workers by a fence), Russia (dejected crowd watching some tanks go by), France (dejected strikers by a fence), and articles entitled "Is Hitler Really Dead?" Neither does the *Crimson* run all those howls in Dear Abby or feature five syndicated columnists all writing on red-hot typewriters. Also it does not copy the big fat papers by including a minimum of ten typographical errors per thousand words. And practically everything in the *Crimson* is worth reading, which is more than you can say for the real estate sections in the *Times*. True, it doesn't have a comic strip, and I think Al Capp, who lectures at Harvard, should waive the royalties and give Li'l Abner to the *Crimson* for free.

In ancient times the *Crimson* had a crew and a baseball team, offered "cups to be played for by competing nines," and challenged the *Advocate* and *Lampoon* to a tug-of-war.

"In the old days," a '92 editor recalls, "the *Crimson* was more of a social than a business organization. The paper was gotten out in a rather happy-go-lucky fashion; sometimes the editors turned up and sometimes they did not. *Crimson* punches were in order at not infrequent intervals, and the whole organization was in the nature of a jolly fellowship."

The *Crimson* has always been very proud of its lightning extras. Way back in 1884 one of its editors wrote "the city dailies gave it credit for getting out extras in the quickest time ever known in the newspaper world. It broke all records by having an eight-page extra, containing a full report of the winter athletic games, running off the press in one-half a minute after the games were over. The extras were in the hands of the students as they came across the yard from the gym."

In 1893 the editors stepped up this pace and an extra after the Pennsylvania football game "was ready for sale within ten seconds after the game was finished." After this triumph someone suggested that the football game be abandoned entirely, and in its place annual contests between the *Crimson* and the Yale *Record* and other rival collegiate newspapers be held instead to see who could get out an extra the fastest and maybe knock the record down to say two seconds, but the idea never took hold with the various student bodies in Ivy-clad circles.

An early upstart competitor to the *Crimson* was the *News*, formed in 1894. Its editors were in the surprising habit of dropping around to the *Crimson* from time to time "in search of news which their menials had been unable to pick up. In order to impress the emissaries of the *News* with the vast resources of the *Crimson*, 'Mac' installed a telegraphic ticker in the office, with an operator's key in the composing room, which he worked vigorously as long as the enemy remained in hearing distance."

Today the *Crimson* also publishes a supplement, *The Harvard Crimson Review*, "The Friday Magazine Section of the Harvard Crimson." Complete with pictures (but no corset ads yet), this is an excellent, readable, and attractive sheet containing thoughtful articles on University and general topics, book reviews, notes on the arts, and a Crimson Crossword, or a particularly insane form of crossword called Puns and Anagrams. ("Every definition in the puzzle is either a pun, which suggests the answer rather than defining it, or an anagram, in which the letters of the answer are rearranged to form a new word." Got the idea? I haven't. Or rather, I have, but I have got to go pick up some razor blades and I'll see you later.)

The Harvard *Graduates Magazine* gives what appears

to be a rather reasonable estimate of the *Crimson*. (The role of the alumni magazine in American literature is to maintain a reasonable attitude at all times so as not to tread on the toes of any alumnus who might possibly be getting in the mood to donate a tuba to the band, a memorial bird bath, or eleven million dollars. This calls for considerable skill in egg-walking and most of the editors go barefoot.)

The *Graduates Magazine* says, reasonably:

"As the college has grown, and become a University in fact as well as in name, the *Crimson* has grown and become more important and more necessary to every student. Whatever may be its deficiencies, it is a thorough news-chronicler. On one hand, it contributes a great deal to the College life of its editors. On the other, it is a daily bulletin and record, which, now that the University has outgrown all unity and coherence, can boast of being in more than one way valuable and useful to its public."

That covers the situation pretty well, but the mildly querulous note about the outlandish size of the University seems a bit premature, written as it was in 1899.

Another famous publication at Harvard is the *Lampoon*, put out by a bunch of jolly fellows dedicated to laffs and to playing practical jokes on the *Crimson*. It is a "funny" magazine printed on nice rag paper but the *Crimson* doesn't think it is very funny and says so quite often. The *Crimson* reviews of the *Lampoon*'s humorous efforts seem to be written by Jack the Ripper. As college humor goes, the *Lampoon* is funny, and it is often a lot better than that. They work very hard at it and, as everybody knows, the harder you work at being funny the oftener you lay an egg. And since there are only about four funny men left in the country and they are all over fifty it is surprising what great material the *Lampoon* sometimes comes up with. Most college laff magazines are best at parody, and the *Lampoon* is not an exception. Last year *Mademoiselle* turned the *Lampoon* boys loose and the regular customers received a parody issue. Among other nifties was a bat on ads for miracle beauty creams, which extolled the virtue of a product called "Reduce-A-Leg." Two before-and-after pictures illustrated its magic limb-slenderizing properties. It was a case of a dame with hippo-style legs Before, and toothpicks After. Maybe this ain't so funny but such is the mental state of the American woman that the *Crimson* offices on Plymouth Street were swamped with legitimate orders for the product in spite of the Mack Sennett illustrations and the wild copy ("In the morning simply wipe away the cream and your legs will be firm, shapely, so tender to his touch").

The same issue had a good slasher by "Leo Lemon" which just about wraps up pretentious criticism for all time.

About an avant-garde play:

The action centers about a group of outspoken and off-beat students sitting around a table in a cafeteria and their collective and ultimately fruitless search for a cup of hot coffee. They are relentlessly rebuffed on all sides by a waitress, the police, and an intruding government tutor. The innocence that they tried to conceal at the beginning is clearly destroyed forever when one of them, asking for a piece of lemon-meringue pie, gets a plate of English muffins instead.

The *Lampoon* dates back to 1876 and is the oldest, and was for a long time after its inception the most successful, college magazine. All college magazines have had a hard time in the past few years and many of them have simply given up. The day of the He-and-She joke has passed and what has taken its place is usually not good enough to hold anybody's interest. Frankly, these magazines make for pretty tedious reading. It is all very well to say that John Marquand and Robert Benchley and Robert Sherwood and George Santayana wrote for the *Lampoon*, but if you go back and look up their stuff, well—I'll tell you what it is—it's college humor.

The *Lampoon* boys recently wrote words and music, performed, recorded, and released a hilarious long-play record album called "The Harvard Lampoon Tabernacle Choir Sings at Leningrad Stadium." The *Crimson* review of it was slightly more fiendish than usual, not so much a review as an assassination; but actually the record was fairly cool. And that's some tribute, because my thirteen-year-old daughter thinks it's The Greatest and I have heard it about one-thousand times, which is far too many times to hear anything, even "Uncle Josh Buys an Automobile" featuring Billy Murray. Jape collector Bennett Cerf's son Christopher was one of the leading talents contributing to the success of this disc. (The *Lampoon* describes it as a best-seller, but I imagine their idea of volume is different from that of the boards of directors of Dot, Victor, Capitol, Decca, etc.) And I bet young Cerf is tired of saying, "Yes, he is my old man."

The *Lampoon* is actually a social club, with headquarters in a curious Dutch castle in Mt. Auburn Street, built in 1910 and paid for largely by an ex-business manager of the magazine, William Randolph Hearst. The mascot is a stuffed ibis which the *Crimson* once pinched, took to New York, and presented to the Russian consul. Wot larks, Pip!

And my sympathies are with the *Lampoon* board in trying to keep an inventory of funny men on hand.

It is terribly difficult to be comical by the hour or by the month. Ask Sid Caesar. He knows.

CHAPTER V

More Dust & Bones:
Cotton & Increase Mather

It becomes difficult to get up early in the morning once a guy starts wearing silk pajamas.
—EDDIE ARCARO

AT THE TIME of Dunster's presidency of Harvard there was a law in Massachusetts forbidding arguing against or voicing disapproval of infant baptism. This is not a topic that gets much attention nowadays, even in Massachusetts, compared to the latest police scandal, but Puritan New England seems to have spent most of its time dotting its theological *is* and crossing its ecclesiastical *ts*.[1] In fact, several citizens who made the mistake of saying "The heck with infant baptism; I think it's a dopy idea"

---

[1] The reading matter in the Colonies was almost exclusively theological. Almost never are the works of English authors of the Restoration and Queen Anne's reign mentioned in native writings. Bliss Perry says that "No allusion to Shakespeare has been discovered in the colonial literature of the Seventeenth Century, and scarcely an allusion to the Puritan poet Milton." In 1723 the Harvard College library, which we might expect to have done better, contained none of the works of Addison, Steele, Bolingbroke, Pope, Dryden, or Swift. Cotton Mather's extensive library held no copy of Milton. In his voluminous works Ben Franklin never once alludes to Shakespeare.

were "deported" to Rhode Island, which was the religious tenderloin of the Colonies and wide open on baptismal rites and pinball games. For some reason President Dunster felt it necessary to take a public stand on his belief—heresy to his contemporaries—that, based on his study of the texts in all the learned languages, infant baptism was "unscriptural." The youngest of his children being about to be tapped for baptism, Dunster refused to permit it and went so far as to create a disturbance at the baptism of another child. This caused a sensation among the brethren. That Harvard's seemingly orthodox and upright President had switched to antipaedobaptism resulted in a horrible uproar, partly no doubt on account of the difficulty in pronouncing the name of his crime, and Dunster was called upon to recant. Being a man of principle, he refused and instead resigned and went to Scituate [2] (1950 population 5993). But he had been at Harvard long enough, fourteen years, to leave his mark. And Harvard still operates under the charter he acquired for it in 1650.

Dunster was followed by Chauncy, and Hoar, and Oakes, and Rogers, which takes us up to 1684. The first of these, Charles Chauncy, came from a prehistoric Hertfordshire family, was a graduate of Trinity College, Cambridge, and arrived in New England also afflicted with powerful convictions on the baptism topic. Chauncy went all out for nothing less than total immersion of colonial infants. Governor Bradford complained that this was "not so convenient in this could countrie," and after a round of censure by his colleagues Chauncy was about to pack up and go back to England when Harvard offered him the presidency. He promptly abandoned his insistence on complete dunking and for eighteen years devoted himself to the college, pious conduct, and the production of six sons (all of whom graduated from Harvard).

It was during Chauncy's reign that one of those noble experiments for the underprivileged was tried out, this time in the form of a college for Indians. Since none of

[2] There is no correct pronunciation of this word.

the Indians in the area had succeeded so far in graduating from the third grade, one would have thought scant need existed for them to have a college. None the less the English Society for Propagation of the Gospel in New England, acting on the same principle that sent bedwarmers to the Fiji islanders, built a two-story red-brick Indian College in the Harvard Yard, with classrooms, books, chalk, beanie hats, printed "Instructions to Freshmen," and quarters for twenty redskins thirsting for the complete story on Aristotle. Altogether, only four or five managed to pass the College Board Exams and gain admittance; of these only one, Caleb Cheeshahteaumuck, managed to garner the sheepskin. The most significant thing Caleb acquired from Christian civilization was tuberculosis, of which he died within a year of graduation, and probably with a headache from all that "*utor, fruor, fungor, potior,* and *vescor* take the ablative," and from trying to figure out how many angels can stand on the head of a pin.

Thanks to the restoration of the Stuarts back in Merrie England, the Puritans had hard times during Chauncy's administration and the Overseers reported to the General Court that their assets as a college added up to "a building, library, a few utensils, the press, some land which cannot be sold, £12 per annum to support four Fellows, and £15 per annum for scholarships."

By 1665 the Indian College had been abandoned and the Indians, who had been borrowed from Fenimore Cooper, were returned to him slightly the worse for wear but speaking proper Bostonian English, which accounts for the fact that all of Cooper's Indians behave and talk not so much like unto Indians as they do Congregationalist ministers. "The press" was set up in the former Indian College, where it functioned not only as the first American university press but also as the only press in the colonies. (This, you recall, was the Widow Glover's press which the college had gained via President Dunster's marriage to her.) Its output was considerable; in addition to printing an Indian translation of the Bible and a primer for

Indian children, it also produced such potboilers as Danforth's *Astronomical Description of the Late Comet or Blazing Star*, Vincent's story of the fire of London and the plague, and other cheery items such as Michael Wigglesworth's *Day of Doom*. The latter was a Book-of-the-Month Club selection, sold 1800 copies in 1662, and ran into two more editions. There is no record of the movie rights.

Chauncy was followed by Leonard Hoar, whose regime was punctuated by "disturbances among the students" until he resigned in dismay to be succeeded by Urian Oakes.

Oakes, a peppery little man, was one of the Overseers and a preacher and agreed to act as President until another could be located, on condition that he not be required to give up his pulpit. Nobody could be found who would take the job and after five years on a pro-tem basis Oakes was elected President, whereupon he died.

Harvard beat the bushes unsuccessfully for a new prexy and was without a President for a year until John Rogers was prevailed upon, cajoled, or bludgeoned into taking the job. Rogers, Cotton Mather says, "was of so sweet a temper that the title of *deliciae humani generis* might have on that score been given him." Or in other words, *e pluribus unum*. Perhaps his sweetness of temper contained elements of timidity or an antipathy toward the harsh voices and rude gestures of college students, for after accepting this high office he was so reluctant to leave his home town of Ipswich that it was a year before he actually appeared in Cambridge. Shortly afterward there was a total eclipse of the sun. His worst suspicions of Cambridge were confirmed and during the eclipse he died, in 1684.

At this point the Mathers entered from stage left and for the next twenty-five years caused more confusion than Clara Bow at a Methodist convention. Increase Mather and his son Cotton Mather were the extremely vocal leaders of the old-line faction in the Puritan church. To say that they held conservative views on church policy barely states the case. They make Godfrey Lowell Cabot [3] look like Trotsky. Each had a temper like a nail keg full of rattlesnakes; they were quick to take offense, eager and violent in controversy, proud—one might even say vain—and ambitious as a Jewish dentistry student. Also they were by far the most cultivated, scholarly, brilliant, and distinguished men of their times. How did they get that way? And aside from having funny names, who were they?

Increase's father was Richard Mather, born in 1596, who began at the age of fifteen to teach school at Toxteth Park, near Liverpool, and subsequently became minister of the Toxteth Chapel. His Puritan leanings soon got him in trouble and in 1634 the ecclesiastical authorities were forced to silence him. Silence being an unendurable condition to the Mather stock, he came to Massachusetts the following year and settled in Dorchester, Mass., formerly known as Mattapannock. Dorchester had been founded by 140 colonists from Dorsetshire, England, who came over on the ship *Mary and John*, and was the largest town in the colony until 1634. The Robert Pierce house, built in 1640, still stands, and in the graveyard is probably the oldest marked grave in the United States, that of Barnard Capen (died 1638), as well as those of William Stoughton, Chief Justice of the court which tried the Salem witches, who founded the first Stoughton Hall at Harvard—and Richard Mather.

Richard Mather was a preacher, writer, translator, and scholar, active in colonial church councils and one of the most famous New England Puritans of his time. His first wife was Katherine Holt, of Bury, England, by whom he had six sons, four of whom became ministers, and one of whom they saddled with the name Increase. His second wife was Sara Cotton, widow of the Reverend John Cotton of Boston.

Increase graduated from Harvard at seventeen in the

[3] Godfrey Lowell Cabot, Class of 1882, had his hundredth birthday on February 26, 1961.

Class of 1656 and took his M.A. at Trinity College, Dublin, after which he was minister for three years to five different congregations in England, returning to America in 1661 to become famous. The first thing he did, however, was to marry Maria Cotton, his step-sister, daughter of the Widow Cotton his father had married after the demise of the Reverend John Cotton. Got all that?

By this marriage Increase Mather became the son-in-law of "The Patriarch of New England," a man who in old rock-bottom theocratic New England had been of almost unbounded popularity and whose influence, "both in ecclesiastical and in civil affairs, was probably greater than that of any other minister." The marriage was obviously made in heaven (Congregationalist heaven); Father Cotton had been twice as religious and famous as anybody at the fair. For his opinions he had been rudely jostled about in England, from which he escaped in disguise (wearing a false nose, a fright wig, and a fake mustache, secured by mail from Johnson Smith & Co., Racine, Wis.) to the hospitality of Boston, landing in the vicinity of Filene's. He was a prolific writer and a prodigious scholar. Among his most famous outpourings was a book for children—not unlike Dr. Doolittle, one assumes, but with a much longer title. It was called *Milk for Babes, Drawn out of the Breasts of Both Testaments, Chiefly for the Spiritual Nourishment of Boston Babes in either England, but may be of like Use for any Children.*

Increase Mather prospered with Maria and his tribe increased, notably with the addition of his son Cotton, named not in honor of Eli Whitney as has often been surmised, but for his grandfather on his mother's side, the eminent divine. Increase became minister of the Second Church of Boston, licenser of the press, and a Fellow of Harvard. Great social and political prestige was enjoyed in those far-off days by the big-time preachers, and as the leader of a large Boston church Increase Mather was at the top of the heap. Thus when he was proffered the office of President of Harvard he accepted on the condition (taking his cue from Oakes) that he be not required to give up his church or leave Boston. Overawed by Mather's pompous bearing and fame, the Overseers accepted, but gave him the appointment as Acting President only.

From 1685 until 1701 the Overseers spent most of their time insisting unsuccessfully that Increase Mather should reside at the college. He wanted both cakes and didn't want to eat either one. The subway had not yet been put in, and to reach Cambridge from Boston meant either a tedious trip through Charlestown via ferry or a long roundabout ride through Roxbury and Brookline. Things being like this, Harvard's President made only sporadic appearances in Cambridge and devoted most of his time to the concoction of inspirational sermons three hours in length for his large Sunday-morning congregation. (The Brookline Country Club golf course was not laid out until 1890, and the Myopia Hunt Club course in 1891.) At one point he was absent in England for a full four years (1688–'92) on a political mission. When he came back he said that now at last he would move to Cambridge, so he was elected President. Whereupon he resumed his ministry in Boston. For the next nearly ten years he kept putting off calling the movers (claiming that he had lost their telephone number), and in fact never did take up residence in Cambridge.

One reason he didn't care to get too close to Harvard was his dislike for college life and his nervous contempt for youth, whom he called "children."

"Should I leave preaching to 1500 souls, for I suppose so many ordinarily attend our congregations,[4] only to expound to 40 or 50 children, few of them capable of edification by such exercises, I doubt I should no do well."

By this time his son Cotton (Class of 1678, A.M. 1681) had become a Fellow of Harvard College and father and son were the leaders of a bitter faction fighting to maintain the old-time religion and the rockbound ministry. The

[4] An interesting supposition. My guess is he counted the house each week like one of the Shubert brothers.

Mathers' concept of Harvard was that it was only to be a farm club leading to the Big Leagues, which was of course the Congregationalist ministry. The Mathers wanted nobody on the Harvard faculty but strict cast-iron Puritans. So they argued about that. And they argued about charters. And they argued about doctrine, the power of visitation, politics. They wrote pamphlets attacking and pamphlets explaining. They were an awful bore.

They were chiefly a bore because times were changing and they were still back on Plymouth Rock. New England was on the verge of the new enlightenment but the Mathers couldn't see it. In the end it was a good thing for Harvard that Increase would not bring himself to cross the Charles River; if he had, with his strong personality and fanaticism, he would undoubtedly have poured Harvard into a sectarian cement from which it might never have extricated itself. Fortunately for the college, during President Mather's peregrinations, things were left in the hands of two of New England's and Nature's noblemen, John Leverett and William Brattle. They were actively in tune with the new spirit of the times, turned on the heat, and brought to an end theological cud-chewing. For the first time Harvard's fame began to spread widely. Leverett subsequently became one of Harvard's greatest and most revered presidents.

The end of the Mathers' influence on Harvard came just after the turn of the century. In 1701 the Overseers put it bluntly to Increase Mather: Either resign the ministry or resign the presidency. Heaving volcanic sighs, after sixteen years on the fence he finally climbed down and trudged unwillingly to Cambridge. Six months of collegiate living among the "children" was such a comedown and "proved so disgusting to eminent Mr. Mather, that he gave it up after Commencement, 1701, and returned to Boston, where the Church (by pre-arrangement no doubt) had kept his seat warm." [5]

Thus ended Harvard's formative period, grown from

[5] Morison.

nothing in sixty-five years to a college capable of award-
ing degrees respected throughout the world and in the
words of himself, Increase Mather, son of Richard, son-
in-law of John Cotton, "*Noble:* for where is the Like in
all the English America. . . . 'T was therefore a brave and
happy thought that first pitched upon this *Colledge.*"

But what of Cotton, that fluffy fellow? What Cotton
wanted was to be President of Harvard. He thought he
had a right to it. Wasn't he the leading intellectual of his
time? Wasn't he turning out several printed works a year
with machinelike regularity? Wasn't it in the stars that he
would be elected to the Royal Society in London? (He
was.) Did he not carry on a constant correspondence with
European scholars? Was he not a paragon of Congregationalist virtue and an authority on ecclesiastical fine
print? His erudition, was it not prodigious? Had he not
condoned the burning of witches in Salem and staged a
private and noble burning of books himself right in the
Harvard yard?

"True. How true," murmured the Overseers of Harvard as they elected Samuel Willard head man in 1701
and John Leverett in 1708. Perhaps it was Cotton's dicta-
torial tone that cost him the one honor he coveted more
than any other. Or, in the words of Duncan Glab, the
popular crooner, "That guy has a lot of personality—all
of it lousy."

But his disappointment over the presidency of Harvard,
his pious attitudes, and the production of over 350 published works didn't interfere with Cotton Mather's home-
work. He had fifteen children.

Cotton's irritation, verging on mania, over the insult to
his pride in being passed over twice as Harvard's President
was slow to cool. He continued to snipe at the college
and as late as 1723 was complaining about total corruption
of the students who, he insinuated darkly, were teetering
on the brink of the hot place by secretly reading such
salacious works as "plays, novels, empty and vicious pieces

of poetry, and even Ovid's Epistles. . . ." [6] An investigation followed these accusations which did indeed reveal numerous collegiate excesses such as visiting one another rather than praying on Saturday evenings. ("Had a pretty cool bull session in Abijah's room last night") and "going into town, on Sabbath mornings, to breakfast" ("Slept late but took a tolerable breakfaste at Hayes-Bykfordes for sixpence").

And even after the beloved President Leverett died, Cotton Mather felt it necessary to describe the man who had reorganized Harvard's finances, secured her first endowed chair, and established for all time the liberal tradition, as "the infamous drone." This endearing phrase was prompted by the fact that Leverett left no published works.

Leverett died in 1724. Cotton Mather was now sixty-one, a seemly age for a college president, and he was more famous than, if just as ornery as, ever. Now, now, he *knew* the Overseers could not pass him by again. And it would be a fitting climax to a life of scholarship and good works (and of intrigue and backbiting, cruelty to those who disagreed with him, and arrogance). If Puritan faces were capable of beaming, Cotton beamed (in the privacy of his chambers) as he contemplated the happy honor: President Cotton Mather of Harvard. Most suitable, most suitable. What they needed out there at the end of the trolley line was a firm hand and a return to the principles of 1636. He danced a brief Congregational jig and planned a good book-burning. First, Ovid's *Epistles.* . . .

But the Overseers did not cotton to Mr. Mather. In fact they were down on him. They had really had enough of his omniscience and felt that almost anyone would be more suitable and useful to Harvard in the role of Presi-

[6] With some pain and embarrassment one can't help thinking of what the Reverend Mather would make of *Tropic of Cancer* by Mr. Henry Miller and the four-column rave review of this strange work in the Harvard *Crimson Review*, Dec. 9, 1961.

dent. They elected Benjamin Wadsworth, minister of the First Church in Boston and a member of the Harvard Corporation.

Mather stopped beaming rather suddenly and wrote in his diary, "The Corporation of our miserable College do again treat me with their accustomed indignity." It was Mather's last chance at Harvard and he had lost. Four years later he died.

One of Cotton Mather's lesser programs that achieved success was the renaming of the Collegiate School of Connecticut. It had been founded in 1701 by a group of conservative Harvard graduates who felt that the old school was going to the dogs on matters of theology. The college was patterned after Harvard. Warm relations existed between the two schools. Their difference lay in the fact that the Collegiate School of Connecticut was strictly dedicated to sectarian righteousness.

In 1718 Cotton Mather suggested a new name for the school.

The name Harvardman Mather suggested was Yale.

THE PENNY ARCADE

At Harvard, learning is kept in cold storage—At the Sign of the Marble Minerva. At Yale the article is served on a hot platter, fresh from the great brain-works which glow continually like a blast-furnace, lighting up the New Haven sky on Winter nights with the radiance of an aurora borealis. No earnest reformer can go to New Haven without feeling a little blue.

"We are democratic," says the Machine with a thousand voices at Yale.

The brakeman, ere he lets you off the train, yells:

> Noo-oo Haven! Noo-oo Haven!
> Democ-ra-see
> with a one, two, three!
> And here you be,
> Right at the great Univer-si-tee!
> Rah-rah-rah, Yale!!

The Cabman who drives you up to the campus repeats the cheer as he slaps up his lame horse, and the colored waiter at the hotel shouts in your ear:

> Lam' chops, po'k chops,
> Coffee or tea, sah!
> Mince pie, apple pie,
> Which'll it be, sah?
> We's democracktick heah, yo' see,
> Eberbody loves de Facultee,
> Yah, yah, yah!
> Rah-rah-rah!
> Yale!

The Democratic Machine will tell you that there are no money-prejudices among the students. I myself have noticed that the railway president's son living in Vanderbilt carries with him no social stigma. He is often as well received, I am told, as any poor student-waiter in the University eating-clubs. If a man runs an automobile and keeps a yacht, his snobbish display of personal property is apt to be overlooked as merely incidental to his many sterling qualities, and any embarrassment he may feel is promptly drowned in a sea of cheers.

This system has led to the Personal Popularity Habit which, as practiced at Yale, has become a violent physical exercise, often more fraught with dangers than the practice and application of football. Only last year the most popular man in his class was slapped on the back until he became a cripple for life.

Everywhere it is a case of Yale-fellow-well-met. The son of Eli is surcharged with temperament, which makes it necessary for him to be yelling, singing, talking, practical joking continually. When there is nothing really important in the way of athletics or ambrosial nights to hold the undergrad's attention, he thinks of his neglected education and buys a "pony" with which he rough-rides for a brief season through Ancient Greece. President Roosevelt has a Yale temperament with a Harvard training, much as Secretary Taft has a Yale training with a Heidelberg shape. And here the question naturally arises: Have our Universities been responsible, after all, for the shaping of our great national figures?

—Wallace Irwin
1907

LADIES PAGE
& HOMEMAKERS DEPT.

Courtesy of *The New York Times*

SUNDAY

Roast pork

Mashed turnips   Harvard beets

Mixed green salad

Cheesecake

HARVARD BEETS

2½ cups sliced cooked or canned beets
⅓ cup sugar
2 teaspoons cornstarch
¼ cup vinegar
1 tablespoon butter

1. Drain the beets, reserving one-quarter cup of the liquid.

2. Combine the sugar and cornstarch and stir in the vinegar and reserved beet liquid (or water). Cook, stirring, over low heat until the mixture is thickened and smooth.

3. Add the beets and butter and cook until heated
Yield: Four to six servings.

CHAPTER VI

Gravy Spots

Nathan threw a piece of bread
And hit Abijah on the head.
The wrathful Freshman, in a trice,
Sent back another bigger slice;
Which, being butter'd pretty well,
Made greasy work where'er it fell.
And thus arose a fearful battle;
The coffee cups and saucers rattle;
The bread bowls fly at woeful rate,
And break many a learned pate. . . .
—The Rebelliad, 1818

"'I found a live worm in my salad about three weeks ago,' Richard P. Holmes, '62, reported to Administration officials yesterday."
—The *Crimson*, Dec. 13, 1961

SINCE IT is in a metropolitan area and has a very hep student body, there is a lot of talk about food at Harvard. Students everywhere have always been notoriously hungry and since 1636 the Crimson lads have been hollering about food and the beverages which accompany it. In this they are merely participating in the great, national, continuous blabber about grub, which reaches its finest form in New York City, where it sometimes takes four people over an hour to decide which thrilling restaurant to eat at.

What this country obviously doesn't need is some more baloney about eating. The way it is right now every time a magazine needs something to put in between the advertisements they jam in some color photos of Robert Preston[1] or some other celebrity in his charming dining room with his favorite casserole flanked with gleaming oversize Brussels sprouts, his grandmother's gravy boat, some ominous bottles of wine, and a lot of neatly folded napkins. In the accompanying copy you can read (if you *can* read) his wife's recipe for a tantalizing cocktail-hour "dip" that all the world of Show Biz is yelling hurray about. *Playboy* magazine features constant dope on how a guy can overcome some long-legged and sexy broad by preparing and serving hot exotic viands in front of the fireplace in his luxurious bachelor apt. This dame is either going to Come Across or she isn't regardless of the menu, but this is not mentioned in the text. Neither are figures given for the number of portions of sweetbreads à la Rasputin that have burned to cinders while the bachelor and the blonde are wrestling on the couch. Actually, since this routine has become obligatory I have given up going out with girls because I've got this pretty crummy furnished flat over the Factory Outlet Shoe Store down by the railroad station and it hasn't got any fireplace and the kitchen looks like the day after the Battle of Manassas Junction. I used to take girls to the Hi Ho Bar and Grill where this fellow plays the accordion on Friday and Saturday nights but nowadays they say "Why don't you

---

[1] Who couldn't hardly buy a subway token without showing his draft card until Leonard Lyons (C. C. N. Y.), Brooks Atkinson (Harvard '17, not to be confused with Henry David Thoreau, Harvard Class of 1837, or Ralph Waldo Emerson, Harvard 1821), Walter Kerr (Northwestern '37), Walter Winchell (Public School 184, 116th St. near Lenox Ave.), and Richard Watts (Columbia '21) told everybody to start liking him on a/c his lead role in *The Music Man*, 1957, by Meredith Willson (an Iowa boy).

ever ask me to your flat and cook me up a meal like them guys in *Dude, Playboy, Nugget,* and magazines of that-there type?" Some of *Playboy's* imitators even have articles on "aphrodisiac" foods to feed the girl friend, but if I was to go that far I figure it would be cheaper to just stun her with a brick wrapped in a bath towel instead.

There are so many cookbooks being printed you'd think eating was the leading national sport. There are also Guide Books to Good Eating which tell you in no uncertain tones which short-order lunch counter in Coal City, West Va., is serving the best vinaigrette these days and what wines to avoid at the same spot. Usually the preferred eatery is one that none of the local Elks would enter unless forced to take shelter from a hailstorm, and in actual fact serves lime-gelatin salad with nuts and very small hunks of marshmallow imbedded in it, tastefully arrayed alongside the lobster tails.

Even *The New York Times* features recipes. Today it is a full page, for example, headed "St. Mark's Place Specializes in Polish-Style Gastronomy" and has four pictures of frightening sausages and a Chas. Addams complete boar's head ready for parboiling plus recipes for "bigos," "babka," and "homemade kielbasa." Not only that, gents, but on the next page of the *Times* are four more recipes: "stuffed eggs au gratin," "tandoori chicken," "strawberry fantasy à la minute" (I'm not kidding), and last of all—well, say, look who's here: "Harvard Beets."

Even *Boy's Life* gives recipes, usually on how to make beanhole beans.

And *Look* magazine (published by Gardner Cowles, Exeter '21, Harvard '25) this week has a full-color feature on how to eat a Game Dinner. In one of the pictures Eddie Albert and his wife are watching Dina Merrill "defy calories." Eddie was born Edward Albert Heimberger and went to the University of Minnesota, where he was a buddy of Roger Roshek's, and it is a rare treat to be able to look at a picture of him watching Dina Merrill eat if you haven't got much to do.

Just to keep in the running, *Life* magazine follows up *Look*'s Game Dinner and goes them one better with not only a Food cover on the magazine but a thirteen-page full-color riot (with recipes) of Christmas puddings, cakes, fondants, sugar plums, cream fillings, *buche de Nöel*, mincemeats, orange sauce, leckerli, kourabiedes, bourbon balls, Spanish almond wreaths, Dutch butter slices, panettone, schnecken, orange honey braid, coconut ice trees, and other goodies subsidized by the Arm and Hammer folks. They go so far as to have these creations photographed by Eliot Elisofon (Fordham '33)—who really knows his way around in the better cake-dough circles—against a background consisting of a "Christmas tree hung with 18th Century Italian terra cotta creche figures and angels in sumptuous silk robes," from the collection of Mrs. Howell H. Howard. Just like down on the farm.

Also *Sunshine and Health*, the ever-popular nudist magazine, besides showing constant pictures of naked ladies and gentlemen playing volleyball and building swimming pools, on occasion plies the reader with health recipes.

In other words, it is almost impossible to pick up a piece of reading matter in this country without receiving unwanted instructions on what or where to eat. It is surprising under the circumstances that from Maine to California it is impossible to purchase an edible piece of toast in a public restaurant.[2]

And don't think that if you "Eat where the truck drivers eat" you can't go wrong, because that is just an invitation to more limp toast, plus watery mashed potatoes served with an ice-cream scoop. Moreover, if you ask for the Home-Made Chili Our Specialty you will be told Thelma makes the chili and it is her day off. Or if you

---

[2] ". . . and many cubic feet of permanently buttered toast."—Clifton Fadiman.

prefer, step behind the scenes at your favorite snobbish French-cuisine-type hash house in New York City where the tab never comes to less than the price of a good used car and look at the half-gallon tin cans of vegetables in the storeroom, and case the deep-freeze dept. They have not heard of a fresh green pea since Luther Burbank died, although the *ris de veau braisée aux fruits de Périgord* is so terrific you are not allowed to eat it at all, but for eleven dollars they will take a portion out of the safe and let you look at it for ten minutes while inhaling through imported gauze.

Having given New York the customary kick in the pants we will now proceed to a culinary tour of the Harvard area, let the gravy fall where it will, usually on the undergraduate's only good necktie. But don't expect too much inside dope, because I am the fellow who goes to the same restaurant every Thursday for five years and at the end of this period all the help still keeps looking at me as though I was going to put some teaspoons in my pocket.

Any discussion of Harvard eating must start off with Locke-Obers' superlative restaurant tucked up an alley called Winter Place, near Tremont Street. If we avert our eyes and avoid thinking about that new addition they put in upstairs, there is not too much that has changed about this temple of culture since the era of the hansom cab. It is a fine and ennobling place, last redecorated in 1886, and its like is not to be found in any other college town in our country. It smacks of ancient times and truly good living, of lobsters off the Portland boat and class, man, class—with the old-time waiters, the slightly musty private rooms with heavy draperies, the red faces of Boston bankers bent over mutton chops,—in fact the whole script was written by Lucius Beebe (Harvard '25, Yale '26, Harvard '27, last seen leaning against a telephone pole in Virginia City, Nevada). He was pretty sore about Prohibition and apropos of same and of Locke-Obers he says:

". . . the most gracious and comforting tavern that

ever survived an era of outrage, pillage, and Federal barbarism, Frank Locke's Winter Place Wine Rooms. It has been variously known as the Dutchman's, as Winter Place Restaurant, as Locke's, and as Locke-Obers, and even, to irreverent undergraduates, as the Nekked Lady, but by any other name it smells the same; fragrant and holy in the souvenirs of many discerning men of several generations."

On a winter night with some good companions, almost nothing could ever be so good again for the Young Man from Iowa as an evening at Locke's and lobster thermidor. Big brothers at Harvard gave their young brothers down from Exeter or Andover a taste of what was to come, if they would only bring up that Latin or Chemistry, by taking them to Locke's and feeding them on Cape oysters, turtle soup, jackrabbit stews, and introducing them to somebody in History and Literature at the next table. All was peace and gleaming silverware and the Young Man from Iowa thought deeply of life, for he had never had turtle soup before or seen such magnificence. It made him think of Dickens and Thackeray and of England and New England. He didn't understand what his brother and his brother's friends were talking about ("And then Frisky said . . . I mean after all, Salvemini? . . . There was a young lady from Wheeling . . . he'll never make *summa* . . . on the way back from Wellesley . . . at the Signet dinner . . . there we were in Tuckerman's Ravine. . . ."), but he knew that something was happening, as he cast furtive glances at the famous barroom nude, that he would be back, that there was a reason for Latin and Geometry and knowing six reasons for the decline of Rome—what it meant was that if you knew the answers you could go to Harvard and eat at Locke-Obers and afterward walk up the snowy Boston Common and from thence to your chambers at Cambridge. And it would all go on forever and ever and there would be A Girl who would also know about Salvemini and Tuckerman's Ravine that you could bring some wonderful evening to Locke's and with whom you could climb the stairs to the ladies and gentlemen's dining room above and share a bottle of hock. (What on earth was *hock?*)

I am sorry to say that life has all been downhill for some Harvard men since their last dinner in senior year at Locke's. The Little League and the Community Chest Drive have not been adequate substitutes.

Down Tremont Street past the Hotel Touraine and left down Stuart Street a half-block is Jacob Wirth Co., a peerless German restaurant with brass rails, sawdust on the floor, and waiters shouting in German. Nothing has changed there in fifty years or more—always the same in Boston. The waiters were all over eighty in my time. A new generation has come, also all eighty or giving that impression, and with them a new generation of students calling for seidels of dark and explaining the motto over the bar: *Suum cuique*—"Every Man for Himself."

No beatniks, no show folks, and no bums, either.

Students have been discovering Jake Wirth's since 1868 and gorging themselves on bratwurst, thick green pea soup in equally thick white soup plates, brisket with horse-radish, beautiful dark rye bread *without* the ever-present New York caraway seeds, New England boiled dinner (incidentally, never offer a girl New England boiled din-ner—somehow it just kills romance; boiled dinner is wife food), fish chowder, and lobster salad, the latter a *Meis-terwerk*.

The Parker House, at Tremont and School Streets in Boston, invented the Parker House roll and is very old Boston, very stately, very quiet and dignified. The service can't be beat. Students do not congregate at the Parker House very much, but visiting fathers and grandfathers take them there for honeycomb tripe à la Parker and the traditional codfish tongues and cheeks. (Sounds pretty awful, doesn't it?) Old grads love the Parker House and on the day of the Yale game the lobby is filled with polo coats, chesterfields, and beautiful ladies in tweeds and furs.

Three blocks away there existed until recently on Harvard Street—directly across from the Howard Atheneum, America's most famous burlesque house, where many generations of prep-school boys got their first and never-to-be-forgotten view of the Eternal Mystery—perhaps the worst beanery on the eastern seaboard. It was known as Joe and Nemo's; the windows hadn't been washed since President Dunster's time (1640–54); and its specialty was hot dogs. Staggering out of the Old Howard, with glazed eyes and feverish pulse, paralyzed by the slapstick buffoonery and the acres of white female skin, the student would totter across the street to Joe and Nemo's and regain his senses with a hot dog and a bottle of tonic, which is what they still call pop in Boston. The Old Howard shut down years ago and recently burned. The entire area is being razed for blocks around by some master plan of city beautification, and where Ann Corio and Georgia Sothern used to wiggle their beaded G-strings, pleasant fountains and shady bowers, Roman temples and marvels of modern architecture will soon arise.

Over on Park Square is Pieroni's Sea Grill, which never seems to make the "Where to Eat in Boston" lists in *Holiday* and *Esquire* but which to one old-time Boston eater is among the best. It is large, bright, and cheerful and has successfully managed to dispense both first-rate seafood *and* Italian food for lo these many years. One has a feeling that he might even get a piece of good toast here. The last time I attended a session at Pieroni's they had collared the only chef in all of Massachusetts who knew what to do about a French-fried potato. I imagine he is gone now, probably to Kansas City where they appreciate such things. Although there are none, one has a feeling of potted palms at Pieroni's, and the turkey trot. Spotless napery. Snappy waitresses.

The Union Oyster House is available at all times at its old stand at 41 Union Street for the best in broiled, baked, stuffed, thermidored, Newburged, fried, sautéed, and stewed lobsters. Also offering daily and Sundays every possible combination of clams, oysters, Cape scallops, mackerel, scrod, salmon, halibut, swordfish, smelts, cod, haddock, sole, blowfish, bluefish, and lumpfish. It's the oldest restaurant within striking distance for a Harvard boy with a date and has had the doors open since 1826. The building was once the home of Louis Philippe and the prices are not going to spoil your fun. Steaks and chops if you don't dig the fins.

All the above-named restaurants plus many others, such as those in Boston's Chinatown, for example, are available to the Harvard student via a subway ride to Park Street and a brief walk. Just keep writing home, boys, and say "Passed Philosophy 102. Send money." You can eat like a king.

But we have not finished with Boston. Across from Faneuil Hall, amid the debris of the wholesale provision markets and surrounded by shabby eighteenth- and nineteenth-century buildings about to collapse with fatigue, up a staircase out of "The Perils of New York," is situated the most curious and to some the most satisfying dining room in Boston. Durgin-Park features long family-style tables and waitresses who rather resent your presence but hurl the food around with amazing dexterity and speed. The menu is strictly basic New England (this "strictly New England" bit may be getting tiresome) and features the usual stews and lobsters, broiled scrod, Yankee pot roast, real "old-fashioned" baked beans, and strawberry shortcake not like Toffenetti's at all but actually just like good ol' Mom used to make. The place is always jammed halfway down the staircase, the noise is deafening, the Indian pudding famous as far as Damariscotta, Maine, and the prices commence low and don't get any funny ideas along the way. No boy from Missoula, Mont., is considered really Harvard until he has been to Durgin-Park. There is no booze, no reservations, and the doors close with a snap at 7:30 P.M.

The last hostelry on my abbreviated Boston list, you will be relieved to know, is not real down-to-earth old traditional New England. A request for old-fashioned

Salem corn dodgers or Indian pudding would result in a police call and soon afterward you would find yourself standing on the sidewalk on Arlington Street wondering what happened. I refer of course to the Ritz, one of the very few fine hotels left in this Republic, despite what Mr. Hilton and those promoters in Miami Beach think of their joints. The management of the Ritz in Boston does not spend twenty thousand per week to bludgeon you with floor shows starring Joe E. Lewis, the Lennon Sisters, and somebody called Paul Anka; instead they concentrate on decorum, service, food, bed linen, well-modulated voices, rooms in which an actor's agent has not thrown a beer bottle at his client, missing him and leaving an interesting stain on the wall, and in creating an all-over feeling that perhaps you are not in the U.S.A. at all but in a good London hotel. The Ritz is one reason why so many shows on their pre-Broadway tryouts choose to come to Boston instead of Philadelphia. The producers and directors certainly aren't fond of Boston audiences, who often sit through shows as though under the influence of pain-killer, or of the critics either, or of the climate (rain, turning to snow, turning to rain), or of the town itself, to whose historic charms they are magnificently and outspokenly oblivious,[3] but they are united in their fondness—amounting to maudlin idiocy—over the Ritz.

The Ritz is sold out for twenty-five years in advance for the Harvard–Yale week end, but I don't think it is much of a haunt of the undergraduate, except for some of those sophisticated New York boys. And I hope I never stroll down Arlington Street and see a new sign up: *Hilton-Ritz* or *Sheraton-Ritz*. Boys, I love you both, but leave the Ritz in Boston alone. We haven't got too much left these days.

[3] "Boston, incidentally, changes with every trip. (For the worse.) Our stage manager was mugged getting the newspapers the other evening. I was followed all the way to the theatre by two junkies, and so on. It's a tacky Irish Sodom and Gomorrah."—from a letter to the author from a producer with a show trying out at the Shubert.

Back in Cambridge, the food quest is more on a catch-as-catch-can basis, as in most college towns. Eating places are numerous, ranging from candle-lit tearooms to the now-famous Elsie's, whose roast-beef sandwiches at fifty cents are probably the best buy in Middlesex County and possibly in any county. Elsie's also has a caviar-and-cream-cheese sandwich of indelicate proportions whose like I have not seen anywhere else. It's a formidable affair and the only sandwich, to my knowledge, to have won a Rhodes scholarship.

At Cronin's resturant, on Mt. Auburn Street, the student from the landlocked reaches beyond the Mississippi can regale himself on Grilled Norwegian Whale Steak, French-fried pots, and chef's salad for $1.50, plus a Full Line of Choice Liquors and Imported and Domestic Beers "At Harvard It's Cronin's."

At Harvard it is also Brigham's, St. Clair's Hayes-Bickford's, espresso joints, several Chinese joints, a Japanese joint, and so forth. Hayes-Bickford nowadays has a lot more girls sitting around nursing cups of coffee than it used to, most of them sporting black stockings and care-free hair. There are several Italian restaurants and pizza outlets, one of them called the Cambridge Tower of Pizza,[4] which features thirty-four kinds of delicious SUB-MARINES and twenty-one kinds of hot sizzling PIZZAS to take out. Finding fragments of cold, unsizzling pizzas around the room on a gray Sunday morning in Cambridge is one of those down-to-earth experiences that prepares the student for the future and drives home the ephemeral nature of sensual pleasures and libertine living more effectively than almost anything suggested to the inquiring mind in the 325 pages of the *Courses of Instruction offered by the Faculty of Arts and Sciences.*

---

[4] Evidently a spelling error. The Tower of Pisa is located in the town and archepiscopal see of the same name in Tuscany, Italy. The campanile in question has assumed an oblique position and attracts many tourists. It was erected in 1174 by Bonanno. The tower was 15½ feet out of perpendicular in 1829, and 16½ feet in 1910.

If you are a dwarf gourmet, or even one of medium stature, there is a French restaurant on Garden Street tailored to your needs called the Petit Gourmet. If you are of normal height you might possibly gain admittance by entering on your knees, like Jose Ferrer (Princeton '33) in his inimitable portrayal of Toulouse-Lautrec. If you happen to come from New York and cannot subsist on anything but French cookery there are also Club Henry IV, which says it is "A Deux Pas de Vous" (how do they know where I am?) and Chez Jean, self-styled "authentique French restaurant."

Last and most heavily patronized are the college dining halls. Although the food in these establishments is substantial and of good quality, no mention of them is found in *Dining Out in America, Where to Eat in New England, A Teen-Age Guide to Soft-Shell Crabs, Indigestion For Everybody, A Gourmet Adrift in Saskatchewan*, or in any of the other standard texts. This cannot be because of poor publicity, because since 1638 the patrons of these fine cafés have been howling their approval at the top of their lungs, staging periodic riots in their enthusiasm for the delectable fare, and even throwing buns at tutors as a blanket ratification of the roast rack of lamb bourgeoisie and the steamed chocolate pudding with foamy sauce. In 1766, for example, gravied mashed potatoes were hurled. In December 1788, "bisket, tea cups, saucers, and a KNIFE were thrown. . . ." In these and other ways the students have always shown evidence of their trust and affection for the college commissary department, hence we are led to doubt the authenticity of an eighteenth-century old grad's reminiscences when he stated: "The Provisions were badly cooked the Soups were dreadful we frequently had Puddings made of flower and Water and boiled so hard we frequently threw them about and kicked them about." The acute student of historic trends may find here not so much a comment on the quality of the food as a hint of the possible origins of football.

In summing up, let us admit that, gastronomywise, Boston has just one shady feature in the over-all national food picture: it was in The Hub where Howard Johnson started it all. Anybody with four kids will know what I mean. But the Harvard student, washing down giant liverwurst sandwiches on pumpernickel bread with foaming seidels of beer at the Wursthaus, is all unaware, in his ignorance of Real Life, of this sinister aspect of Things to Come.

He'll find out:

"But Karen dear, we just *stopped* at a Howard Johnson's only forty-five minutes ago. . . ."

THE PENNY ARCADE

What the College Incubator Did for One Modest Lambkin, by George Ade

from "Breaking into Society"

One Autumn afternoon a gray-haired Agriculturist took his youngest Olive Branch by the Hand and led him away to a Varsity. Wilbur was 18 and an Onion. He had outgrown his last year's tunic, and his Smalls were hardly on speaking terms with his Uppers. He had large warty Hands, which floated idly at his sides and his Wrists resembled extra Sets of Knuckles. When he walked, his Legs gave way at the Hinge and he Interfered. On his Head was a little Wideawake with a Buckle at the Side. Mother had bobbed his Hair and rubbed in a little goose grease to make it shine. The Collar that he wore was a size 13, and called the Rollo Shape. It rose to a Height of a half inch above his Neck-Band. For a Cravat he had a piece of watered Silk Ribbon with butterflies on it.

Wilbur had his Money tied up in a Handkerchief and he carried a Paper Telescope, loaded down with one complete

Change and a Catalogue of the Institution showing that the Necessary Expenses were not more than $3.40 per week.

As the train pulled away from Pewee Junction, Wilbur began to Leak. Salt Tears trickled down through the Archipelago of Freckles. He wanted to Crawfish, but Paw bought him a box of Crackerjack and told him that if he got an education and improved his Opportunities some day he might be County Superintendent of Schools and get his $900 a Year just like finding it. So Wilbur spunked up and said he would try to stick it out. He got out the Catalogue and read all of the copper-riveted Rules for the Moral Guidance of Students.

The Curriculum had him scared. He saw that in the next four Years he would have to soak up practically all the Knowledge on the Market. But he was cheered to think that if he persevered and got through he would be entitled to wear an Alpaca Coat and a Lawn Tie and teach in the High-School, so he took Courage and began to notice the Scenery.

Wilbur was planted in a Boarding-House guaranteed to provide Wholesome Food and a Home Influence. Father went back after making a final Discourse on the importance of learning most everything in all the Books.

Nine Months later they were down at the Depot to meet Wilbur. He had written several times, saying that he could not find time to come Home, as he was in pursuit of Knowledge every Minute of the Day, and if he left the Track, Knowledge might gain several Laps on him. It looked reasonable, too, for the future Superintendent of Schools had spent $400 for Books, $200 for Scientific Apparatus, and something like $60 for Chemicals to be used in the Laboratory.

When the Train suddenly checked itself, to avoid running past the Town, there came out of the Parlor Car something that looked like Fitz, on account of the Padding in the Shoulders. Just above one Ear he wore a dinky Cap about the size of a Postage Stamp. The Coat reached almost to the Hips and was buttoned below. The Trousers had enough material for a suit. They were reefed to show feverish Socks of a zigzag Pattern. The Shoes were Very Bull-Doggy, and each had a wide Terrace running around it. Father held on to a Truck for Support. Never before had he seen a genuine Case of the inflammatory Rah-Rahs.

Wilbur was smoking a dizzy little Pipe from which the Smoke curled upward, losing itself in a copious Forelock that moved gently in the Breeze. Instead of a Collar, Wilbur was wearing a Turkish Towel. He had the Harvard Walk down pat. With both Hands in his Pockets, the one who had been pursuing Knowledge teetered towards the Author of his Being and said, "How are you, Governor?"

Father was always a Lightning Calculator, and as he stood there trying to grasp and comprehend and mentally close in, as it were, on the Burlap Suit and the Coon Shirt and the sassy Pipe, something told him that Wilbur would have to Switch if he expected to be County Superintendent of Schools.

"Here are my Checks," said Wilbur, handing over the Brasses. "Have my Trunks, my Golf Clubs, my portable Punching-Bag, the Suit-Case and Hat-Boxes sent up to the House right away. Then drive me Home by the Outside Road, because I don't want to meet all these Yaps. They annoy me."

"You'd better git out of that Rig mighty quick if you don't want to be Joshed," said his Parent. "Folks around here won't stand for any such fool Regalia, and if you walk like a frozen-toed Hen you'll get some Hot Shots or I miss my Calkilations."

"Say, Popsy, I've been eating Raw Meat and drinking Blood at the Training-Table, and I'm on Edge," said Wilbur, expanding his chest until it bulged out like a Thornton Squash. "If any of these local Georgie Glues try to shoot their Pink Conversation at me I'll toss them up into the Trees and let them hang there. I'm the Gazabe that Puts the Shot. Anyone who can trim a Policeman and chuck a Hackman right back into his own Hack and drive off with him doesn't ask for any sweeter Tapioca than one of these Gaffer Greens. The Ploughboy who is musclebound and full of Pastry will have a Proud Chance any time that he struts across my Pathway. In my Trunks I have eight suits a little warmer than this one and 47 pairs of passionate Hose. I'm out here to give the Corn-fields a Touch of High Life. It's about time that your Chaws had a Glimpse of the Great Outside World. Any one who gets Fussy about the Color-Combination that I spring from Day to Day will be chopped up and served for Lunch. To begin with, I'm going to teach you and Mother to play Golf. If these Mutts come and lean over the Fence and start to get off their Colored-Weekly Jokes we'll fan the Hill-side with them."

"What do they teach up at your School—besides Murder?" inquired Father. "I thought you wanted to be County Superintendent of Schools."

"I've outgrown all those two-by-four Ambitions," was the Reply. "I'm going to be on the Eleven next Fall. What more could you ask?"

That very week Wilbur organized a Ball Team that walloped Hickory Crick, Sand Ridge, and Sozzinsville. He had the whole Township with him. Every Cub at Pewee Junction began to wear a Turkish Towel for a Collar and practice the Harvard Walk.

MORAL: A Boy never blossoms into full Possibilities until he strikes an Atmosphere of Culture.

CHAPTER VII

"What? That Barbarian!"

*"Who plays opposite you at end? Do you find you
can get down well under the ball to tackle the fullback? How are you tackling?"*
   —THEODORE ROOSEVELT TO KERMIT, OCT. 13, 1902

ALTHOUGH the torrent of Harvard jokes
rolls ever onward, for some peculiar reason the
masses, washed and otherwise, keep electing Harvard men
to the national Presidency. They even elected Jack Kennedy, who was not only a Harvard man, a member of
the Hasty Pudding Institute of 1770, and a Bostonian
(enough already to make Westbrook Pegler turn permanently purple), but an egghead who "wrote a book,"
and whose wife talks French right out loud and knows
Oleg Cassini, the inventor of the electric toaster, personally. In spite of these drawbacks, any one of which would
kill a person's chances for a night watchman's job in any
state in the Union, Mr. Kennedy was elected President
and shortly afterward Richard Nixon's house in Brent-
wood, California, almost burned down. Joe E. Brown's
homestead *did* burn to the ground in the same holocaust,
including his trophy room—which he called his "Room
of Love" and in which were Tris Speaker's shoes, Mickey
Cochrane's glove, Babe Ruth's bat, Jack Dempsey's trunks,
Bobby Jones' driver, Bill Tilden's racquet, and Frank

Wyckoff's shoes. Mr. Nixon sprayed his own roof with a garden hose although he had no trophies inside except some old bundles of Campaign Promises tied up with ribbon.

As of September first, 1961, the United States had had a Harvard man in the White House in Washington for exactly one third of the twentieth century. This has not had any notable effect on the football team, but it has been profoundly annoying to many people regardless of their collegiate affiliations or lack of same. Or irregardless, which is now in the dictionary.

The other, or non-*Crimson*, twentieth-century Presidents were certainly an assorted lot. In order of their appearance and disappearance.

WILLIAM McKINLEY. Nobody can remember much about McKinley except that he got shot. School kids do not like McKinley because they can never learn to spell the assassin's name correctly which was Czolgosz. You can't hardly blame them.

TAFT went to Yale and could only see his shoes when they were off his feet.

WOODROW WILSON went to Davidson College, the University of New Jersey, the University of Virginia, and Johns Hopkins—and also taught at Johns Hopkins, Bryn Mawr, Wesleyan, and Princeton, and was the President of Princeton. This record makes him unquestionably the champion bigdome and outstanding egghead President. As might be expected, he did not understand very clearly what the man on the sidewalk had on his mind.

WARREN G. HARDING was better-looking than Francis X. Bushman. However, Francis X. Bushman would have made a better President. Harding once told William Allen White, the Emporia Eagle: "My God-damn friends, White, they're the ones that keep me walking the floor nights." Alice Longworth, the famous expert on hybrid corn, said of this Ohio President, "Harding was not a bad man. He was just a slob."

Naughty naughty, Alice; mustn't tease little Warren.

CALVIN COOLIDGE usually was sleepy after lunch and took advantage of it. The décor in the White House, or Casa Blanca, never bothered him none as long as there was a couch handy to lay down on.

HERBERT HOOVER was born in West Branch, Iowa. He is best known in the haberdashery field for popularizing the "Hoover Collar," and is said to have been the inspiration for Cluett, Peabody & Company's "Arrow Collar Man."

HARRY TRUMAN fooled them all. They thought he was a dumbbell from Missouri but he had the last laugh.

DWIGHT EISENHOWER was educated at West Point, although he also has an honorary Harvard LL.D. ('46). Eisenhower did not keep his book dealer very busy and had so little interest in the performing arts that he never attended the theatre or a concert during his two-term reign. He was a mystery man and a recluse and indulged in no outdoor sports. His press interviews are used in college English courses as examples of the finest prose since Addison and Steele.

These are the non-Harvard Presidents, and as can be seen they are widely assorted as to background and talents, accents and styles of dress and preferences in entertainment and tobacco, draperies and ladies' hats, and in their worldly ambitions. (At least one had a rather unique goal: that of drawing a perfect royal straight flush. He never succeeded.)

The rest of the Presidents since 1900, three of them in number, were Harvard. And two of them made more noise and were the cause of more fist fights than the other eight put together.

Two of them were Roosevelts, and we will go into the other one later. Between them the Roosevelts witnessed the finals of no less than twenty Championship District of Columbia Easter Egg hunts out on their lawn, and 7300 mornings in the White House looking for a new razor blade. The number of dismal formal parties they attended staggers the imagination and makes everybody except

Perle Mesta and the caterers' union swoon with the horrors. Each Roosevelt had an enormous grin which was supposedly infectious but which caused easily irritated members of the opposition to leap in front of speeding trains and hurl themselves from tall buildings with annoyance. One of them anticipated Ernest Hemingway in the false-hair-on-chest department and spent many golden hours perforating wild animals with high-speed rifles and posing, staring straight into the camera like Rudolph Valentino, with one foot on the carcasses. He is well known for his "Big Stick" policy which originated from his running out of ammunition one time and liquidating two musk-oxen, twenty-three lemmings, and an Indian guide with a handy club. He attempted a come-back on the Bull Moose ticket in 1912 but was defeated in heavy voting by cinnamon bears, elks, mountain goats, white-tail deer, and other members of the newly formed and short-lived "Animal Party."

The other Roosevelt collected stamps and provided endless merriment among his ill-wishers because he said "My friends . . ." No one has ever been able to figure out what was so funny about this, but at one time in the U.S.A. any party cut-up could have the gang in stitches merely by saying "My friends . . ."

Frank smoked his cigarette through a long cigarette holder like Theda Bara and got away with it.

Teddy was a Republican who acted like a Democrat and Frank was a Democrat who acted just terrible.

From a safe distance, let us turn our Boy Scout two-cell flashlight on Theodore Roosevelt, President. If we get too close we might get hurt.

He was born in a brownstone house full of gloomy furniture at 33 East 20th Street in New York. His father belonged to one of New York's wealthiest families. He was born "at quarter of eight in the evening of October 27, 1858, as carriages took operagoers to the nearby Academy of Music, where the celebrated Mlle. Piccolomini was to appear in Donizetti's 'The Daughter of the Regiment.'"

So far, so good. When little Theodore was five years old Abraham Lincoln journeyed to Gettysburg, Pa., and gave his little talk. When he was about eight years old he was walking up Broadway to get some strawberries and saw a dead seal laid out on a slab. (Even today there are quite a few dead seals on Broadway.) "That seal filled me with every possible feeling of romance and adventure." Romance and adventure in his case meant killing some seals for himself, but since live seals were scarce in his neighborhood and since he wasn't old enough yet to punch that splendid target, J. P. Morgan's nose, he took to robbing birds' nests and capturing birds.

"The robin's and catbird's nest I pushed from limbs with sticks. All of a sudden we saw high in the barn . . . a swallow's nest. We got it with a ladder." "I saw about forty swallows. I caught most of them."

Commenting on this, a biographer refers to the youth as a "lover of nature." Now when *I* was a youthful naturalist it was not considered cricket to knock down birds' nests and kidnap birds. You were supposed to leave them alone and study their quaint antics without wrecking their home life.

Little Teddie, as he was called, had asthma. "I had an attack of the Asmer but I did not go to New York." He was a sickly child and unable to attend regular schools, but had tutors instead.

When he was eleven he and his family made the Grand Tour of Europe. He was sick or ailing much of the time. "I was very sick last night." "I had a miserable night." He was a great diarist and wrote down opinions, lists, plans, and programs for self-improvement. He stuffed more and more birds, animals, and salamanders.

By the time he was seventeen he was writing down his physical measurements and physical conquests. "Race between Johnny and Theodore. Theodore won." "Wrestling Theodore beat Elliott." "Theodore and West wrestling and boxing Theodore won."

Meanwhile he continued with his "nature studies." In

1876 he wrote his sister: "I am writing in a rather smelly room as the fresh skins of eight night herons are reposing on the table beside me." This writer, who is penning these words while suffering from a serious flesh wound inflicted by a vicious chipmunk, suggests: Wouldn't it have been sporting to leave seven of these night herons standing on one leg someplace and just knock off *one* to smell up the room? But he was a pathological game hog. He couldn't help himself. In 1909 on his safari in Africa he killed 296 animals. "That barbarian!" one Harvard professor said when Roosevelt's name was tentatively brought up for consideration to succeed Charles William Eliot.

While all the night herons and friendly toads in the neighborhood breathed a sigh of relief, Roosevelt easily passed his entrance examinations for Harvard and arrived in Cambridge in the fall of 1876, where he immediately became the outstanding Freshman Oddball of the Year. Complete with side-whiskers.

He didn't like his room in the Yard because there were too many guys frolicking around, some of whom went so far as to drink beer and sing songs, so he moved out and into a room two blocks from the Square on the corner of Holyoke Street. His sister came up to Cambridge and chintzed up this room for him and he wrote her as follows:

Sept. 30, 1876

My Darling Sister,

I have just received your sweet letter. Darling Bamie, you will not miss me more than I miss you. . . .

Here we see how times have changed. Undergraduates nowadays do not address their sisters in tones of such affectionate warmth for fear of being hauled off to the neighborhood analyst. But today we cannot comprehend the almost hermetically sealed closeness of Victorian family life, or the results of it in maladjusted adults, spinster daughters, and desolation and grief in separation.

More of the same letter to "Bamie":

Ever since I came here I have been wondering what I should have done if you had not fitted up my room for me. The curtains, carpet, furniture—in short everything is really beautiful; I have never seen prettier or more tasteful wall paper. When I get my pictures and books, I do not think there will be a room in College more handsome or comfortable.

Quite a contrast, one might imagine, from the sentiments of those crude beer drinkers in the Yard.

To his father he wrote: "I do not think there is a fellow in college who has a family that love him as much as you all do me."

One blushes today, not at his feelings or at the picture of family warmth, but at his putting it down on paper in a letter. We just don't do that any more. But he always put down just what he thought, and the fact that he was now at Harvard did not restrain him from expressing himself in exactly the same terms as if he were confiding in his diary at the age of twelve. Later on he was to call Woodrow Wilson a "trained elocutionist," "neither a gentleman nor a real man," a "Logothete," "utterly and coldly selfish," and said that "In time Wilson will be the most damned man in America since the days of Buchanan and Andrew Johnson." Concerning these utterances, in a letter to Rudyard Kipling, he said with the naïveté of a child, "I do not believe I have spoken intemperately!"

In his freshman year, 1876, Roosevelt was considered freakish and eccentric, or "a good deal of a joke." His room soon became filled with "stuffed animals and mounted birds perched on desk and table, and here and there a pair of antlers." There was also a cage with live snakes, turtles, and other study aids.

"Indifference" was at its height at Harvard. Actually it finds its modern counterpart in a social behaviorism described in the vernacular as "playing it cool." Roosevelt did not lounge about in a droopy attitude playing it cool. Instead he dashed about like a dog with a tin can on his tail. One of his classmates said that at a time when "it was not considered good form to move at more than a walk, Roosevelt was always running." At a time when good form also dictated a minimum of study, Roosevelt actually read books other than those required by his courses. He also lifted weights, rode, jumped rope, boxed, rowed, sparred, measured his biceps, did pushups, and rushed about the Massachusetts countryside on field trips, disrupting the meditations of purple grackles, semi-palmated plovers, and blackburnian warblers. He went to Maine and shot at things and he wrote, "I do not find it nearly so hard as I expected not to drink and smoke." (Thirty-seven years later he stated, "I have never drunk a cocktail or a highball in my life.") He arose at 7:15 and hurled himself in all directions until he went to bed, usually at eleven o'clock.

His marks in that freshman year showed a high of 92 in German and a low of 58 in Greek, with grades in the middle seventies in between. This remained his range throughout his career at Harvard. And yet in his autobiography he says, "I was given a Phi Beta Kappa 'key.'" One gathers that the standards of this august organization also have changed. Or as Dean Bender recently stated in regard to the increasingly high admission standards, it is likely that neither of the Roosevelts or John F. Kennedy could have gained admission to Harvard under the present requirements.

In his sophomore year some of the boys began to call him Teddy and he began to feel at home. He sent to New York for his silk hat and entered the gay social life of Cambridge and Boston and it was very gay and very fancy. He had plenty of money and "a good horse and cart," joined the *Advocate*, and was elected to Porcellian, then as now the most exclusive and mysterious of Harvard's clubs. (Neither FDR nor Kennedy made it. Perhaps they turned it down? No, one really doesn't turn down Porcellian, I suppose, like Sinclair Lewis and the Pulitzer Prize.)

Perhaps he was not a snob, but what does one make of this: "I most sincerely wish I knew something about the antecedents of my friends. On this very account I have avoided being very intimate with the New York fellows."

Listen, buddy—take off your silk hat and say that again. And Smile.

On October 18, 1878, in his junior year, he met Miss Alice Lee, a cousin of his Harvard classmate Richard Saltonstall of the Saltonstalls. Never has a college student been bitten quite so smartly by the Love Bug. For the remainder of his Harvard life he was a frenzied, lovesick, relentless, palpitating mass of Collegiate Love Goo. His rifle, shotgun, and sidearms grew rusty, his specimens and antlers grew dusty, and while the Lesser Scaup Duck frolicked unmolested he pursued Miss Lee through the parlors of Boston, around and around tennis courts, and up and down Beacon Hill. At dances he brought her ices and low-pressure glasses of punch, and at picnics he protected her from vicious Massachusetts ants. He drove a dog cart through Harvard Square and up to Chestnut Hill for sweet Alice's amusement. He even "shocked the Porcellian Club into disbelief when, seemingly forgetful of the traditionally unbroken rule, he took Alice to lunch with him at the Pork house. Harvard men will believe anything about the Roosevelt of those years, but this Porcellian men still deny."

He was a terrific prude. One of his cousins married a French actress and he wrote in his diary, "He is a disgrace to the family—the vulgar brute."

And he lavished upon himself praise for his immaculate condition which falls strangely on modern ears, tuned as they are to a daily barrage of sex braggadocio.[1] "Thank

---

[1] "As for Radcliffe girls, almost all the articles agree that after an initial freshman year carnival of dates, they are anxious to enter into an affair."—"Harvard Romances as Others See Them," *The Crimson Review*, Nov. 10, 1961.

"Virtue, as a matter of fact, is pretty non-U all over the world. I don't mean simply that it's not worth competing for, I mean it's a positive disadvantage to have it."—John Crosby in the *Herald Tribune*.

Heaven," he murmured to his diary, "I am at least perfectly pure."

But he was coming along fast.

Tormented by his "sweet love," he told his diary that when he was alone with her he could "hardly stay a moment without holding her in my arms or kissing her; she is such a laughing, pretty little witch."

Watch that lust, there, man.

Alice, whose pictures show her to have been truly a rare beauty, finally gave in, and on October 27, 1880, four months after graduation, the Reverend J. A. Buckingham married them in the Brookline Unitarian Church.

But before the nuptials, Teddy had another fling with his firearms. In August after graduation (he graduated twenty-first in a class of 161, the same rank a former failure in the leather business in Galena, Illinois, Ulysses S. Grant, had made at West Point), he and his brother Elliott hied themselves to Minnesota and Iowa to hunt. He told his mother it would build him up. "We have had good shooting and I feel twice the man for it." "We are travelling on our muscle and don't give a hang for any man." To build himself up and increase his purity he took the gift of life away from 203 animals on this little jaunt.

Twenty-one years later, on January 14, 1901, in one of his letters to his children from Colorado:

. . . This time, after a couple of hundred yards, the dogs caught him, and a great fight followed. They could have killed him by themselves, but he bit or clawed four of them, and for fear he might kill one I ran in and stabbed him behind the shoulder, thrusting the knife right into his heart. I have always wished to kill a cougar as I did this one, with dogs and the knife.

God in heaven, what a letter to write to one's children, and Great Prince of Peace and Mercy, what an ambition!

Not much of Harvard rubbed off on Theodore. He came fully intending to become a scientific naturalist, but when he discovered that at Harvard zoology did not mean bully evenings around the campfire with some regular fellows and days spent in decimating the animal kingdom, he lost interest. As he says in his autobiography: ". . . at that time Harvard . . . utterly ignored the possibilities of the faunal naturalist, the outdoor naturalist and observer of nature. They treated biology as purely a science of the laboratory and the microscope, a science whose adherents were to spend their time in the study of minute forms of marine life, or else in section-cutting and the study of the tissues of the higher organisms under the microscope."

In fact, the poor saps didn't even know a Winchester Model 95, .405 from a Daisy Air Rifle.

Four years at Harvard do not indicate now, and did not mean then, that the graduate's opinions in comparative literature will ever afterwards be spellbinding in their sophistication or originality. Harvard didn't really give Roosevelt "an awkward view of literature," as one writer has said, it gave him no view at all. Here are some of Theodore Roosevelt's literary evaluations:

Of Emile Zola: "Of course the net result of Zola's writings has been evil . . . the lascivious, the beast side. . . ."

Of Walt Whitman: ". . . warped. . . ."

Of Longfellow: ". . . he knew that cowardice does not promote peace. . . ."

(*Take that, Wilson.*)

Of Dickens: ". . . Thackeray was a gentleman and Dickens was not."

Of Tolstoi: "First as to Tolstoi's immorality. Have you ever read his 'Kreutzer Sonata'? The man who wrote that was a sexual and moral pervert. It is as unhealthy a book, as vicious in its teaching to the young, as Elinor Glyn's 'Three Weeks' or any other piece of pornography." [2]

[2] For the true nature of Miss Glyn's piece of pornography, see "Cloudland Revisited: Tuberoses and Tigers," by S. J. Perelman (Brown '25).

But hold, enough! If he didn't buy any of these writers, what writers did get the nod from this Harvard recipient of a Phi Beta Kappa key? Yes, he did have favorites; one was a kiddies' paper called *Young People's Magazine* ("good reading") and another was *The Virginian*, by his Harvard buddy Owen Wister.[3]

What did Harvard think of Teddy? President Eliot was horrified by his crude and aggressive political shenanigans and considered him a thorough jingoist with a "chip on the shoulder attitude of a ruffian and a bully," and a "degenerated son of Harvard"—also a warmonger. And probably not as much of a gentleman as even Charles Dickens. Harvard in general also took a dim view of their celebrated graduate's adolescent enthusiasm for games like "Let's All Dress up in Funny Costumes and Play Soldier," as in the famous Rough-Riders-in-Cuba charade, which nonetheless captivated the American audience almost as much as Floyd Collins' getting stuck in a cave was to do not so many years later.

The Theodore Roosevelt Memorial Library is housed in Harvard's Widener Library. This is one of the most fantastic collections in the world devoted to one individual. It contains over 10,000 books and microfilm of over 125,000 letters, as well as 5000 photos and cartoons. Almost every mention of Theodore Roosevelt that was made in any medium during his lifetime and since is represented.

And what did Teddy think of Harvard? Of his four years in the halls of learning he said: "I have certainly lived like a prince. . . . I have had just as much money as I could spend. . . . I have kept a good horse and cart, I have had half a dozen good and true friends . . . a lovely home; I have had but little work, only enough to give me an occupation, and to crown all infinitely above everything else put together—I have won the sweetest of girls

---

[3] In those days a good man could find trouble anywhere. Of Thoreau's *Walden* John Greenleaf Whittier declared: "A wicked and heathenish book."

Commonwealth of Massachusetts.

Middlesex, SS.
District of Newton. }

To Richard F. Bissell

of Mercer, Cambridge in said County GREETING:

IN THE NAME OF THE COMMONWEALTH OF MASSACHUSETTS

L. S.

YOU are commanded to appear before the District Court of Newton, in the District of Newton, in said County of Middlesex, on the 26th day of May current1899, at nine of the clock in the forenoon; to answer unto the COMMONWEALTH OF MASSACHUSETTS, upon the complaint, in behalf of said Commonwealth, under oath of Alfred W. Russell, of said Newton, made before said Court, charging you with the offence of

OPERATING AN AUTOMOBILE AT UNREASONABLE SPEED

which complaint will then be heard and tried before said Court. Fail not of appearance at your peril.

Witness, WILLIAM F. BACON, Esquire, our Justice of our said Court, and the seal thereof, at Newton aforesaid, the 19th day of May in the year of our Lord one thousand nine hundred and thirty -nine99

James F. Gallagher
Clerk.

Charles J. Cody
Police Officer of Newton.

. A true copy. Attest:

L. S.

Commonwealth of Massachusetts

MIDDLESEX, SS. THE THIRD DISTRICT COURT OF EASTERN MIDDLESEX, HOLDEN AT CAMBRIDGE, IN THE COUNTY OF MIDDLESEX, FOR THE TRANSACTION OF CRIMINAL BUSINESS.

To Fredreck E. Bissell

of Cambridge in said County of Middlesex.

You are hereby summoned in the name of the Commonwealth of Massachusetts to appear before said Court to be holden as aforesaid on the seventh day of June in the year of our Lord one thousand eight hundred and ninety-nine, at nine o'clock in the forenoon, then and there in said Court to answer to a complaint this day made on oath before said Court, charging you with

playing ball on the Lord's day

Hereof fail not at your peril.

WITNESS, CHARLES ALMY, Esquire, at Cambridge aforesaid, this fifth day of June in the year of our Lord one thousand eight hundred and ninety-nine.

Herbert J. S. Claire Ass't.
CLERK.

A true copy, attest.

James H. H. Heath Police Officer of Cambridge.

for my wife. No man ever had so pleasant a college course."

Gay college years! Scott Fitzgerald, Wherever You Are, please note.

THE LINE-UP

Relations between the Cambridge constabulary and the Harvard student have never been conspicuously warm. The originals of the two appended historical parchments, which may help to document this fact, are available for further study in the archives of the author under the heading *Crime, Family*.

CHAPTER VIII

Sports & Pastimes

I will not enter the debate as to whether football or baseball is our great national sport. The sad fact is that it looks more and more as if our great national sport is not playing at all—but watching.

—JOHN F. KENNEDY '40, LL.D. '56

One day I hit the third double of my career—counting high school ball—and then I was picked off second base. Manager Joe McCarthy asked "what happened out there?" and I said "I don't know, I've never been out there before."

—VERNON ("LEFTY") GOMEZ

THE IVY LEAGUE may be under a soggy overcast of suspicion on social and intellectual grounds among the deep thinkers from the provinces, but when it comes to the subject of sports as practiced on these hallowed playing fields, scorn changes to derision, derision to sneers, sneers to rude catcalls, and ends with the hurling of mud, bricks, stones, and textbooks on animal husbandry and painless embalming. To the 296-pound tackle on the Iowa football team (for some occult reason he is a Negro and so are six other members of the team, although there is no visible Negro population in Iowa, and Duke Ellington's band cannot get rooms at the hotel—to this folk hero whose exploits are soberly recorded weekly like those of an eminent statesman, there is nothing quite so comical as motion pictures of the Harvard-Yale game, or the Dartmouth-Cornell game, or any other of those examples of children at play. Who can blame this athlete with rippling muscles and impervious torso as he sits there staring almost in disbelief at this facsimile of the game he plays if he smiles indulgently and recalls the lines of Oliver Goldsmith (the whole Iowa team is very keen on Goldsmith):

> *By sports like these are all their cares beguil'd,*
> *The sports of children satisfy the child.*

Not that Coach shows the team such comedy films, as he is afraid they might get the giggles and fall off their folding chairs and hurt themselves on the cement floor. But they occasionally see them in the newsreels, where they cause more merriment than the chimps' tea party at the Bronx Zoo.

Even in the East it is fashionable to chuckle indulgently at the antics of the Ivy elevens. No party in Westport or New Canaan is complete during the football season without good old Frank, formerly from Lake Forest, martini in hand, telling the folks about the Big Ten and how the game is really played "out there." Sportswriters who have been feeling lately that their stuff has been falling off can always snap back with a humorous piece about the pigskin frolic last Saturday down at Princeton. And even in Boston, right in George Apley's front parlor, a hush falls over the post-game group of tea drinkers when some avid Brahmin fan (who has been reading those New York papers again [1]) pronounces the solemn words *Ohio State*.

[1] Not many Bostonians err in this direction: "Three years ago I got on a plane at Boston destined for New York. The man in the seat next to me wore on his watchchain a Porcellian Club emblem. He had that unmistakably sound and salubrious look of a proper Bostonian. We introduced ourselves. He was a distinguished Harvard graduate, in middle life, engaged in running a large investment trust, bearing one of the best Boston names, active in the life of Harvard. He was reading a Boston *Herald* and I had managed to secure a *New York Times*, which having read, I offered to him. He hesitated. "Thank you," he said, "but I think I'll stick to the *Herald*. If I read the *Times* I get sort of mixed up."—*A Casual Past*, Francis Biddle, '09.

"Well anyways," says Kay Apley (she finally divorced old Harry Pulham and married George Apley's grandson while he was in the Lower Form at St. Swithin's)—"anyways, Harvard didn't look as bad as last year."

Whereupon everybody nods cheerfully and begins sneaking whiskey into their teacups.

Has everybody lost their minds? What is sport, anyway? Was the battle of Waterloo won on the playing fields of Eton or by two professional teams called Manchester United *vs.* Liverpool and the Rest of Liverpool? I doutcha.

Let us peer into the Century Dictionary, Volume Two:

"*Sport*, n. Diversion, amusement, or recreation; pleasant pastime; a particular form of pastime; esp., a pastime pursued in the open air or having an athletic character, as hunting, fishing, racing, baseball, tennis, golf, bowling, wrestling, boxing, etc."

Now whether the bruisers on the payroll out in the Big Ten or down in the Kumquat Bowl or the Cotton Pickers Bowl or the Integration Bowl or any of the other vessels of greater width than depth maintained on a strictly commercial basis for the greater glory of education like it or not, *this* is what Harvard considers "Sport." Everybody at Harvard can play at sports, diversions, and pleasant athletic pastimes if he wants to. Only if he wants to. Like everything else at Harvard, nobody is standing behind you with an axe saying Do this and Do that, Think like this, don't Think like that or People Won't Like You. But if you want to, it's all there, from fencing, squash, and tennis to crew, football, and all the rest. (Say, I never hear too much about the Oklahoma tennis team, what are they, a bunch of bigdome sissies out there?) And as for playing on teams, thanks to the House Plan at Harvard there are teams (with a plural). Not just "the team" that everybody stands around gawking at as though they were going to do a levitation act or play on the musical saw.

I have a young friend who was the captain of his prep school basketball team and who went to one of the Big

Ten schools. When he responded to the call for candidates for the basketball team he found only five students had appeared out of a student body of 12,200, of whom 7990 are men.

"What's the idea?" he asked one of the other guys as they departed.

"Oh, of course the *team* has already been hired," replied the other.

So he gave up the whole idea and spent the winter as a spectator and in cheering The Team, which consisted of a number of lads with bruises all over their foreheads from bumping into the ceilings of public buildings and day coaches.

Harvard has its House Plan and Yale has its Colleges. Each House or College has its teams and they play inter-college games. This means that on a single week end, while *The Game* [2] is going on and Yale is fumbling and the Harvard center is shooting the ball over his punter's head and into the stands, and while both teams are trying out plays that don't work and bumping into each other and generally carrying on as if they were in a crowded subway and wished they were home, meanwhile there are ten or more other Harvard-Yale games going on, between the Jayvees, the Freshmen, and the Houses. This is college football, this is amateur athletics.

Of course I am not convincing anyone because in our country the mad desire for professionalism stops at nothing. Nobody pays any attention to the cute kid who sings for free at the Elks Club banquet. They don't know whether she's flat or sharp or playing the kazoo. But as soon as she is signed by Manny Glick and associates of

[2] *The Game*, among Harvard and Yale graduates, refers only to the annual Harvard-Yale football classic, played on alternate years at the Yale Bowl, which is roughly sixty-five miles from the Yale campus, in New Haven, Conn. (pop. [1950] 9444), and at Soldiers Field, on the banks of the Charles River, in Cambridge, Mass.. (pop. [1950] 120,740).

When she was three years old, Brenda Diana Duff-Frazier Kelly Chatfield-Taylor's father, a loyal Yale man, went off to The Game and, it is recorded, "never came home, although Yale won."

Hollywood, California, they name a street for her. Just wait and see, the next of our Great American Institutions to go professional will be the Little League. These kids play very crummy ball compared to the Yankees and pretty soon a reaction is going to set in and we are going to see some of the shorter members of the Three I League having their expenses paid at the William Cullen Bryant grammar school and smoking cigars in the boys' toilet and arguing with teacher about their contract.

Unbelievable though it may seem to the boys filling out their football pool cards these days, Harvard used to be a power in football and the Harvard-Yale game was observed with awe by the outlanders as a top sporting event instead of a social gathering. Harvard, Yale, and the other Ivy teams were regularly represented on the All-American teams. And that brutal formation, the flying wedge, was invented by Harvard.

The flying wedge created such mayhem on the playing field that President Eliot asked President Hadley of Yale to a meeting to see what could be done in the way of reducing the casualties. Walter Camp, the Yale coach, suggested opening up the game by penalizing the mass play. Percy Haughton, the great Harvard coach, suggested the forward pass. This is only one of Haughton's innovations which contributed to the game as it is today, and to the continual bewilderment of the saucy co-eds in the stands. His name may have been Percy but he was one of the greatest football coaches of all time. If you think I am prejudiced, listen to what Charles A. Wagner has to say. He is also prejudiced.

"Percy Haughton was without question the greatest creative mind of American football. Other names may challenge the designation, or draw more familiar recognition; still others may, through the circumstance of promotional prestige, be called forth above his own on the roster of regency. It is fable. Haughton was the supreme artist of American football coaching. He approached his art with the deviousness of a Leonardo; all science, all knowledge, even life itself was the slave of his creativity."

Haughton, who made both the Walter Camp and Casper Whitney All-American teams in 1898, returned to Harvard as football coach in 1908. A slow tear will trickle down the cheek of the old grad of those years as the names of some of Haughton's Harvard Heros come to mind: Charlie Brickley, Eddie Mahan, Percy Wendell, Fred Bradlee, Sam Felton, Ham Fish (yes, the very same Hamilton Fish), Tacks Hardwick, Don Watson, Minot, Cutler, Eddie Casey. . . .

Haughton's teams in eight years won 85.54 per cent of their games, lost 8.43 per cent, and tied 6.03 per cent. As a player he was a flash at both fullback and tackle, and his punts averaged 60 yards. One of his punts went for 85 yards, possibly with a full gale from the sea behind it.

"Football is poetry," Haughton said. "The same rhythmic skill, the same startling and significant expression."

You can always tell a Harvard man—from the way he talks.

Harvard has twelve major sports, five minor sports, innumerable unclassified sports (swallowing live goldfish has been abandoned but a minor letter is still awarded for accuracy in dropping paper bags of water out of windows). Athletics are financed out of the educational budget and not by gate receipts and the college has one of the finest athletic plants in the country. The goal of the program is athletics for all. There are team sports and individual sports such as squash, tennis, gymnastics, poker, billiards, pool, and sculling. At Harvard if you do not care for "games" you can go down to the Weld boathouse and take out a single scull and row all by yourself on the Charles, contemplate infinity, enjoy the out-of-doors, and build up your puny body all at the same time. You will eventually get as good as Grace Kelly's father Jack, who was the U.S. national sculling champion, Olympic champion in 1924, and the greatest oarsman in U.S. history, or

as skillful as the Princess' brother "Kell" who won the
Diamond Sculls.[3] After that you can very easily get a job
in almost any brokerage house in the country. The Weld
boathouse contains sixty wherries and singles and fifteen
eight-oared shells for intramural rowing. Across the river
is the varsity Newell boathouse, which offers two four-
oared and fourteen eight-oared shells, six eight-oared
barges, and a rowing tank. None of the following colleges
has ever beaten Harvard in a crew race: Iowa, Illinois,
Ohio State, Minnesota, Michigan, Michigan State, Oklahoma, Indiana, Kansas, Colorado, Missouri, Southern
Methodist, Texas A & M, Baylor, Duke, Louisiana State,
Texas Tech., Purdue, Nebraska, Muhlenberg, or Knute
Rockne. Rowing would not interest most of these colleges because there are no oarsmen in the steel mills for
hire and it is a poor spectator sport (except at New London where it somewhat resembles the Derby at Epsom
Downs). And it is a terrible drag for the sports writers
as there is no blood,[4] no contract holdouts, no individual
eccentricities to belabor, no virtuoso performers to hot up
the typewriter over—just eight guys in a boat.

The noble and honorable art of rowing is an extremely
ancient one. Originally a means of propulsion through the
water, it soon developed into a sport.

The waiting crews are crowned with poplar wreaths;
Their naked shoulders glisten, moist with oil.
Ranged in a row, their arms stretched to the oars,
All tense the starting signal they await.
Together at the trumpets' thrilling blast
Their bent arms churn the water into foam;
The sea gapes open by the oars up-torn;

[3] Father Kelly was not permitted by our English cousins to compete
in The Diamond Sculls as he was not a gentleman and "worked
with his hands."
[4] ". . . trudged over to the stadium this afternoon and watched The
Team, which consists of several herds of wild animals from the
plains, memorize another Golgotha against the brethren from South
Bend. Tonight the field of glory is littered with bones."—Letter
from Cletus Barff, Iowa '63.

With shouts and cheers of eager partisans
The woodlands ring, the sheltered beach rolls up
The sound, the hills re-echo with the din.

What have we here, a description of the Poughkeepsie regatta, or perhaps Harvard *vs.* Yale on the Thames at New London? But why no mention of the boat train, loaded with cheering spectators and martinis? Dear reader, the above graphic bit of sports reporting is not from the gifted Remington of Grantland Rice or John Lardner, may they rest in peace, but by that ever-popular ace scribe, Publius Vergilius Maro (70–19 B.C.), known to the sports world of today as Virgil. It is from a Friday column of his called the *Aeneid*.

From William of Malmesbury we find that Edgar the Peaceful had himself rowed in state by tributary kings on the river Dee, while he himself held the coxswain's seat.

Eton had a ten-oared boat, *The Monarch*, in 1811, plus three eight-oars. The Oxford-Cambridge race, perhaps the world's greatest sports classic, at least as regards the number of Lords, Dukes, and other British curiosities contending, was first rowed over a two-mile course at Henley in 1829.

It was only natural that Harvard, patterned as it was after Oxford and Cambridge, and situated directly on a stream of suitable depth and size, should imitate her English counterparts in aquatic pursuits. The Charles River, flowing by her door, was a tidewater river (it is no longer) of navigable depth for commercial vessels. Until 1826 the college maintained the sloop *Harvard*, which made periodic trips down east, bringing firewood for the college directly to their own pier.[5] From the earliest times students skated on the Charles, swam in it, and occasionally drowned in it. One must presume that some informal boat-

[5] Nathaniel Bowditch, the *Practical Navigator*, was elected to the Corporation in 1826. Finding the college finances in severe disorder, he insisted on a rigid economy program. The good sloop *Harvard* was sold and the firewood purchased locally and colorlessly at much lower cost.

ing took place and that perhaps a student or two had knocked off the classics long enough to drop a baited hook in the water.

But real boating, organized boating, did not begin until 1844 when a regular boat club was formed by members of the class of '46 with the six-oared *Oneida*, "a plumb stem, undecked lapstreak, thirty-seven feet long, three and a half foot beam." [6] A race was held with two Boston crews on the Back Bay and turned out to be such a lark that other clubs sprang into being and boating, if not "crew" as we understand it today (although they did have races), was fairly launched at Harvard.

Competitive rowing had already been going on for quite a while in the U.S.A., as had organized rowing for pleasure. In 1811 and again in 1823 the ferrymen of Whitehall in New York City defeated crews from Long Island and Staten Island on the Hudson, and in 1824 they outrowed the crew of the British frigate *Hussar* in a four-mile race which ended at the Battery. This race created international excitement and heavy betting.

The first amateur boat club was the Castle Garden Boat Club Association of New York in 1834. Another early club which survives today was the Detroit Boat Club, founded in 1839. The purpose of most of these clubs was social, with hauling on the sweeps only a part of the fun. There were banquets, balls, toasts, picnics, and parasol-waving by the ladies. Also rowing.

The oldest college contest in the United States is the Harvard-Yale crew race. It antedates football by seventeen years. It's been going on for 110 years.

The first formal intercollegiate boat race was rowed in August 1852, between Harvard and Yale at Center Harbor on Lake Winnepesaukee in central New Hampshire. The Harvard craft was old faithful *Oneida* and one wonders how this thirty-seven-foot-long boat was transported and who footed the bill. Harvard beat three Yale boats in the morning and after lunch beat Yale again by four lengths

[6] Morison. *Three Centuries of Harvard.*

over a three-mile course. This was an eight-oared race with coxswain.

"Rowing has always stood high at Harvard, and the boats have been manned by men of admirable quality," says John Hays Gardner in an Oxford University Press book published in 1914. This volume dates from the Pleistocene period of simple book titles and is not called *Also But Not Yet the Ibis Cries*, or *The Roman Spring of Ernest Albert Hooton*, but simply *Harvard*. There is another book in the same series with the plain and unadorned title of *Vassar*. Not *Vassar, a Study in Contemporary Upper Level Behavior Patterns*, or *Why Can't Vassar Girls Read?* —just plain *Vassar*. Makes a person shudder.

Among other "men of admirable quality" who rowed on Harvard crews was the great Charles William Eliot, well-known in Minden, North Dakota, as the editor of the "Five Foot Shelf of Uncut Books" and further east as Harvard's greatest President, who turned down the Ambassadorship to England twice and whose sidewhiskers were as famous as Lincoln's warts.

"Hurra Hurra!! Hurra!!! We've beaten the entire crowd tremendously—" he wrote his girl friend, Ellen Peabody, in 1858 "—and made the quickest time ever made round the course. 19 min. 22 sec. was our time. . . . We beat by 1 min. 58 sec. which is a very large difference. Ellen, it was perfectly splendid—we had the sympathy of the entire crowd, and what a crowd it was!" The moment we appeared the people began to clap and hurrah—we looked 'flash,' I tell you. . . . Then we saw the men we were to row against—great stout Irishmen with awful muscles— as Crowninshield said, his heart was right in his mouth. . . ."

This was the Boston Regatta of June 19, 1858, rowed against six other crews from Boston, New York, and St. John. Aside from the fact that future President Eliot, rowing not as an undergraduate but as an Assistant Professor of Mathematics and Chemistry, was sweating at the sweeps that day in the winning boat, the race is of historic interest to loyal sons and lovers (of crew) for two other reasons: it was rowed by Harvard in a new boat from the boat-builders of St. John, New Brunswick —the first real shell to appear on the Charles,[7] and it was also the first occasion on which the crimson was displayed as the Harvard color. For the occasion Mr. Eliot and his friend Crowninshield, who rowed at stroke, decided to add a little of the above-mentioned "flash" to their usual costume, which was simply their underwear. So they went over to Hovey's store and picked out "six China silk handkerchiefs of a brilliant crimson," which were tied around their heads. The color became popular with the other Harvard teams and was used henceforth, although not officially recognized by the Corporation until 1910.

"Professors Peirce, Agassiz, and Huntington were all in Boston to see the race," Eliot says to the girl friend, "and came out to Cambridge in a state of exultation. Huntington cheered and shouted to such an extent that he was as hoarse as a crow today."

Harvard has always given a good account of itself on the English Thames; for example in 1959 in the Henley Regatta it won both the Grand Challenge Cup and the Thames Challenge Cup. On the American Thames at New London it holds a very slight edge over Yale in total victories.

Actually, there has always been a slightly salty flavor among segments of the Harvard community. There was Nathaniel Bowditch, and there was Richard Henry Dana, who left Harvard as an undergraduate and shipped out on a Boston brig to spend two years before the mast. We might also mention Harold Vanderbilt ('07, Law School '10), and Charles Francis Adams, Rear Admiral (retired) Samuel Eliot Morison, official Historian of Naval Operations World War II and noted authority on maritime

[7] Perhaps it is not polite to mention this but if the Harvards were racing in a light shell and the bulging Irishmen in the heavier old-style boats, might it not have contributed to their victory?

affairs (and practically everything else), Assistant Secretary of the Navy Franklin D. Roosevelt, and lastly, the hero of Blackett Strait in the Solomon Islands, home-town boy Lieutenant (JG) John F. Kennedy of PT boat 109. (Cheers from gallery. Sound of hautboys and side drums.)

Harvard men are constantly pacing the quarterdeck and issuing tots of grog for all hands in the most exalted yachting circles. On January 18, 1962, George R. Hinman, '33, a former commodore of the New York Yacht Club, was elected president of the North American Yacht Racing Union to succeed J. Amory Jeffries, '16. F. Gregg Bemis, '22, M.B.A. '25, was elected a vice-president (Bemis Bags, Cohasset Yacht Club), George Roosevelt, '09, an ex-commodore of both the New York Yacht Club and the Seawanakha Corinthian Yacht Club, was elected secretary. Yachting, like Newport, ain't what she formerly was; but yachtsmen still manage to run a close second to golfers in the Conversational Boredom Sweepstakes, what with their blown-out spinnakers and self-bailing jib-booms.

The English game of "rounders," slightly modified and now known as baseball, or *beisbol* if you live south of the border, came to Harvard during the Civil War, although its actual beginnings in this country are shrouded in mystery. The Abner Doubleday-Cooperstown myth seems to have been completely blown up by now although it will no doubt go on forever like the one about Betsy Ross and the flag. Abner supposed to have simply invented the national pastime at Cooperstown, New York, in 1839. But modern sleuths have discovered that he probably was not even in Cooperstown in 1839 but down at West Point learning to be a colonel. You might as well say he invented Gilette Blue Blades, Mel Allen, and Luke Appling. Way back in the eighteenth century in England, Lady Hervey mentions "baseball" in her *Letters*. Under date of November 8, 1748, she amuses herself with a passage baiting Frederick Prince of Wales and indicating that in her opinion he was of a childish and retarded frame of mind:

"The Prince's family is an example of cheerful and

innocent amusement . . . they divert themselves at base-ball, a play all who have, or have been, schoolboys, are well acquainted with."

Jane Austen also mentions baseball in *Northanger Abbey* (1798).

George Ewing, a soldier at Valley Forge, writing in 1788 from that place, mentions "playing at base."

In *The Boys' Own Book* (1828) a description of the game closely paralleling the early American game is given.

Samuel Hopkins Adams discovered a newspaper dated in the 1820s with a mention of the Rochester baseball club, which had fifty members, in spring practice for the season. (And making dates with the waitresses.)

Oliver Wendell Holmes, Harvard 1829, said that he played "a good deal of baseball" while at Harvard.

All this certainly seems to dent the Cooperstown theory, which is too bad because they have such a nice museum up there, with Moe Berg's sliding pads autographed in nine languages.

Both Cuba and the Soviet Union reject all the standard theories and each claims to have invented it along with fire, the wheel, etc.

CUBA ADDS HER CLAIM AS
HOME OF BASEBALL

Special to the New York Times.

WASHINGTON, March 11—Cuba, like the Soviet Union, has put a claim on the invention of baseball.

A recent speech by Premier Fidel Castro and a subsequent editorial in the official newspaper *Revolucion* declared that *pelota*, as baseball is known in Cuba, "Is not a Yankee creation."

It is, however, the country's most popular sport and Dr. Castro, who occasionally goes to bat himself, announced that "the first inhabitants of Cuba played it, with the name of *batos*." *Revolucion* explained that the game was invented by the Indians who lived in Cuba before the Spanish conquest.

Soviet publications for several years, most recently last

month, have asserted that baseball was descended from an old Russian game called *lapta*.

Last week Premier Castro introduced the fourth strike to baseball at a game in which he went to bat.

Anyway, Colonel Doubleday had nothing to do with baseball at Harvard, for by that time he was very busy at Gettysburg, Pa. Heaven only knows what kind of "baseball" Oliver Wendell Holmes played at Harvard in 1829, but organized team ball was first played in Cambridge by some students who entered from Phillips Exeter Academy. They called it the "New York" game, presumably operating under the set of rules laid down by the Knickerbocker Baseball club of New York in 1845. The diamond was on Cambridge Common and in the first varsity game Harvard drubbed Williams 35 to 30 for a game total of sixty-five runs scored. (A pitchers' duel.) The score suggests that the hassocks were groaning, the sacks were loaded, the willow was wielded, the apple was pounded, the sphere took a ride, the pellet was blasted, and that circuit clouts exploded. Three years later witnessed the initial contest with the Elis. Again it was a case of four-ply blows but only forty-two runs were scored with the Crimson racking up 25 to 17 for their rivals in blue from the Nutmeg state.

For some reason nobody pays much attention to college baseball and about the only sizable crowd it attracts is the one on Class Day when the Twenty-fifth Reunion boys come rolling in in their funny hats after a big lunch and eight martinis apiece. Comical remarks such as "We want a touchdown!" fill the air and during the third inning old Bob Stottlebower is carried under the stands so the kiddies won't see him and get the wrong impression of their future Alma Mater. At the seventh-inning stretch half of the wives leave and go back to Thayer Hall to lay down and think of home. That night nobody knows what the score was.

Speaking of baseball, I don't know what Cotton Mather

would make of it but square old Harvard owns a piece of the St. Louis Cardinals. By an anonymous gift the University owns 10,000 shares of Anheuser-Busch stock.[8] Anheuser-Busch, in turn, owns the St. Louis Cardinals, having purchased the club from Fred Saigh for about $3,750,000.

Says the *Crimson* (in March 1953), "Harvard's stock is listed as worth $250,000.00 but is worth much more than that. Probably Harvard's interest in Anheuser-Busch is the equivalent of at least 1/15th and maybe more than 1/10th of the price paid. . . .

"Some questions must be faced:

"What minor league classification will the Harvard baseball team be put into?

"Will Harvard players be subject to annual player draft?

"Can the Cards send us players on option?"

And will the Harvard Corporation be known as the "New Gas House Gang"?

Will President Pusey journey to St. Louis annually to throw out the first ball, check the hot-dog quality, and give the grounds crew a pep talk?

Superannuated Cardinals will probably seek out Cambridge in which to make their homes and with time hanging heavily on their hands will probably take to attending lectures. Spittoons will have to be provided in the lecture halls for these heroes emeritus unless they can be induced to switch from plug tobacco to Copenhagen. (Will the *Crimson* go Pro-cuspidor or violently Anti-cuspidor?)

It is impossible to go into an analysis of each and every sport indulged in at Harvard. Suffice it to say there are "facilities and organization for every level of athletic

---

[8] Actually 9738 shares in June 1961, at which time Harvard's Food, Beverage, and Soap Common stocks consisted, in addition to the Budweiser-Michelob-Bavarian suds holdings, of the following: 2005 General Mills, 34,637 National Dairy Products (worth $998,407), 9046 Procter and Gamble, 2000 E. A. Stuart and Company, 9800 Unilever, Inc. (worth $1,011,185).

ability. . . . There are 49 tennis courts, 71 squash courts; the Indoor Athletic Building which contains two swimming pools (there is another in one of the Houses), three basketball courts, and rooms for wrestling, boxing and fencing. . . . Just across the Charles on Soldiers Field are 79 acres of playing fields. Dillon Field House is there and the Briggs cage and the stadium, which was the first college stadium built (1903). A new enclosed artificial-ice hockey rink was completed in 1955."

In addition to the standard sports there are also varsity teams in sailing, skiing, lacrosse, and rugby. There is also occasionally informal cricket, bowling on the green and maybe even curling, cockfighting, falconry, and tossing the caber. That form of organized murder known as hurling is restricted to contests, and brutal ones, by Irish teams in Boston on Sunday afternoons. Although Averell Harriman (Yale '13) was a champion croquet player, there are no facilities for this game at Harvard. Still, I have a well-heeled classmate who played polo. (Mr. Harriman was also an internationally known polo player, but how did he get in here?)

"But skiing!" you're saying, "where do they practice— in the slush in Mount Auburn cemetery? Ridiculous!" (Please stop pounding on the table. And I'm not deaf, you know.)

I don't know *where* the ski team practices, but in the winter of '35–'36 I used to drive out on wintry afternoons to Concord, with N. Blatchford, IIIrd (who was wandering through Sociology with Sorokin and Boldyreff), and ski on Ponkawtassett Hill where Ellery Channing used to live. My brother's 1932 Ford phaeton had very leaky side curtains. We also took the "Snow Train" on Sunday from the North Station, which whisked us to the mountains where there were much bigger trees to crash into. We were a pretty sorry lot by modern standards. Parallel skiing had not been invented. We used the Hannes Schneider method in which you assumed a crouch like Heinie Engel or some other famous wrestler approaching his adversary and about to fall into a forty-minute toe-hold. We had no steel edges or safety bindings. We made our own wax from a secret formula, the principal ingredient of which was melted phonograph records. There were no ski lifts. The girls wore their brothers' mackinaws and baggy blue Melton ski pants. The trails weren't overrun with Kanonen bearing German accents and having complexes like baked apples covered with maple syrup. Stretch pants hadn't even been invented. How rectangular can you get?

That was skiing at Harvard back in the Alf M. Landon days and it is no wonder Scotch Fitzgerald got irretrievably loaded and disorderly when he went up to the Dartmouth Winter Carnival to make that movie. He just took one look at the girls' sporty outing costumes and had to have thirty-four martinis at once.

Harvard recently received a somewhat bizarre challenge from some roughnecks across the seas:

TO THE EDITORS OF THE *CRIMSON*

Four or six members of the Oxford Tiddlywinks Society (all-England champions and holders of the Prince Phillip Interuniversity Trophy) are planning a tour of the States from July to September 1962. We are keen to accept any challenges from your side of the Atlantic and particularly like to play a series against the Ivy League. Any help or publicity you can give us would be much appreciated.

Yours faithfully,
Elizabeth Kind
(Hon. Sec. O. U. T. S.)
St. Hugh's College, Oxford

We understand the Harvard Athletic Association declined this challenge after a *sub rosa* investigation which disclosed the fact that the Oxford Tiddlywinks Society is noted for its all-out, no-holds-barred, brutal style of play. The report also implied that of a six-man team (none of whom weighs less than fifteen stone), at least one is a rank professional. It was felt best to avoid an unpleasant international incident.

Before we leave the stadium and trudge tired but happy across the Larz Anderson bridge for hot buttered rums and indigestible canapés let us return, at the risk of inducing tedium,[9] to the subject of Harvard football.

While we raise our hammered silver flasks from Shreve, Crump and Low and watch the Yalies trying to tip over the Harvard bass drum (a source of further irritation to the Elis because it is the Biggest Drum in the Ivy League and possibly the Biggest Drum in captivity), I am going to turn the meeting over to John M. Barnaby, '32, Harvard coach of tennis and squash. Although in 1961 Harvard trounced, drubbed, cudgeled, stomped on, ran roughshod over, and dismembered and ground into the Connecticut greensward a very irritable Yale team to the dulcet notes of 27 to ought, the *Crimson* was displeased again. (I wonder if they love their mothers?) In another slashing bit of two-fisted journalism they described the Crimson victory as a "horror show," a "debacle," and, finally, reaching for the journalistic stars: "slop." They were also dreadfully concerned and made quite ill by the fact that the Varsity Club dared to hold a Victory Dinner, which they described as a "sickening congratulation fest."

Tennis and Squash Coach Barnaby, relaxed and happy on the Monday morning following the game, as all Harvard men from the Back Bay to the steaming jungles of Amazonas were after that splendid and spiritually uplifting Saturday, picked up the *Crimson*. He noted in the Classified Section that a ride was wanted by "2 gorgeous girls and 1 ugly guy to St. Paul or thereabouts." He saw that "Dr. Timothy Leary will address the Social Relations Graduate Colloquium on 'The Inner Utopia' at 4 P.M. today in room 327, Emerson Hall." He read that the Catholic Student Center lecture by Prof. Christopher Dawson had been postponed. He observed that a "Rolls Royce 1934 Sports Saloon, Hooper body, owner driven,

[9] "Football bores me!"—F. E. Bissell, Jr., '31, M.A. '35.

sea green, push button chassis lubrication, overhauled, rebored, beautiful condition" could be had for $2750.00 firm from Mike Liles, Hastings 43. He made a mental note of the Harvard-Radcliffe Verein Turmwaechter Filmabend scheduled for 7:30 P.M.

He then turned to page three and read the article above mentioned, entitled:

IVY LEAGUE HITS ALL-TIME LOW POINT

Within a period of less than sixty seconds Coach Barnaby's blood pressure had reached an All-Time High Point. Smoke was seen to curl from his ears, sparks whistled from his nostrils, and tongues of blue flame flitted about his lips. Seizing a convenient sheet of asbestos, he penned a letter to the *Crimson* which was printed on the following day.

And I think that all of you Old Campers will agree with me when I say that I feel this letter by Coach John Barnaby expresses better than I can the high ideals of sportsmanship which I like to think is the keystone of life here at our beloved Camp Wipigaki in the Pines by historic Upper Moose Lake. And in the Varsity Game of Life let us all remember. . . .

(Cries of "Let's hear the letter!" "Quit shoving, Schroeder!" "Pipe down, you guys!" "Who's got the marshmallows?" Etc., etc.)

IN THE MAIL

IVY LEAGUE FOOTBALL

TO THE EDITORS OF THE CRIMSON:

I write in reply to Michael S. Lottman's article of Thursday, December 7, concerning the Ivy League.

I have never before written in this vein, although I have naturally disagreed with the *Crimson's* view on occasion during my coaching career.

I have been active in and an observer of Ivy athletics for some thirty years. I think I know a little of what I am talking about. I seriously question whether Mr. Lottman has anything more behind his views than a penchant for destructive cynicism plus a habit of self-indulgence in this direction, minus a sense of responsibility in making use of our much heralded freedom of the press. To back this up:

First, he says the Ivy League is a dying concern. This just plainly is not true. The fact is that most people in athletics admire Harvard's "Athletics For All," and the athletic picture at more and more schools is trending toward the Ivy type; intramural provision for all the students plus, at the top of each sport, an intercollegiate team that grows from and represents the normal student body as contrasted with the big time team which is always composed of a special group financed by athletic money, not educational money.

The Ivy League, based on this thinking, is to be judged not by the standard of top-notch performance in the stadia, but by the question "Does this type of program contribute more or less to the educational process?" Quite obviously it contributes more; because at an Ivy college, anyone with reasonable ability and the will to work at a sport can go out for that sport and will be given a chance and some coaching. At any college where top-notch performance is guranteed continually by "athletic scholarships" (what a contradiction those two words make anyway!) the student body as a whole is automatically excluded from the intercollegiate program. Leaving aside the irrelevant consideration that the Ivy League performance sometimes falls short of pleasing "true football fan" Lottman, which type of program makes sense, educationally, for the students?

It is a fact that in the minds of thoughful people everywhere, the benefits of our program are more than worth the loss in N.C.A.A. prestige and also justify the fact that not all games are superlative entertainment.

Second, he says we cheat. We claim not to recruit, but do; claim not to practice, but do. I say, let him cite chapter and verse and back up that dirty crack with specific proof, or let him publicly retract what he said—and on the front page in large type. Over several centuries, Harvard has stood for one thing if for nothing else—integrity. I, for one, consider this

sort of mud slinging to be inexcusable and unworthy of any representative of Harvard. I also think it marks the lowest ebb in my experience in *Crimson* editorial responsibility. Let every officer of the *Crimson* bear in mind that tolerance of such greasy practices reflects on them as well as on Lottman. When does freedom of expression become license? When will the *Crimson* regain its proper status as being a reasonable representation of Harvard student opinion?

What are facts? Harvard could—easily and quickly—have a "great" football team if it wished to make this the objective. This is so obvious—with Harvard's prestige and money—that it can stand as a statement of fact. Why don't we? Because it would mean compromising more important educational values.

It is true we try to interest football players in Harvard, *provided* they qualify in general as satisfactory Harvard prospects. We also go after outstanding boys who do all sorts of other things—debators, musicians, etc. It is a fact (not a speculation) that we lose many football players because we won't offer them a lot of extra financial incentive. Are we so poor? No—Harvard gives more financial aid annually than any other college. We merely refuse to set the athlete on a special financial pedestal. To equate our normal search for talent of all sorts with the usual meaning of the word "recruit" is such a distortion of the truth that Lottman's use of the word is at least inexcusable if not worse—or is he really that ignorant of the subject concerning which he does not hesitate to damn and dogmatise?

My teams at Harvard are not recruited. They are legitimate members of the student body. Sometimes they commit the awful crime of playing below the level of Australian tennis and Pakistanian squash—but we still consider our activities moderately worthwhile. Some people even like to watch. Looking objectively at football, I personally submit the suggestion that Captain Pete Hart, who I am told began at 165 pounds and worked like a dog to build himself up to become a regular, then captain—this boy got as much or more out of football at Harvard than any paid athlete anywhere any time. I even got a kick out of it myself. This is the true and proper function of college athletics—beneficial experience for student participants. Any bored spectators have the privilege of stay-

ing away, from the games, from the dinners, and from unconstructive criticism that hurts some and helps none.

John M. Barnaby '32
Coach—Tennis and Squash

Considering that the Harvard athlete is also carrying a full study load under conditions of stiff scholastic competition in a college where intellectual pursuits are the essential business at hand, he bears some relationship to Dr. Johnson's woman preacher:

"Sir, a woman preaching is like a dog walking on his hind legs. It is not done well; but you are surprised to find it done at all."

If Harvard plays football like a dog walking on its hind legs, instead of carping let us be grateful that they are playing at all. After all, the boys have other fish to fry. But they *do play*. We have no record at hand of Mr. Khrushchev's athletic background, but President Kennedy while at Harvard played on the Jayvee Football team,[10] and he is still passing the ball around on the lawn with relatives, friends, and Clansmen. This seems to astonish everybody, although the President who preceded J.F.K. spent hundreds of hours playing golf and shooting at birds. Or as Bob Hope says:

"Listen, touch football is not a sissy sport. Up there in Hyannis Port, roughing the passer is a federal rap."

President Kennedy sometimes notes parallels between football and politics, but not in the inspirational hit-the-line-hard vein of Teddy Roosevelt.

In the fall of 1961 Notre Dame's football team bested Syracuse 17–15 on a disputed ruling by a referee which was followed by howls of indignation from the losers.

Speaking at the National Football Foundation's annual banquet shortly afterwards, President Kennedy said:

"Some Republicans have been unkind enough to sug-

---

[10] Kennedy also was on the Winthrop House hockey, swimming, and softball teams, and in addition his Class Biography contains the note: Golf (1).

gest that my election . . . was similar to the Notre Dame–Syracuse game. But I'm like Notre Dame. We just take it as it comes along. We're not giving it back."

A certain Mr. H. Jones, from the Middle West, writes me on football as follows:

"The Wisconsin freshman team this year had a line averaging 260 lbs. One of the boys weighs 300, is 6'4", and is as fast as an angry grizzly bear.

"Somebody on the Ohio State Alumni Association had a letter published this fall saying it would be cheaper to hire a pro team than pay our $416,000.00 in athletic scholarships to students who really don't have to take any courses which could be called real education.

"The only courses a football player could pass at Harvard (not necessarily because of stupidity, but because of no time for anything else) would be in the Divinity School, which is not open to undergraduates."

I've always shied away from the Divinity School myself, on account of all that Hebrew syntax. And I am not perfectly sure that a three-hundred-pound football player would just breeze through Church History 123: "Readings in the Vulgate and Medieval Latin Literature"; Theology 171; "Theological Anthropology"; or Church History 201: "Ecclesiastical Historiography." I am trying but I find it hard to picture some fullback in ivy-covered Eliot House thumbing the pages of the *Harvard Theological Review* and getting all wrapped up in such articles as "Oxyrhynchus Papyrus 655 Reconsidered," by Robert A. Kraft; "Theological Tendency in the Textual Variants of Codex Bezae Cantabrigiensis," by Eldon Jay Epp; or "Dryden's Apparent Scepticism in Religio Laici," by Elias J. Chiasson. It's true that Elmer Gantry got through Divinity School but I don't think it was Harvard though I am not sure. I suppose I could call Burt Lancaster or Shirley Jones, but they are probably both in Rome. I seem to be about the only one left these days who is not in Rome.

"Mack Lewis, of Iowa, only a substitute center," our

Mr. H. Jones continues, "resembled a dinosaur. When he centered the ball, instead of looking between his legs and quailing with fear, Mack snapped the ball with his right hand, glowering at the opposing guards, and as he snapped the ball took a step forward and knocked the opposing center flat on his ass with the open palm of his hand—activity which went unnoticed in the railroad boxcar shunting noises and thunder of play rolling up into the stands from typical Big 10 blocking and tackling."

No, we certainly can't see anything like this when Harvard takes the field. But if we demand to see hired professionalism in action let us thumb through the catalogue of the Faculty of Arts and Sciences, stroll up to the Yard, and attend a few lectures. These are Harvard's professionals. That is why the 35,000 top-standing high school students in the country recently voted Harvard as the "college they would most like to attend." Harvard's professionals, her faculty, are not rewarded by invitations to the Rose Bowl but with Nobel prizes, Fellowships, Presidencies of Universities and Large Corporations, domestic and foreign honors, and occasional invitations to occupy the White House and rearrange the furniture.

Francis Bacon, in discussing the subject, says:

"Studies serve for delight, for ornament, and for ability. Their chief use for delight is in privateness and retiring; for ornament is in discourse; and for ability, is in the judgment and disposition of business; for expert men can execute, and perhaps judge of particulars, one by one; but the general counsels, and the plots and marshaling of affairs come best from those that are learned."

No mention of football.

John Milton says:

"I call a complete and generous education that which fits a man to perform justly, skilfully, and magnanimously all the offices both private and public of peace and war."

No complaints about the team.

T. E. Huxley says:

"Education is the instruction of the intellect in the

laws of Nature, under which name I include not merely things and their forces, but men and their ways; and the fashioning of the affections and of the will into an earnest and loving desire to move in harmony with those laws."

No squawk there about being stuck with seats on the five-yard line again.

What the hell is football anyway? Scott Fitzgerald wondered if it was a symbol of the "eternal violence of life," or of "the eternal immaturity of the race," or even of "the failure of culture within the walls." But after the soul-searching he ends up blubbering about it, calling it "beautiful" and "the most intense and dramatic spectacle since the Olympic games." Eventually he bursts into uncontrollable sobs:

"The death of Johnny Poe (a Princeton football hero) with the Black Watch in Flanders starts the cymbals crashing for me, plucks the strings of nervous violins *as no adventure of the mind that Princeton ever offered*." The italics are mine but the sentiment, thank God, is his.

I make the mistake of reading the newspapers, or daily horror sheets. What with East Berlin, Georgie Sokolsky's alarms, Castro dictators and Castro convertible beds, Jack Paar's ill nature, landslides in Peru, train wrecks in Holland, rats in Harlem, planes blowing up, governments you never heard of falling down, and Zsa Zsa Gabor—why it fairly makes a person's hair stand unbecomingly on end. And football doesn't help 1 bit. So who needs it? I'm through with it.

The hell with football.

Still, we did beat Yale.
27–0.

CHAPTER IX

The Author in the Guise
of an Anthropologist

Their faith in education was so full of pathos that one dared not ask them what they could do with education when they got it.

—HENRY ADAMS (CLASS OF 1858)

HOW I WANDERED into Anthropology at Harvard is a bit hazy. I had always intended to concentrate in American History and Literature, largely because I admired Huck and Jim and the Mississippi River Valley. The connection may seem remote. It was: I had never heard of the Transcendentalists; all American poets, even Walt Whitman, bored me; I didn't know a Whig from a Know-Nothing—what could I have been thinking of? What I was thinking of apparently was Grant before Vicksburg, the lead mines at Galena, Captain Daniel Smith Harris and the "Grey Eagle" on the Upper Mississippi, my grandfather's Victorian house in Dubuque, the Ryan Hotel in St. Paul, the Bellevue and Cascade, Iowa, narrow-gauge railroad, rafting on the Chippewa River, and "Frank on a Gunboat" by Harry Castlemon. My readings in American literature had been largely confined to a number of works never gnawed over and worried by Van Wyck Brooks and De Voto. More than likely the department of American History and Literature at Harvard is still ignoring the authors on my list. I refer to such noble contributions to the stream of American literature as "George At the Wheel," by Harry Castlemon, "Four Afloat" and "Four in Camp," by Ralph Henry Barbour, "Swatty" (laid in Muscatine, Iowa, a river town), by Ellis Parker Butler, "Sube Cane," by Edward Bellamy Partridge, "Rudder Grange," by Frank Richard Stockton, "A-Rafting on the Mississip'," by Charles Edward Russell, and "Old Times on the Upper Mississippi," by George Byron Merrick. You can tell these are important writers because they all have a middle name and use it.[1] Another significant volume, thus far overlooked completely by Harvard, the *Saturday Review*, Mary McCarthy, and H. R. Trevor-Roper, is "The Motor Boat Boys' River Chase," by Louis Arundel (M. A. Donahue and Co., Chicago, 1914). In its depiction of six chums afloat and ashore in the period of pre-World War I teleological idealism and neo-realist pseudo-pragmatic "historical discipline" we find a cogent correspondence with a rare and ever-familiar reality.

Aside from these classics, my readings in American letters at Exeter had been confined to *Ethan Frome* and *The Scarlet Letter*, neither of which put me in a very feverish condition.

True, I was somewhat of an authority on Melville, having seen John Barrymore and Dolores Costello silently in *The Sea Beast* four times at the Majestic Theatre in Dubuque, Iowa, in 1926, followed four years later by two viewings of John Barrymore and Joan Bennett in *The Sea Beast* (with sound), once in the Thompson Gymnasium at Exeter and once in the Gem Theatre in Bellevue, Iowa.

---

[1] Frank Sullivan says of Wendell Phillips that "he was about the only Bostonian of his time who wore no middle name and was therefore considered half naked. Even Mark Twain, when he went to visit Howells in Boston, registered as Samuel Longhorne Clemens."

Barrymore's address at that time was 6 Tower Road, Hollywood, California, while Norma Talmadge was living at 1038 Beach Road, Hollywood.

In my freshman year at Harvard I took Geology, a stiff course but one made interesting, up to a point, by Kirtley Mather ("down down down in Mothurr Earrth's Interriorr" . . . "these schisty forrmations" . . .). When showing slides of gneiss, gabbro, or Roxbury conglomerate there were often figures in the picture, usually ladies and gentlemen in turn-of-the-century garb, and Mather always raised a howl by stating parenthetically: "These people we see here absorrbed in this interrresting loess deposit arre not memburrs of my immediate family." Aside from such merry moments the course was a head-buster, especially the lab work in Peabody Museum. Nothing that I did in Geology lab ever worked, ever came out right. On a dreary afternoon when all of Greater Boston lay under a sodden blanket of mist, fog, and soft coal smoke and there was a new Dick Powell and Ruby Keeler film directed by Busby Berkeley that I wanted to see playing a matinee at the Uni Theatre on the Square, I would be found in the Peabody Museum scratching rocks together and trying to identify them. It seemed a useless sort of occupation. The possibility of ever using these techniques in the future seemed very slim, my goal in life during my freshman year being that of Motion-Picture Theatre Manager. For in the words of Walter A. Cutter, in his well-known essay "Psychology of the Theatre": "The individual theatre is the outpost of the industry and the manager is the visible representative."

The career shaped up as the ideal one to me, and during English 28 lectures I used to think up new and daring gimmicks for attracting hordes to my film house. I also spent considerable time thumbing a pamphlet put out by the National School of Motion Picture Theatre Management. And I pored over books from Widener Library on the subject that discussed the pros and cons of various soap-dispensing devices for the rest rooms, and how to handle a kiddies' matinee.[2]

I have forgotten most of whatever I once knew about John Dryden (Trinity College, Cambridge, Class of 1654), John Milton (Christ's College, Cambridge, Class of 1629), John Donne (Oxford 1587, Cambridge 1590), John of Gaunt, John of Brienne (Emperor of Constantinople), and John Zapolya (born at the castle of Szepesvar in 1487, appointed to the voivody of Transylvania in 1511, crowned king of Hungary on Armistice Day, November 11, 1523)—but I have not forgotten the aphorisms I soaked up as a youth at Harvard from the *Ace Motion Picture Handbook For Managers and Operators:*

Whatever the character of theatre seats, they must be firmly fastened to the floor.

Where a single musician (piano player) is employed it is of the utmost importance that he or she be "on the job" from the time the picture starts until it stops.

The TICKET SELLER should be a bright and attractive young lady, neatly dressed and wideawake.

An affable manager is an asset to any theatre.

The cost of a vaudeville act should run not more than $25 for each actor per week.

At any rate, my experiences in Geology and in the great gloomy pile of the Peabody Museum had nothing to do with my switch from American History and Literature to Anthropology and three more years in this same great gloomy pile. It was all my brother's fault.

[2] See *Building Theatre Patronage*, by Barry and Sargent (illus.), 1927, as an example. Perhaps one quote from this work will whet your appetite. From the chapter entitled "Outdoor Advertising" I select one out of 81 promotional suggestions.

"71. *Deaf Man.* A stunt that stops traffic is a man with an ear trumpet listening to a friend telling about the great picture to be seen at your theatre. If the men are good actors, it does not in the least suggest an advertising stunt, and it can be worked repeatedly, especially in trolley cars."

David Merrick, are you listening?

I finished the freshman year in Geology with dogged distaste. In my map of the Boston area on the final examination I remembered where to put the Squantum tillite and the Medford diabase, but got derailed someplace in the Ordovician System, flubbed up a whole raft of brachiopods, cystids, blastoids, ostracods,[3] and bryozoa, and ended up with a D for the course and a profound sense of relief that I would *never* have to enter the Peabody Museum again as long as we both should be in existence.

So my brother and I went home to Iowa for a summer of low water on the Mississippi. I was still heading for American History and Literature so I went down to the Carnegie-Stout Public Library and promised them I would be a "Clean-Hands Reader" if they would let me borrow *Main Currents in American Thought* by Vernon Louis Parrington, who was born on the Burlington Railroad at Aurora, Ill., and taught for twenty years at the University of Washington where he was hailed by the staff of the Bremerton Navy Yard as the Van Wyck Brooks of the Ponderosa Pine Belt. Of this glutinous work the *World Book* says: "Its critical understanding and fresh readable style has not been equalled in any similar work."

As a future alert Motion Picture Theatre Manager perhaps I wasn't in the mood for Parrington. Perhaps it was natural stupidity. The book seemed to be written in my native tongue but I could make nothing of it. I reread sentences to see if I could figure out what they meant. I couldn't. What a shock. What the hell was I getting into? Panic.

I complained to my brother Fred, whose middle name is actually Ezekiel. He was a tutor in History and Literature and an Instructor in History 1 at the time. He lived in Eliot House and was pals with Frisky Merriman, F. Otto Matthiessen, DeVoto, Merk, Harry Levin, Murdock, Whitehead, Perry E. G. Miller, Karpovich, McIlwain, Ted Spencer—you name them, he knew them. T. S. Eliot

[3] An "ostracod" is an unpopular codfish.

had just spent a year as a Visiting Something and lived in Eliot House and my brother knew him, too.[4] I asked the oracle if he could understand Parrington.

"What do you mean 'understand' him?" he said. I should have known better than to ask a Phi Bete a question like that.

"Well, I can't understand what the hell he's talking about. Emerson and all that."

He mulled this over for a while.

"You know what you ought to do," he said. "You ought to get into Anthropology."

"Yeah?" I said. "What's that?"

My brother is a compelling momentary enthusiast. He tells you that everybody should walk from Seattle, Washington, to Juneau, Alaska. He pictures crisp mornings on the trail, sizzling rainbow trout at dusk, amorous Indian maidens in scanty clothing, man-to-man talks with the Royal Mounties, dance-hall girls in beaded dresses, gold dust, the lure of the Open Road, the hush of the pines, the call of the moose, election to the Explorers Club, color pages in the *National Geographic*, lecture tours, bejeweled matrons offering their favors in rotation. . . .

When you stagger in six months later covered with deer-fly bites, broke, suffering from six Indian diseases and minus an arm which you left with a kodiak bear rather than argue about it, the following dialogue takes place:

"Say, you don't look so fine. Where have you been?" he says.

"I did like you said. I walked from Seattle to Juneau."

"Yeah? What kind of a crazy stunt was that?"

"It was pretty neat. I met this Indian girl, see. Say are they ever friendly up there. Good looker, and boy, what a pair of eyes. So I said to her, 'Listen, honey, how about you and me . . .'"

[4] Mr. Eliot left a coat hanger in his closet when he departed which can be seen today in the Author's Collection of Harvardiana. Admission 25¢. Closed Mondays.

"Yeah, yeah," he says. "Listen, let me tell you about my trip to Milwaukee. I met good old Carl Mueller. Remember Carl? He's got this 1914 Locomobile roadster. Undershot valves, reversible camshaft, 35⅝ X 15¼ tires, snakeskin upholstery, sliding doors. Boy, he's got it made. What a car. Finest piece of machinery I ever saw. I'd give my right arm for a car like that."

Since you haven't got a right arm any more to give, you borrow some money and give that to Carl instead and buy the car. So what happens?

"Where'd you get the heap?" says my brother.

"Why from Carl Mueller. You got me so fired up I went over and bought her."

"Does it run?" he says. "Listen, let me tell you about my trip to Ottumwa . . ."

One of my brother's buddies was Lloyd Cabot Briggs. His mother was a Cabot but he was an anthropologist.[5] We called him "Beaver," which had something obscure to do with his youth at Milton Academy. He's still a practicing anthropologist and lives in North Africa, in Algiers. Probably has a harem, the bastard, while I spend all my time driving kids to music lessons. Anyway Beaver had brother Frederick all hopped up on anthropology via witty anecdotes, curious limericks, strange sex practices of the Hottentot, inside dope about fossil mandibles, and glowing reports on sibfriends and infibulation in the tribes along the Ucayali River.

"Why don't you read *Up From the Ape?*" my brother said in a tone that implied that a refusal to do so would confirm a somber but friendly suspicion that I was not interested in the right things.

So I returned Parrington to the library and have not seen him since. Smiling wanly at the librarian, who asked me

---

[5] His father was the eminent Boston psychiatrist L. Vernon Briggs, who testified that Sacco and Vanzetti were sane. On one occasion Dr. Briggs left a package containing feces for laboratory analysis on the front seat of his Rolls-Royce. When he came back, the package had been stolen by a sneak thief, who got quite a surprise.

how I liked it at Yale, I withdrew from the premises with a copy of *Up From the Ape,* by Earnest Albert Hooton, Professor of Anthropology at Harvard.

Hooton, who died in 1954, had a son named Newton Hooton. But aside from that, Hooton was a brilliant and world-renowned physical anthropologist, a writer, and an endlessly entertaining lecturer. Physical anthropology concerns itself not only with dolichocephalic and brachiocephalic skulls of man and their meaning, the number of precise degrees the arm bones are twisted and such lore, but also with heredity, cell development and evolution, anatomy, physiology, zoology, embryology, paleontology, and other assorted, related ologies. Anthropology is the science of Man. Not individual Man, but Man in groups, races, and peoples. Physical anthropology, sometimes called "somatology," is not concerned with man's customs, arts, and material culture, but with his bodily inheritance.

Hooton was an "ape man." His specialty was the primates, the highest zoological order of mammals, to which all of us glorious human beings belong, together with our cousins the monkeys, apes, and lemurs. Within his specialty Hooton was particularly entranced by the chimps, gibbons, gorillas, orangs, and even the mysterious spectral tarsier. He was endlessly amused and bemused by the anthropoid apes, so remarkably like ourselves, behaving unlike other animals and in many respects like men. Hooton's great appeal, especially to a fathead like me, was that he had a sense of humor, a commodity rarer than perfumes of Araby in academic circles. I have known plenty of scholars and they can be good companions, but oh how arid an existence some of them live. They can't understand anything. How can you take a man seriously who can behold Major Hoople leaning on a snow shovel, and produce no more facial expression than if he were looking at some trigonometry tables, can read a piece by Benchley or S. J. Perelman with the vacant response of a hibernating opossum, or observe the pained expression on Jack

Benny's face without a flickering twitch of human understanding?

I am not suggesting that Hooton was a Fred Allen, but he had a wry and dispassionate view of the human race, possibly because he viewed people not as God's anointed but as primates.

Up From the Ape was written in an easy and informative style and the subject matter seemed fascinating. Parrington was out. New England's dopey old Indian summer was out. The American Claimant and the Plight of the Farmer and the Son of the Middle Border were out. The Rising Middle Class was out and so were Bronson Alcott, the History of Standard Oil and *Leaves of Grass*. Anthropology was In. Hand in hand with a happy chimpanzee I would stroll thru the piled-up femurs and fragments of brain pans under the paternal eye of genial father Hooton. And besides the friendly anthropoids there were Mayan temples waiting for me to discover in the Guatemalan jungles, Inca breastplates of gold, a joint dig in the Easter Islands perhaps, with attractive girl anthropologists from . . . (from where? Stanford? University of Chicago? Columbia?)—and perhaps a year in the Tuamotu Archipelago doing a definitive bit of research on marriage customs. (The chief would insist that I take not one but *both* of his daughters to wife. On a temporary basis of course.)

So when we had straggled back to a hot September Cambridge I went around to see Professor Alfred Marston Tozzer (A.B. '00, Ph.D. '04), the eminent Mayan scholar and authority on Chichen-Itza, who was then head of the Department of Anthropology. Here I was back in that great pile of bricks again, in the Peabody Museum.

"You wish to change your field of concentration from History and Literature of America to Anthropology?" the kindly professor queried. "Why?"

"Well, you see my brother . . . uh, I mean I read *Up From the Hoot*, by Earnest Ape this summer and. . . . There's all those apes and stuff like that. . . . I mean it sounds pretty . . . well . . . interesting and like that . . .

take like Tarzan for example," I said. "Hooton—I mean Mr. Hooton—I mean Professor Hooton lectured to us in Geology last year. He was real keen—I mean right on the ball with the bones. . . ."

Tozzer should have tossed me out onto Divinity Avenue but instead he let me in. I didn't even resemble the ape—"inventive but cultureless," as the great Alfred Kroeber says.

And that is why I happen to have a degree in Anthropology instead of one in American History and Literature, and explains why I am an authority on pictograph "love letters" of the Yukaghir tribes in Siberia [6] instead of on Celia Thaxter, the poetess laureate of the Isle of Shoals. To show you what I got into, one of these love letters, which are scratched on a piece of birch bark by Yukaghir maidens as it is the only way a young girl in those parts is allowed to tell a fellow she thinks he is mighty cool, is translated thus:

Each youth his mate doth find; my fate alone it is of him to dream who to another wedded is, and I must fain contented be, if only he forget me not.

This may have suffered a bit in the translation, as it was translated by Jochelson (a political exile in Siberia under the Czars) into Russian first and then into English. All the ingredients of ethnological scholarship are contained herein, however, and by comparison Cotton Mather is breezier than George Ade.

With my uncanny penchant for self-torture, having gotten into the Department of Anthropology (sealing up my college career via the casual reading of one book) I proceeded to take all the wrong courses within the field.

I never saw Hooton again, for one thing, except in the

[6] For more information see Waldemar Jochelson, "The Yukaghir and the Yukaghirized Tungus," the Jesup North Pacific Expedition, edited by Franz Boas; *Memoirs of the American Museum of Natural History,*" Vol. IX (N.Y., 1926) pp. 434-436; 444-450.

corridors or hurrying through the rain, until my oral exams three years later when he said:

"I see you have had two years of Russian language. Why is that?"

"I thought it would be fun," I said, "to know an off-beat language like that."

"What connection is there," he asked, peering at me through his thick lenses, "between Church Slavonic and old Finno-Ugrian?"

"I don't know," I replied cheerfully. "Professor Cross just taught us how to read and write."

"Hum," he said.

(Yes, I passed my Orals.)

First off, I had to take Anthropology 1, which covered the entire subject of Man and his works in all ages and climates from the primeval ooze up to Herbert Hoover. All in one full course. It was like a Burton Holmes lecture plus thumbing back issues of the *National Geographic*. As soon as you got interested in the archeology of Mesopotamia, you were whisked off to New Mexico and "The Zuñi Origin Myth: The Origin of Corn." It was all most perplexing, and rather like being nine years old and confronted with a five-pound box of candy.

Actually I got a degree in Anthropology (having passed my Senior Oral Exams I was even excused from final exams), and only actually took three courses labeled "Anthropology," and since two of them were half-courses I really only had *two* courses in the field.

The joker was, the field is so broad, that dozens of other-departmental courses are "related." This enabled me to absent myself from the Peabody Museum for months at a time. I don't recall even being in the building in my senior year.

In my junior year, when I should have taken Hooton, I shied at a tin can in the road, jumped three fences, and landed in The American Indian. Let me give you a tip: If you are worried and distraught, keyed up and filled with tensions so that you can't sleep and are using those pills, toss the pills out the window and get a copy of *The Sun Dance and other ceremonies of the Oglala Division of the Teton Dakota*, by J. R. Walker. Within minutes you will be in a coma so deep that the *World-Telegram* will send a reporter and a photographer to work up a front-page story. When you have recovered consciousness after ten days, during which time psychologists have been sticking pins in you with no response, pick up *Types of Haida and Tlingit Myths* by John R. Swanton, and despite your recent slumbers it will be another instantaneous case of nighty-night.

My tutor was giving a course in Africa so I took that. It was a slight improvement over the Oglala; and I wrote a complicated and erudite paper on the food supply and medicinal remedies of some tribe in Nigeria as well as a definitive report on the Masai. Ever since my paper on the Masai no anthropologist has dared to touch the subject. ("It's been done. That Bissell paper. Remember? 1935? Princeton, I think, or possibly University of Chicago. Completely authoritative. Amazingly thorough.") But I should have been taking that course on Asia. I was always going to the wrong ball park.

In the American Indian course we chipped flints in laboratory. The object was to make an arrowhead, or a spearhead, or dammit, *something*. It was worse than Thurber's lab work in Botany and his troubles with a microscope. We had plenty of instruction on how to chip these flints ("a sharp blow at the percussion point," etc.) but I never succeeded in making anything that looked more remarkable than a piece of flint somebody had been pounding on. I think the Indians bought their arrowheads from an arrowhead factory someplace that has yet to be discovered. Possibly in Pittsburgh or Detroit.

I got a final mark of A in Classical Archeology, from Professor Chase. My father insisted that Chase had gotten my mark mixed up with somebody else's. But it was no fluke. I *liked* the course, and I *liked* little white-haired

George Chase ('96), and I *liked* the Topography and Monuments of Athens, the History of Greek Vase-Painting, Mycenae and Tiryns. Besides, the course was given in the Fogg Museum, where we were surrounded by Renaissance artifacts that fell pleasantly upon the eye. Professor Chase, who was Dean of the Faculty of Arts and Sciences, Hudson Professor of Archeology, Curator of Classical Antiquities, and a member of the Corporation of the Yenching Institute, once became so deeply engrossed in his studies in Widener Library that when he finally returned to reality he discovered that the library was closed and locked for the night with himself inside it. He was rescued by the Yard police.

I also knocked out an A in History of Religion with Professor Arthur Darby Nock, Frothingham Professor of the History of Religion, now Senior Fellow of the Society of Fellows, a man of fantastic erudition but withal a sprightly lecturer with a merry wit. Nock hauled in visiting lecturers; thus it was that I had an opportunity to get an inkling of what was going on in the back room in Sanskrit studies, Semitic studies, Oriental studies. Nock was an Englishman and an oddball, the absent-minded professor type, just loaded with knowledge.

Nock *looks* like the Frothingham Professor, changes his two pairs of glasses constantly while lecturing, speaks in an almost unintelligible English of his own devising, frequently beaming and ejaculating "Ha" or "Ho" when a point he has made amuses him, and can be seen shuffling into Harvard Hall on wintry mornings wearing a plush hat of the type favored by Sunday-School superintendents in the 1910 period. At this writing he is still going strong. Hooton rather frightened me. Roger Bigelow ("Frisky") Merriman was twelve feet tall and terrified me. But Nock didn't. A Jewish classmate taught me how to write two sentences from the Old Testament in Hebrew and I rang them in on my final exam. Nock must have known that I wasn't a student of Hebrew, but he didn't say anything. I think he enjoyed the joke.

"Why can't that boy ever get an A in something sensible?" was my father's comment on this triumph of mine. Once when I was going through my Proust Period, father picked up *Swann's Way* and after reading ten pages by the eminent stylist and *Prix Goncourt* twentieth-century literary champ, delivered himself of a terse two-word critique: "Smart aleck." Yet thirty-five years previous to this edict he had been taking courses at Harvard from William James, Santayana, Munsterberg, and Josiah Royce. *Slava bogu!*

Russian language with Prof. Sam Cross was fun. This was before everybody was looking under the bed for Communists and there were no political implications to taking Russian—it was just another language course, with a powerful literary background. It was small—I believe there were not more than seven or eight in the class, whose motives remained obscure. Mine was curiosity and the desire to be "different," which has characterized a good many of my projects before and since.

Prof. Cross had succeeded the wholly amazing Professor Leo Wiener (father of Norbert), a nonacademic scholar in whom were combined an alert and inquiring mentality with an uncanny aptitude for languages. Professor Grandgent said of Wiener that his "polyglot and iconoclastic activity carried him far beyond the confines of Slavic, carrying light and havoc into realms so remote as to generate faith in almost impregnable security."

I am not sure what that means but it certainly gives forth an impressive rumble. At any rate Wiener's linguistic feats were so extraordinary they resembled those of mathematical geniuses (or freaks) who multiply combinations of twelve-digit numbers in their heads and give the answer in thirty-two seconds.

Professor Samuel Hazzard Cross (A.B. '12, A.M. '15, Ph.D. '16 died 1946, Cambridge, Mass.) was a delightful, rather roly-poly gent with a clipped gray mustache, who met with us in Sever Hall. We sat at the old-style tables which consisted of a narrow plank deeply incised with initials, names, mottoes, scores, and dates back to 1900, carved by former generations of artistic students.

A Radcliffe girl in classes at Harvard was somewhat of a rarity in those days, but we had one in Slavic 1a. Although she did not seem to wash her hair "several times a week" as Nora Sayre tells us she did ("The Radcliffe Girl," *Holiday*, December 1961), our Radcliffe girl lent a special aura to the course. Not that we ever spoke to her. That would have been going too far. When she picked up her books at the end of the hour and disappeared into the teeming corridor I wondered where she was going. I didn't even know where Radcliffe was. Until 1959 I had the idea that Radcliffe was over behind the Divinity School someplace.

One of our number had a distinct and almost unfair advantage over the rest of us struggling Anglo-Saxons bewildered by the Slavic vocabulary and syntax. This was "Mr. Bogunieski." I think he was a day student, a commuter. He had figured out a way to pull down an easy A. The mysterious Russian language, highly inflected, with its verb forms called "aspects," its peculiar absence of articles, and its vocabulary which suggests nothing to Western eyes and ears and must be learned by rote, was as easy for Mr. Bogunieski as falling off a troika: Mr. Bogunieski spoke Polish at home.

Mr. Westbrook Pegler's favorite President, Franklin D. Roosevelt ('04), had just brought about the recognition of the Soviet Union, and when the new Ambassador Troyanovsky visited Cambridge, Professor Cross took our class to meet him. We all shook hands and while we stared at him tongue-tied he addressed us warmly in Russian, of which, since it was not from Dostoievsky, Lermontov, Fonvizin, or Saltykov-Shchedrin, we understood very little. It is a beautiful language and I hope I will not have to take the Fifth Amendment for saying so. I must confess that I am very fond of borsch, too, although I never order it when in Washington, D.C. I mean, why go looking for trouble? As a matter of fact I have a plan for "burying" Khrushchev with the help of heavy earth-moving equipment to be supplied by the LeTourneau Corporation and dropped on Moscow from planes lent by Ozark Air Lines.

All in all, as I look back through the years of alternating despair, triumph, and broken shoelaces since I left Cambridge, I think I fared better in Anthropology than I would have in American History and Literature. The type of scholarship that all too often surrounds literary studies is as far from my natural instincts as life in the chill and arid altiplano of the Andes. And fancy literary criticism leaves me tired and lonesome. For one Dwight Macdonald or Edmund Wilson there are always six thousand earnest obfuscators busily working over their little essays, striking out sentences and recasting them into more stupefying patterns of unintelligibility.[7] De Voto, good friend though he was, almost drove me away from Sam Clemens forever with his *Mark Twain's America*, a viscous gruel requiring litmus paper and the Oxford Dictionary. All the fun and all the elation evaporate from poetry when you start blabbering about it. Max Eastman, for example, in his *Enjoyment of Laughter* succeeded in casting a thick yellowish cloud of mustard gas over the entire subject of "humor," meanwhile draping a sodden blanket of dreary ideas over every comical notion from Aristophanes to Ogden Nash and Joe Frisco. It so happened that I eventually became a writer, after thirteen postgraduate years of bumping into the furniture while wandering through the marts of trade. Edward Weeks ('22), editor of the *Atlantic*, in 1949 discovered me arguing about piece rates in a garment factory and gave me orders to stop doing that at once and become a writer. So I did. If I had been in American History and Literature at Har-

---

[7] Says Clifton Fadiman (Columbia, '25), "A company of mandarins seems to be engaged in the unearthing of ever-new symbols, tensions and ambiguities in the most surprising literary areas. . . . A consequence of this intramural traffic in subtleties is a growing reluctance to read serious literary criticism."

—*Holiday*, May 1962.

vard I suppose I would have ended up an anthropologist and be sorting Aurignacian flints right this minute.

Harvard always offers a racy variety of selections on the intellectual bill of fare. And there was an excitement in the air, not from pep rallies but from the sound of typewriters at open windows, applause from lecture halls, from seeing Alfred North Whitehead strolling through the Yard, from argument, debate—and always talk and more talk about courses. They say the theatre is exciting, that Positano is exciting, that the Revere Beach roller coaster is exciting. Nothing except being in love is as exciting as being an undergraduate at Harvard. In addition to the courses I have mentioned I was also able to sandwich in a full course in Philosophy, one in French Literature, a survey course in English Literature, and a course in Sociology with Professor Sorokin. (Years later I swiped his name, pinning it on the hero in a frolic called *Pajama Game*.) Of science I confess I know no more than I did when I left Exeter, where I learned how to make laughing gas. Thus I find myself embarrassingly ignorant of the technologies required in blowing up cities filled with men, women, children, and dolls, and other inspiring feats of our enlightened age. I am, however, working closely with a Committee whose aim is to humiliate the Russians by being the first to land a complete set of the works of Tiffany Thayer on Arcturus. That'll show them a thing or two and we figure it will only cost the taxpayers $18,911,-098,263.98, plus Federal Entertainment Tax and postage.

My head finally got so stuffed with knowledge that I had to go in to Filene's basement and buy a new hat off the "Slightly Imperfect" table. And I even gave up my ambition to be a genial neighborhood movie-house manager and conduct Bank Nite.

Instead I went to sea, as all young men must do, and saw the Parthenon for myself.

CHAPTER X

A Cheering Interlude
for Yale Readers

(If any have got past page two)

IT SEEMS to me that the institution Harvard is more designed to turn out clergymen than able and informed citizens. . . . The manner of dress and the manner of conducting oneself and of being polite in society, etc., are sciences to which not the least attention is paid; and the outward appearance of the students is the most slovenly that has ever been seen in students of this kind. The President is lean, austere, and of an insufferable circumspection.

—Diary of Francisco de Miranda, 1784

In the midst of the lull the cheer captains called on the Yale crowd. Then they dropped their megaphones and lifted their arms. As one man that vast gathering in the Yale stand suddenly barked:

" 'Rah, 'rah, 'rah! 'Rah, 'rah, 'rah! 'Rah, 'rah, rah! Merriwell! Merriwell! Merriwell!"

—*Dick Merriwell's Colors,*
or All for the Blue,
by Burt L. Standish

> One night, while sleeping,
> I dreamed a dream so sweet.
> I thought that all my schoolmates
> Again I did meet.
> The first young college mate
> To grasp me by the hand
> Was that young athlete,
> Frank Merriwell so grand. . . .
>
> —Jack Lee, Stamford, Texas
> January 13, 1906

According to the late Dr. Arthur Adams, for thirty-five years guiding spirit of the New England Historic Genealogical Society, and an authority on heraldry, Elihu Yale had a very good coat of arms, but John Harvard had none.

Who Killed Society?, Cleveland Amory

William Randolph Hearst, ex-business manager of the Harvard *Lampoon*, is not thought of very highly in some circles.

The edifices used for the under-graduates Chambers and for the lecture rooms are by no means handsome. They are very ugly red-brick houses standing here and there without order. There are seven such. . . . It is almost astonishing that buildings so ugly should have been erected for such a purpose. These . . . stand on a large green, which might be made pretty enough if it were kept well mown like the gardens of our Cambridge colleges; but it is much neglected.[1]

—Anthony Trollope

[1] A quite different viewpoint of these "ugly red-brick houses" is seen in *The Bostonians*, by Henry James. Basil Ransom is discovered walking through the Harvard Yard with Verena Tarrant (James always pins names on his characters as though he was writing for "Chatterbox"). Of the structures in the yard:
"Basil Ransom . . . admired them all, and thought several of them exceedingly quaint and venerable. The rectangular structures of old red brick especially gratified his eye; the afternoon sun was yellow on their homely faces; their windows showed a peep of flower pots and bright-coloured curtains; they wore an expression of scholastic quietude, and exhaled a tradition, an antiquity . . ."

DICK MERRIWELL'S COLORS

TIP TOP WEEKLY

An Ideal Publication for the American Youth

No. 687   JUNE 12 1909   5 CENTS

AT THIS MAGNIFICENT
SPORT THOSE YALE
ENTHUSIASTS OFF THE
LAUNCH WENT FAIRLY
WILD WITH DELIGHT

Sign on a home in Verona, N. J., belonging to John B. R. Anderson, who works for U.S. Steel:

FOR SALE
ACCEPTABLE COLLEGES ONLY
HARVARD UNACCEPTABLE

(Mr. Anderson went to Lehigh and is a Republican. "Acceptable colleges," said Mrs. Anderson, over the telephone, "I guess would be just colleges that he would pick out, colleges that regular guys went to and not eggheads and stuff.")

The politics of the managers of Harvard University are opposed to those of the great body of the American people. She is the aristocratic college of the United States. Her pride of antiquity, her vanity of preeminence and wealth, are likely to prevent her renovating her principles and management, so as to suit the wants of the period. . . . The sons of the wealthy will therefore flock to her. . . . The attainments usually made within her walls are inferior . . . her professors [are] accustomed to lecture and examine the students and nothing more. The indolent and the careless will therefore flock to her. . . . The middle and lower classes . . . the strength and hope of the nation, avoid Harvard.

—Harriet Martineau, 1838

. . . I think and I am sure that I owe my life to Burt L. Standish and *Tip-Top Weekly*. Reading "Dick Merriwell" has influenced me to give up smoking corn silk, whips, and grape vine. . . .

Leo O'Connor
—Letter to *Tip-Top Weekly*, June 12, 1909

We went to [Harvard College], expecting to see something unusual as it is the only college, or would-be academy of the Protestants in all America, but we found ourselves mistaken. We found eight or ten young fellows sitting around, smoking tobacco . . . the whole house smelt so strong of it that I said "It certainly must be also a tavern." We inquired how many professors there were and they replied not one, that there was not enough money to support one. . . . They knew hardly a word of Latin. . . . They took us to the library, where there was nothing particular. . . .

—Journal of Jasper Danckaerts, 1680

Sabin W. Carr, a Dubuque, Iowa, boy, and a Yale man, won the pole vault for the United States at the Olympic Games of 1928, soaring over the stick at 13 feet 9½ inches. Several girls in Dubuque were in love with him but nothing came of it as they never got to meet him.

The stroke went up again. Harvard imitated Yale but in the middle of her boat one man showed signs of distress. On the other hand, every Yale man was rowing as if he felt as fresh as he had at the start.

The whistles began to shriek, and a tumult of sounds filled the air.

"Yale wins!" shouted Hal Darrell, waving his hat.

"Yale wins!" cried Rob Claxton. "Good old Yale wins!"

"They've got 'em!" screamed Charley Fair, lifting his sister in his arms that she might see the better—"They've got 'em, Polly! They're still gaining!"

"Oh Charley," said the little girl trembling in his arms, "isn't it fine that you're a Yale man!"

"The finest thing in the world," he answered.

Amid the shrieking of whistles, the wild cheering of the multitude, and the booming of cannon, Yale crossed the line, a winner.

Dick Merriwell's Colors, or All for the Blue

As an alumnus of Harvard I have little to say which is favorable—about Harvard, that is. When as a fledgling student of the great University, and confronted by my own personal problems, I sought help,—I received none from Harvard. Of course, I have never forgotten this, and being cast in the human mold, perhaps never will. Since Harvard was mostly anonymous to me in respect to help, I shall continue to remain so to her.

I was in the service, the Infantry. I wound up my army career as a corporal, *sans esperance*.

I was advised, since I had no personal "connections," to enter the "lowest" branch of our government service, namely, the Post Office Department, where I remained these eleven arduous years as a letter carrier with a Harvard background, and an alumnus of Boston Latin School to boot.

—From a 25th Annual Report

CHAPTER XI

That Big Long Century

Humanitys culture consists in setting down in circles and passing the word around about how darned smart humanity is.

—ARCHY

WHERE were we? Oh yes . . .

We left Harvard in the hands of President Wadsworth, elected in 1724. Cotton Mather, "neurotic, irritable, vain, and ambitious," [1] was in decline and died in 1728. He took the count swinging, though, one of his last cheerful campaigns being an unsuccessful attempt to divert the lavish financial attentions of Thomas Hollis from Harvard to Yale.

Wadsworth, and Harvard, were thus finally free to operate without a constant noisy running comment on the moral turpitude of the student body and the general ineptitude, slackness, falling away from principle, and black decadence of everybody and everything connected with "our miserable Colledge." The General Court gave Wadsworth a substantial raise in pay, plus some fringe benefits, and also voted the sum of £1000 for the construction of the first presidential house. "Wadsworth House," a commodious clapboard structure, was finished in 1727, with an orchard adjoining, and across the road a field in which

[1] Kenneth B. Murdock ('16, Ph.D. '23).

freshmen were required to make hay foi the President's horse, whose name was Dobbin and who served to the age of twenty-three, when he was turned in on a new model. The house still stands, square in the middle of things, somewhat bewildered, poor thing, by the masses of brick and stone which have risen around it, and by the bizarre conversations of the students who pass its doors. Instead of being lulled by the drowsy hums of bees from the rose garden it is assailed by the backfires of mo-peds and the squeal of defective brakes. In 1775 the house served as the military headquarters of General George Washington [2] (no college affiliation).

Harvard was nearly one hundred years old but still in knee britches. If the Congregationalist pressures of that old-time religion had slackened somewhat, there was still plenty of Latin, Greek, and God on the daily agenda. Fines were still imposed on collegians caught in the act of speaking English within the college enclosure, and turtle-neck sweaters were taboo. The student body was still small, but had been increasing steadily. Forty-five graduated in 1725. But the enrollment did not grow much during this exciting century, as we might have expected it to, and the largest class graduated up until 1810 was only sixty-three. The "cross-section" we hear about so much today had certainly not come about—almost all the students came from Massachusetts and New Hampshire, with an occasional venturesome lad from the Carolinas. The entering age, which had hovered around fifteen (and younger) rose to an average of seventeen. The boys were drawn from many walks of life, and proud magistrates' sons from Boston mingled with farmers' sons from the rocky pastures of New Hampshire, but lest anybody get any funny ideas the catalogue was still printed with the names of graduates in order according to the social rank of their families. Not until the new republicanism of the age made itself felt in 1773 was the list put into alphabetical order.

[2] 1732-1799. Family lineage direct to Sulgrave, Northamptonshire, England. No Boston connections, unfortunately.

With respect to student manners and customs, a new spirit of freedom was breaking through and the authorities were hard pressed to hold ardent spirits in check. Puritanism was on its last legs. Like students in all ages, our boys chafed under restrictions they considered out of date. They not only chafed, they erupted. They behaved at times, in fact, not unlike a troop of merchant seamen on the loose in Singapore after a long passage. They cut loose with a variegated set of misdemeanors— from stealing chickens, playing stud poker, and gargling rum to profane swearing, rioting in the night, and wenching in the Olde English manner. Morison tells us that there was a tavern on the road to Charlestown where students of a sophisticated and worldly frame of mind "made rendezvous with ladies of easy virtue," and that "in 1770 2 women of Ill Fame were discovered to have spent the night in a certain college chamber." Both these methods of filling in study breaks are apparently still in favor with college students, the record being held by our rivals, Yale, who, imbued with team spirit as always, recently staged an episode involving merely one young lady, which resulted in the expulsion of no less than twenty-one Elis. This is not only an Ivy League record but may give the Big Ten something to shoot at.

The popular mixed beverages favored in student orgies were punch, negus, and flip. "Negus" is, or was, port or sherry wine plus hot water, sugar, nutmeg, and lemon, which drove the cold out while laying the groundwork for ulcers and gout. This concoction was invented by an English colonel in the days of Queen Anne, named Francis Negus, who dreamed it up one afternoon after a miserably cold and unsuccessful rabbit hunt. The summer version, substituting ice for hot water, is a "cobbler."

"Flip" is egg, sugar, and wine or liquor, according to one authority, and beer or ale spiced and heated with a hot iron according to another and you can have both of them.

"Punch" goes back to the Saxon wassail bowl and in

various eras has consisted of a mixture of most everything including the kitchen sink and Congoleum rug. One variation was called "syllabub" and was made by milking a cow into sweetened beer.

Hard liquor consumed by Crimson tosspots bent on demolition of the motor functions and visions of Xanadu were "rum," "Rhum," and "rumm." A manuscript written in 1651 and now in the archives of Trinity College, Dublin, says the chief "fuddling" in Barbados at that time was "rumbullion, alias kill-divil and this is made from sugar canes distilled, a hot, hellish, and terrible liquor." This was the chief ingredient of colonial punches. There was a distillery making whiskey on Staten Island in 1640 but the New England drink was rum. Scotch whisky, a temperance beverage currently in great favor in the Ivy League, was not popularized in England until John Haig, James Buchanan, and Tommy Dewar invaded England with a whirlwind sales campaign in 1880 that eventually brought about annual sales of twenty-one million gallons, half of which comes to the U.S.A. and one quarter of which is consumed before, during, and after the Harvard-Yale game.

The martini, which has contributed even more to marital discord than "working late at the office," was not invented until after the Revolution. It consists of a glass of gin to which is added the contents of one small Chinese firecracker. It is generally credited with being the cause of both World Wars and the eruption of Mont Pelee in Martinique in 1902.

At least one professor fell a victim to the grape. Isaac Greenwood, the first Hollis Professor of Mathematics, and a valuable, dynamic figure in the spreading of scientific knowledge in New England, had a weakness for the bottle. He was appointed in England by Thomas Hollis himself, who grew somewhat discouraged over his choice when he discovered that before taking ship for Boston the new appointee had not only tossed away £300 in conviviality but also purchased "three pair of pearl grey stockings."

Greenwood buckled down on arrival, however, and for ten years, beginning in 1728, between private and semi-private battles with brother kill-divil, did his best to keep New England abreast of the new age in science. He wrote papers on meteorology, mine damp, the Aurora Borealis, and Dighton Rock. (I don't know what the problem was there at Dighton Rock. I don't even know where it is. I hope they have got it fixed.) He gave lectures and demonstrations and wrote *Arithmetick, Vulgar and Decimal,* which was the first vulgar book to be published by a native son in the colonies. It was immediately banned by the Watch and Ward Society of Boston. After toppling off the wagon several times and receiving several warnings, he was finally separated from the college in 1738, and succeeded by John Winthrop.

Meanwhile the boys were introducing live snakes into tutors' rooms and setting off squibs in the Yard.

Winthrop raised Harvard's prestige in the scientific world to the first rank. His experiments in electricity, navigational geography, meteorology, and seismology were talked about in all the scholarly world. Even Ben Franklin, who had previously taken a fairly dim view of Harvard "fops," now joined the Harvard Boosters Club. Some of the scientific instruments donated by Franklin are still at hand and getting pretty dusty. By the end of the century Harvard had established itself in the horrible world of science. Yale, concerned as it was with righteousness and ecclesiastical matters, had fumbled the ball and did not even name a chair in Natural Science until the eve of the Revolution, finally getting around to it in 1770.

An innovation during this period was the teaching of a modern, or speakable, language. A musical-comedy-type Frenchman named Monsieur Louis Hector Piot de l'Angloiserie had been imported to Boston, where he busied himself explaining the French subjunctive and useful phrases such as "I covet the Indian pudding of my uncle" to young ladies on Beacon Hill who did not want to be caught with their pantalons down linguistically in case they received an invitation to a house-party at Versailles. In 1733 M. de l'Angloiserie, who suffered severe migraine headaches from hearing his name mispronounced several hundred times a day, began visiting Cambridge thrice weekly to give private French lessons. After only two years the strain began to tell on him and he commenced to see things that weren't there and also claimed he had established a direct communication with the Other World. As the college already had a complete inventory of Divine Visitations in a cold-storage warehouse in Somerville they canceled his commuter's ticket and found a substitute. These informal instructors, one of whom was Albert Gallatin, continued to arrive and depart until 1787, when a permanent instructor in the French language was appointed, Joseph Nancrede. He was the first modern-language instructor in any American college.

A student named Bird called one of the Overseers "a dumb dog that could not bark" to his face, and was court-martialed and drummed to the city limits. Rum sociables, singing of ribald songs, and penny ante continued in the Yard.

Exclusive emphasis on religious studies lost its drive. Presidents of the college found it increasingly tiresome to expound the Scriptures to the students daily. None of the boys objected when the practice faded away. The long-forgotten English language was again a subject of scrutiny in syntax and exercises in style, and Exhibitions in oratory were held twice or more times a year. PLAYS were performed. Telescopes were peered through. MUSIC was played. And by 1755 the study of Hebrew had been scratched as a required course.

Other signs of the times were the abolishment of corporal punishment, largely as a result of a lawsuit in 1733 by William Vassall, a student, against Daniel Rogers, a tutor, for assault and battery, or a hell of a beating. Those healthful Puritan thrashings were thereupon abandoned but the management was still permitted to release themselves from nervous tension by "boxing," or socking any student who annoyed them a sharp blow on the ear.[8] There was also a regular list of fines printed in the College Laws covering offenses such as breaking open doors or picking locks, blasphemy, fornication, using distilled spirits, punch, or flip, neglecting declamation, going on roof of Old Harvard Hall or cutting lead from same, and entering meetinghouse before the bell, plus many more. The cash amount of these penalties varied from 2 shillings for tardiness at lectures to expulsion for fornication, forgery, and other "atrocious crimes." It was the century of freedom, however, and by 1759 student prohibition was repealed and Cambridge tavernkeepers have been wreathed in smiles ever since.

Hollis Hall, where Charles Townsend Copeland lived at number 15 from 1904 to 1932, was built in 1764. "Copey," as he was known to many generations of students, was extremely friendly to the boys. He came right out and admitted that he liked the students. He liked to have them around. He took an interest in them. This so astonished everyone that he became in his lifetime an institution, sort of a Yankee Mr. Chips, only by no means so groggy and drenched with treacle. But he did maintain the Mr. Chips tradition by falling asleep while you read your literary effusions out loud to him. Emerson and Thoreau, the famed Transcendentalist halfbacks, also lived in Hollis Hall. It has Ivy on it.

"Old Harvard Hall," which had been built in 1677 to replace the sagging and dilapidated original building, was in January 1764 the center of Harvard College. You might go so far as to say it *was* Harvard College, for it contained the entire college library of five thousand volumes, all the "philosophical apparatus," portraits of former presidents, as well as a collection of oddments rivaling Barnum's Dime Museum, among which we may mention a

---

[8] The thumb screw and the Iron Maiden had long since been outlawed. The only place they survive today is in the New England prep schools.

choice relic called in the inventory "piece of tanned negroes hide." The fine old building, four stories of brick with a gambrel roof and twelve gables, was the focal point of all important meetings, deliberations, and celebrations, served not only as library but also for lectures and learned dissertations, had known the style of Increase Mather's shoe buckles and heard the voices of Oakes, Leverett, Brattle, the immortal tutor Flynt, and Sever and Wadsworth, and Judge Sewall, and visiting celebrities and great noblemen, the unfortunate Greenwood and the glittering genius Winthrop, platoon after unending platoon of students year after year—some grand, some awkward—and regiments of mothers and fathers and giggling sisters and small round brothers. It was a link with the now fast-fading times of old, with the ancient colonial beginnings.

There was a smallpox epidemic in Boston in January 1764, and the General Court had moved out to Cambridge and had been holding sessions in "Old Harvard Hall." The Court adjourned for the night on January twenty-fourth and its members dispersed to their various lodgings for their evening pipe and bowl of punch. The janitor was not too sharp about his duties that cold evening and sometime during the night an untended fire in the library got out of hand and before you could say "D——n George Grenville!" the entire building was ablaze. In the midst of a raging snowstorm coming in from the direction of Newburyport, frantic efforts to save the proud temple of culture were made by legislators, tutors, and students under the direction of seventy-five-year-old President Holyoke, but all to no avail and on the grimmest morrow that Harvard had ever faced, there was naught of John Harvard's books but a smouldering pile of rubble. All was lost. Ah, what a heartbreaking sight:

> The roofs, the walls, and in one ruinous heap
> The ancient dome and all its treasures lie!

The townspeople came to see the dreadful view on that cold and snowy Massachusetts morning. The high and the mighty and the grand left their Georgian mansions on Brattle Street and came through the snow to look calamity in the face. Through the snow came tavernkeepers and tradesmen and had their look and shook their heads. Small boys threw snowballs into the ruins and heard them hiss on the hot bricks of the seventeenth century. Fair Harvard had never known such a disaster, nor has she since.

But this was the age of action and resolution (as King George was soon to discover). While lamentations still filled the wintry air the Massachusetts General Court, assuming complete responsibility for the loss, voted to replace the structure. Friends of the old college rushed into the breach with whatever they could spare and much they could not spare. Alumni stripped their shelves of books. Packets of books began to arrive from all friendly quarters, from rich Boston merchants, from bone-poor country parsons, from Portsmouth, Dover, Concord, Keene, Saco, Andover, Newburyport, Ipswich, Portland, Hampton Falls, Lowell, Brunswick, and Exeter, from Springfield, Greenfield, Newfields and Old South Byfield, from Rockingham Center and Pow Wow River, from Philadelphia and North Carolina, and the West Indies and London. Such a rallying around the old Crimson flag was never seen. Dr. Benjamin Franklin sent "valuable" scientific instruments. Thomas Palmer of London sent over twenty volumes of "Roman antiquities." And likewise from across the seas, though King and Court contributed nothing, Boswell's "worthy booksellers and friends," the Messrs. Dilly, sent a replacement copy of Longhorne's *Plutarch*.

(*First Librarian:* How's the new copy of *Plutarch*?
Second Librarian: It's a dilly.)

"The Archbishops of Canterbury and York subscribed and used their influence in favour of the college," and Cowper's "virtuous and faithful Heberden," "*ultimus Romanorum*, the last of the learned physicians," donated three guineas. And to top it off, the Province of New Hampshire voted to foot the bill to completely restore the library.

Within two and a half years the Harvard Hall we know (well, not quite but almost) had arisen on the very site of the old. The books were back, and the lilacs were in bloom.

"If every building in the yard were to burn down," George Lyman Kittredge said a century and a half later, "and you had your library, you'd still have a university."

Amen. Harvard University today has the largest college library in the world.

In addition to Massachusetts, Holden, Hollis,[4] and Harvard halls, the eighteenth century saw one other essential structure rise in the Yard. It stands no longer and its architectural features remain obscure, though its dimensions were twenty-four by twenty-five feet. To some it may have been the most important building of all. This was the new brew house, built in 1762.

And then came the beginnings of War, with nearby Boston the first seat of resistance. In 1768 the students boycotted the British textile and haberdashery trades by voting unanimously to "take their degrees in the manufactures of this country" and revealed themselves at Commencement in Yankee garb. Still, there were plenty of aristocrats with Tory sympathies in the ranks. And since student opinion is always of the violent variety, it is easy to picture the noisy Revolutionary bull sessions and requests to "Step outside and repeat that asseveration, Frothingham, you d——n Tory."

The Reverend Andrew Eliot (A.B. 1737) wrote that "the young gentlemen are already taken up with politics. They have caught the spirit of the times. Their declamations and forensic disputes breathe the spirit of liberty . . . they have sometimes been wrought up to such a pitch of enthusiasm, that it has been difficult for their tutors to keep within due bounds."

'Twas ever thus, and ever shall be. Even today the boys

---

[4] "Hollis remains to this day the best-looking of the college buildings."—CHARLES W. ELIOT

work themselves into a weekly lather over liberty: liberty to take dolls on band trips to Princeton in the bus, liberty to use typewriters and smoke hashish during exams, liberty to present a dramatization of *Lolita* at the Loeb Theatre, etc.)

A group of Tory students almost caused a premature Bunker Hill in March of 1775 by bringing tea into the dining hall to infuriate their patriot classmates. The effect of this ill-timed jest was so immediate and so explosive that the Faculty, fearing riot, mayhem, and cracked pates, issued an edict barring tea from the premises:

Since the carrying India Teas into the Halls is found to be a Source of uneasiness and grief to many of the Students, and as the use of it is disagreeable to the People of this Country in general; and as those who have carried Tea into the Hall declare that the drinking of it in the Hall is a matter of trifling consequence with them; that they be advised not to carry it in for the future, and in this way that they, as well as the other Students in all ways, discover a disposition to promote harmony, mutual affection, and confidence, so well becoming Members of the same Society: that so peace and happiness may be preserved within the Walls of the College whatever convulsions may unhappily distract the State abroad.

Things were getting very hot and Cambridge was in the middle of it all. From 1770 to 1773 the General Court of Massachusetts held all its sessions in Harvard Hall. British troops were occupying Boston and the legislators were allergic to the particular shade of red garments worn by His Majesty's police. The Harvard authorities may not have been very keen to find themselves overrun by the predecessors of James Michael Curley and his cronies, but it was a great lark for the students (and how educational!) and the local cigar stores and wig cleaners-and-dryers, not to mention saloonkeepers, thought it was just fine.

By April 1775 scarcely a farmer was then alive who was not in Cambridge with his bedroll and flintlock. The whole area was teeming with high-spirited rustics encamped not only around Cambridge but even in the buildings of Harvard Yard. The times were so badly out of joint that the Overseers of the college had the year before voted to cancel public participation in that noisy frolic known as Commencement. And in 1770 a college military unit had been formed that drilled in nifty uniforms and cocked hats and who polished off "three or four buckets of rum toddy" after each performance. What with the Quartering Act, the Stamp Act, the Townshend Acts, the Boston Massacre, the Tea Acts, the Intolerable Acts, and the Pullman Strike, everybody's nerves were mighty jumpy and the weather report did not look too good, either.

At this point General Thomas Gage, in command in Boston, who was trying as best he could to avoid trouble, made a slight tactical error and started a War. On April 19, 1775, he sent Major John Pitcairn and a thousand men out for a day in the country at Lexington and Concord. The first object of this outing was to destroy military stores being hoarded in these sleepy villages by the patriot militia, and the second was to kidnap two Harvard men sequestered there, John Hancock (A.B. 1754) and Samuel Adams (A.B. 1740). Adams and Hancock shared the leadership of the Massachusetts Whigs and had for several years been putting sandburs under the royal saddle and treating the King's Men to the Beantown hotfoot. General Gage (actually he did not become a General until 1782, long after he had been bounced back to England following the Battle of Bunker Hill) decided he would like to have both Hancock and Adams more centrally located, in Boston say, locked in the men's coatroom at the Hotel Touraine, for example.

When the rattle of gunfire began that morning, six Harvard lads hastily abandoned declining the paradigms of the Greek nouns and verbs and joined the minutemen. One of them was sophomore Edward Bangs, who wrote the original "Yankee Doodle." He was behind the stone walls, saw the farmers of Middlesex County, Massachusetts, gathering at crossroads and in farmyards, and joined them in making the lobsterbacks' day an interesting and active one, so they would have something to write home about.

Later in the day, which proved decidedly tiresome to the British troops, 273 of whom had a contrasting shade of red added to their uniforms, Lord Percy came through Harvard Square with reinforcements.

"I say, you chaps," he said, addressing several undergraduates discovered lounging in front of Ye Olde Poole Hall smoking cubeb cigarettes, "could one of you sturdy lads direct me to a neighboring hamlet called . . . er, ah . . . Lexington, I believe it is?"

"I'm from Fitchburg," replied Northey, '76 [Hockey (2) Glee Club (3) Fall Dance Committee (2) Cercle Français (3) Cheer Leader (1) Iroquois Club.]

"Lexington? Why man that's in Kentucky," ejaculated Fairbank, '77 [Student Council (2) Kirtland Latin Prize, Chess Club (2) Christian Fraternity (3) Golden Branch Debating Society (3) Herodotan Society (2) Spee Club].

"But . . . I thought . . ." sputtered Lord Percy, for he was indeed taken aback at the unexpected turn things had taken.

And just as Shreve, '75 [Varsity Crew (3) Varsity Lacrosse, Manager, Der Deutsche Verein (3) Outing Club, Chapel Monitor, OK Society], was about to give Lord Percy faulty directions which would have led him and his troops not to Lexington but to Kurtz' Diner in Exeter, New Hampshire, who should appear on the scene but Tutor Isaac Smith (A.B. 1767).

Again milord spoke, addressing Tutor Smith.

"Where is this here Lexington at?" he queried sternly. Tutor Smith replied with alacrity.

"My Christian upbringing rules out prevarication," he stated. "In short, I cannot tell a lie. There is the road to

Lexington," he said, indicating the thoroughfare in question. "Just follow them car tracks."

In the weeks that followed, Tutor Smith's popularity among students and colleagues waned to such an alarming degree as a result of this episode that he fled the unfriendly atmosphere of the Yard and sailed for England. Eleven years later he was back, all was forgiven, and he ended up College Librarian.

Lord Percy did not reach Lexington. As he approached the outskirts of town he met his British comrades, whose one idea at that moment was to get out of there. Lord Percy covered their calamitous retreat, being entertained over the entire route by the minutemen.

Near Porters Station, Major Isaac Gardner of Brookline was killed; a member of the Harvard Class of 1747, he was the first Harvard man to fall in the War of Independence. In the same skirmish John Hicks of Cambridge died. His house is now the Kirkland House Library, fronting the rumble of traffic and the subway yard wall on Boylston Street.

In the days that followed the shooting by the rude bridge at Concord and at points between there and Charlestown, Cambridge became a regular military headquarters for the siege of Boston. School let out early that year. Things were getting much too hot for either students or instructors to give their proper attention to ethics and Chaldee. College sessions ended on May 4, 1775, and reconvened in October, not by the Charles River in Cambridge, but hard by the confluence of the Sudbury and the Assabet, at Concord. The professors and students lived in taverns and private houses, while classes, recitations, and prayers were held in Concord meetinghouse, schoolhouse, and courthouse. It was a much-reduced student body. Some of the boys were in the Army; others, feeling that Harvard in Concord was not Harvard at all, resigned. Some no doubt decided the times were entirely too upsetting to their awakening sensibilities and that time off to "find themselves" was imperative.

Scene: Leverett House, Fall of 1961
Father: Where's your friend Gaylord?
Son: Oh he's taking a year off to find himself.
Father: Do you want to take Langworthy to lunch?
Son: He's in China this year.
Father: What's he doing in China?
Son: Well, he's finding himself too.
Father: *O tempora! O mores!*
Son: I suppose that's Latin.
Father: Let's go to lunch.

Probably the only persons to benefit by Harvard's exile to Concord were the local maidens and the dealers in bonnets, laces, ribbons, Hoyt's German Cologne, hair curlers, whalebone, autograph books, smelling salts, and sheet music.

In Harvard's absence the college buildings were taken over for the use of the troops. On June 15, 1775, as John Hancock flushed with jealous mortification, the Continental Congress had voted George Washington leadership of the American troops. His headquarters were in Craigie House. It was then known as the "Vassal house," having been built by John Vassal in 1759. It was the stateliest of all the stately mansions on "Tory Row" (now Brattle Street). But it had become too warm in Cambridge for the Vassals, and they had fled to Boston with many others on the Row.

And on July third, at the gates of Harvard College, as the troops paraded on Cambridge Common, George Washington, drawing his sword and wheeling his horse under the famous elm tree, took command of the patriot army that would hurl the tyrant George's detestable minions from our shores. In the following March he seized Dorchester Heights commanding Boston, and mounted cannon that he had had dragged over the icy roads all the way from Ticonderoga. The British, feeling a want of hospitality, departed from Boston leaving two hundred very useful cannon and innumerable small arms and munitions to the Lowells, Cabots, their friend God, and the Irish. His task accomplished, Washington left to take up the defense of New York. The day before he left, on April third, the College Corporation and Overseers voted him an honorary LL.D., and presented his diploma to him in his headquarters at Craigie House. In other words, the Father of His Country was a Harvard Man.

In June of 1776, while the young ladies of Concord twisted their curls and pouted in their doorways, Harvard picked up the College Clock and other scholarly impedimenta and traipsed back to Cambridge, with the college fire-engine at the head of the baggage train and two love-sick sophomores bringing up the rear. Sixteen hundred and eighty rude soldiers had been quartered in the college buildings and in addition to the disappearance of half a ton of lead from the roof of Harvard Hall (which had been converted into bullets) most of the interior woodwork, brass doorknobs, and box locks had evaporated. Copies of Fordyce and Locke and Jean Jacques Burlamaqui's *Principes du droit politique* and letters from home and sweethearts had been used to kindle fires, pillows had suffered from bayonet practice, and Vassar pennants had been commandeered as neck scarves and chest warmers, and the place was a considerable shambles. But everybody was glad to be home (except those two love-sick sophomores, who immediately hired a gig and returned to Concord that evening to a taffy pull and charade party).

Harvard staggered through the war under difficulties of every kind. Food was scarce, and due to the mismanagement of funds by the college Treasurer, none other than John Hancock, money was scarce. Students of the right stripe were also scarce and the enrollment dwindled. Such students as put in an appearance seem to have been a sorry lot and new forms of experimental dissipation were the lab work of the day (or should I say night).

But these trials passed with the end of the war and the beginning of the grand and virgin Republic. By 1800 the college assets were in the close neighborhood of $200,000, an increase of $150,000 since 1777. Cultural subjects far different from those at the beginning of the century dominated the curriculum, and the behemoth Science was roaring through the Yard.

The student body was feeling its oats and indulging freely in sports, games, musical entertainment, and other non-Calvinist pursuits. The first clubs had been formed, some for definite purposes such as debating, others purely social. There was the Speaking Club, whose guiding spirit was Samuel Phillips, founder of Phillips Andover Academy (a penal institution not far from Exeter, N. H., home of the revered Exeter Brass Works).

Phi Beta Kappa, originally a fearsomely secret society at William and Mary with rituals not unlike those of the ancient Mayans (moon worship, human sacrifice, etc.), was imported to Harvard in 1781. During the season the baseball scores are posted daily in its luxurious club rooms. A complete display of post cards, novelties, and souvenirs is for sale at the cigar counter.

The exclusive Porcellian Club was founded in 1791 by a group of bon vivants favoring a diet of roast pig. The Porcellian is much more exclusive and holy than Skull and Bones at Yale. If a Bones man is in the room and the words *Skull, Bones,* or *Skull and Bones* are mentioned, he is required to leave the room. (As a result many Yale men have flunked out of medical school due to the frequent necessity of departing from the anatomy lectures. Also, as is well known, no Bones man of Yale has ever witnessed the finale of Hamlet, as they all have to exit to the lobby in Act V, Scene 1: *"Hamlet:* That *skull* had a tongue in it, and could sing once: how the knave jowls it to the ground, as if it were Cain's jaw-*bone. . . ."*) But if someone mentions *Porcellian, Pork,* or even *Baked Stuffed Pork Chop* in the presence of a Porcellian man, he is required not only to leave the room but to leave college and enter a rest home maintained for the purpose by the Club in Athol, Massachusetts.[5]

In 1795 Hasty Pudding was founded, a "jolly amalgam of literary, convivial, and patriotic elements." [6]

Some of the students held horse races on the Common. They went to balls in Boston, and the Theatre. Featherbeds and looking glasses were not unknown in college rooms—and likewise chafing dishes, corkscrews, punchbowls, pipes, tea sets, pictures of actresses, and copies of frivolous English magazines.

The old primitive Calvinism was gone from the scene, and Unitarianism, at the opposite pole of theological belief from the fundamentalism of the founding fathers, held sway over Harvard. The Calvinists gnashed their teeth.

Students became so bold as to petition President Langdon to resign for incompetence. Insolent puppies! But Langdon complied, and retired to Hampton Falls, N.H., not far from the Hampton Beach *FUNARAMA* [7] and Buzzell's Karmelkorn and salt-water-taffy emporium.

A Harvard professor demonstrated that earthquakes were not caused by divine wrath. Sacrilege!

A maidservant in President Locke's household was great with child. The President took the blame and resigned his high office.

Crimson undergraduates debated such topics as "Whether it be fornication to lye with ones sweetheart before marriage."

After a visit to a "rural charmer" in Concord, student Joseph Dennie of the class of 1790 reported that he "enjoyed the luxury of her lips" and "received a lesson on the celestial globes."

[5] And then there is the old one about the Porcellian stroke of the Harvard crew. The joke goes: "Sure, he's democratic. He knows all the guys in the boat except the three up front."
[6] Morison.
[7] Owned and operated by Joe Dineen (Harvard '36).

This same young buck's tutor in Groton, the Reverend Daniel Chaplin (A.B. 1772) read "Rabelais, as well as Cruden's Concordance," and was "as expert at a jest as at a sermon."

Looking down from Heaven at the Harvard scene, Cotton Mather observed it all, and saying, "I told you so" (in Latin, Greek, and Chaldee) he busted his golden harp over long-suffering St. Peter's head.

"De way dat man do carry on," was this worthy's comment, for to Mather's chagrin, due to a mixup at the Back Bay Station, he had been consigned to a Heaven under the management of the Rejuvenated Saints of Africa.

And thus the century ended.

THE PENNY ARCADE

The poem which follows, "The Lay of the Lone Fish Ball," was for half a century a favorite comic song at Harvard. It was the age of the comic song and this one was written by George Martin Lane, Class of 1846, Professor of Latin. Mort Sahl and Bob Hope have ruined this kind of joke for us latecomers, but the writer has met old grads from the turn of the century who still think "We don't give bread with one fish ball" the funniest joke line they have ever heard in their long lives.

The Lay of the Lone Fish Ball

There was a Man went round the Town
To hunt a Supper up and down:
For he had been right far away
And nothing had to eat that Day.
He feels his Cash to count his Pence,
And all he had was just Six Cents.
"Wretch that I am, it happens meet,

"Why did I leave my Kirkland Street!
"None but a Fool a Wife forsakes,
"Who Raspberry Jam and Waffles makes.
"If I were now safe out of Town,
"I'd give my bran new Dressing Gown.
"But yet I'll make a start and try
"To see what my Six Cents will buy."
He finds at last a Right Cheap Place.
And stealeth in with bashful Face.
The Bill of Fare he runneth through,
To see what his Six Cents will do.
The cheapest of the Viands all,
Was 12½ for Two Fish Ball!
The Waiter roars it through the Hall;
The Guests they start at "One Fish Ball!!"
The Waiter brings One Fish Ball on,
The Guest he looks abashed down.
The Scantness of the Fare he sees;
"A Piece of Bread now; if you please."
The Waiter roars it through the Hall,
"We don't give Bread with One Fish Ball."
Then whoso orders One Fish Ball
Must get Bread first or not at all.
And who would Two with Fixin's eat,
Should get some Friend to stand a Treat.

CHAPTER XII

"That Man in the
White House"

Nothing dangerous yet,
look out for tomorrow!!

IN THE 35th Anniversary Report of the Harvard Class of 1904, published in 1939, one of its members answered a question in the blank form sent out by the Class Secretary as follows:

> *Question:* Any public service performed?
> *Answer:* President of the United States.

This answer no doubt thrilled the hearts of many of his classmates but it was only the cause of still another bitter attack of nausea to an even greater number, who had been suffering these attacks periodically since March 4, 1932, in company with hordes of other Harvard men. For seven long years of uninterrupted agony, they had retched almost daily from all the combined tortures of fear, hatred, contempt, frustration, and abject loathing. These passions had afflicted them with stomach ulcers, heart attacks, facial tics, trembling hands, strawberry rashes, falling hair, spavin, springhalt, heaves, spots in front of the eyes, rhinophyma, and hives. Franklin D. Roosevelt, former editor of the Harvard *Crimson*, now not only the Happy Warrior but the Hilarious Warrior, had caused broken engagements, civil war within ordinarily peace-loving family circles, rifts between friends that would never heal in a lifetime, insults hurled that would never be forgotten, clumsy fist fights in respectable clubs, disinheritances, broken trusts, tears, lovers' quarrels, husbands sleeping on couches, dismissal of faithful retainers, allowances cut off, witchhunting, burning of books, apoplexy, even suicide and murder. Family dinner parties ended in brawls, and pro-FDR wives ejected anti-FDR husbands from the nuptial sheets and vice versa. Thinking to brighten up the conversation and display their wit, young men told an "Eleanor story" and had their faces slapped and rings thrown at them.[1]

In Kansas a man went into the cyclone cellar and said he wouldn't come out until Roosevelt was gone. While he was down there his wife ran away with a drummer in the infants' knitwear game. In New Jersey, infuriated by a presidential "fireside chat" over the air waves, a man threw his radio out the window, striking a passerby on the head; en route to the hospital the ambulance carrying the victim crashed into a produce truck, damaging over $250 worth of valuable vegetables. In Ohio a prominent banker, after watching W.P.A. workers leaning on shovels, threatened to eat some worms and die.

And it was to go on and on. For six more years.

Who was this man? Was his name really Rosenbloom? Did he actually have a facsimile opium den in the attic of the White House? Was his stamp collection in fact only a blind for a nationwide smuggling ring? Was Harry Hop-

---

[1] One of the most curious features of the era from a socio-historical point of view was the birth, growth, and endurance of the "Eleanor story." This bizarre form of social behavior manifested itself in the endless repetition of purportedly humorous anecdotes aimed at debasing the integrity, not of the Chief Executive, but of his wife. Many of the individuals seized with this inexplicable and uncontrollable mania exhibited no other abnormalities in their psychological makeup.

kins related to Klim Voroshilov? And what of the dog Fala? Was this slippery canine taking bribes from the Amalgamated Clothing Workers as was bruited about behind closed doors of the N.A.M.?

Reader, seek not the answers to these grave questions within these pages. We avoid whenever possible the murky alleyways of politics.

Franklin Roosevelt's early interest in excitement and bold, dangerous living are revealed in a letter, written in pencil on pencil-ruled stationery, which he wrote to his mother on Janury 1, 1888, when he was five years and eleven months old:

> Hyde Park, N. Y.
> Telegraph Station, Poughkeepsie
>
> my dear mama
> we coasted! yesterday nothing dangerous yet, look out for tomorrow!!
> your boy
> *F*

Opponents in later years learned to "look out for tomorrow."

An only child, his affection for his parents was unusually strong. He addresses them variously as "My darling mumpkin and Pop!" "Darling Mumpy," "My dear Mammy," "Dear Mumsy and Pupsy," "Dear Mommerr and Popperr." After he went away to prep school and college these childish salutations changed to "Dearest Mama and Papa" or "Dear Ma and Pa."

He was educated by tutors and entered Groton School in Groton, Massachusetts, in the fall of 1896, his first experience with the rough-and-tumble of living in a group with his contemporaries. Groton had been founded twelve years previous by the Reverend Endicott Peabody, a pillar of rectitude who ran the school somewhat on the lines of a concentration camp with games. The boys slept in cubicles, everybody had to get out and get kicked playing violent games in which they were joined by the Reverend Peabody, there was much Chapel and hard study. It was a Christian education based on the English public-school idea of lumps for everybody. Everybody had to take a cold shower every morning and presumably none of the small grubby sins of schoolboys ever took place at Groton. But it was chiefly Peabody himself "who put his stamp on the school, infusing the routine and the discipline with an awful moral significance." [2]

Franklin tried hard to fit in. His school spirit and loyalty were immense. In his letters home he faithfully reported all scores of athletic contests with details on the games. ("Yesterday our team played the English High School eleven, a lot of toughs again. They disputed every point of the game and made Mr. Peabody quite angry.") He played games himself with enthusiasm. ("My head is a little banged up, but otherwise I am all right.") He was manager of the baseball team and on the Debating Society, won a Latin prize—but somehow one feels that he was a bit apart. It takes great practice to build a public personality in prep school. The standards of schoolboy admiration are so elusive. Individuality is greeted with jeers and quirks of personality are pounced upon. It seems that Franklin in his later years at Groton developed "an independent, cocky manner, and at times became very argumentative and sarcastic. In argument he always liked to take the side opposite to that maintained by those with whom he was talking. This irritated the other boys considerably." [3]

[2] Schlesinger, *The Crisis of the Old Order.*
[3] James L. Goodwin, a classmate.
A considerably nobler version of FDR at Groton appears in *The Story of Young Frank Roosevelt*, evidently written by either Horatio Alger (who went to both Harvard and Harvard Divinity School), Harry Castlemon, or Oliver Optic, under the pseudonym of Wayne Whipple (copyright 1934): "As he went from class to class, from lecture to library, he excited the envy of the dumbbells by his apparently easy mastery of his various courses, but his perennial smile soon overcame any feeling of jealousy and his modest good-nature and energy in games and sports kept him from being labelled a 'book-worm' or a 'greasy grind.'" We can safely assume from this that he also quite often found rich old gentlemen's pocket books and returned them, refusing any reward.

Well it's certainly no way to win the poll on Most Lovable Sixth Former. You start arguing with a bunch of Grotties and telling them that people from Illinois should be allowed the vote the same as if they lived in Massachusetts and right away you are going to get a reputation for being a nut. On top of that if you don't apologize for coming from New York why you won't have anybody to sit with at the St. Marks game. Then you are in trouble because the Groton–St. Marks game, although nobody more than twelve miles away has ever heard of it, eclipses all other activities of the human race.

The Reverend Peabody is credited with the astonishing statement that to be a headmaster you had to be "a bit of a bully." Another Grotonian, Averell Harriman ('09) said of him, "You know he would be an awful bully, if he weren't such a terrible Christian."

In such an atmosphere Franklin spent his school years, bombarded by the constant arrival of presents from home from a doting mother, and he graduated in June 1900, "feeling very blue" about leaving, and after buying a new bicycle. "I am going to buy a new bicycle! A Columbia chainless for $60 . . . shall need a good wheel in Cambridge next year, I thought this a chance, as the wheel costs ordinarily $75."

A week later, after graduation ("scarce a boy but wishes he were a 1st former again") he loaded the new Columbia on car 500 of the Boston and Maine at North Station from whence he departed for the summer on Campobello Island.

On September 25, 1900, he was in Cambridge, unpacking in his luxurious three-room suite in Westmorly Court smack in the middle of the Gold Coast.[4] The next day he went in to Boston to see about his trunks and prepared for the academic season with the purchase of a pair of evening shoes and a derby hat. He went to see Archibald

[4] The "Gold Coast" was an area on Mt. Auburn Street consisting of very fancy and expensive privately owned apartment houses for well-heeled Harvard students.

Cary Coolidge about his courses and set himself up with the following rugged schedule:

French 2-C: Prose and poetry. Prof. Marcou and Dr. J. D. M. Ford.

Latin B: Livy, Horace, and Terence. Prof. Morgan.

English 28: History of English Literature. Dean Briggs, Barrett Wendell, George Lyman Kittredge, and George Pierce Baker.

History 1: Medieval and Modern European History. Professor Coolidge.

Government 1: Prof. Silas Macvane and Abbott Lawrence Lowell (later President).

Geology 4 & 5: Dean Shaler.

This ex-freshman's mind reels at the thought of such a schedule. And in addition to this load, he vied with the butterfly in his social life. He also bounced around like a ping-pong ball in extracurricular endeavors. Perhaps scholastic standards have changed?

What was it like, this turn-of-the-century world at Harvard, in Cambridge, in Boston?

Charles William Eliot was in his fourth decade as President of the college and he still had his sidewhiskers.

A fifteen-jewel dust-proof watch with a Waltham movement, double-cut expansion balance and Breguet hairspring could be purchased for $5.25.

A man's fur coat of natural black Bulgarian lamb skins came to $24.

A cheap genuine brass bed cost $15; a massive one, with artistic scrollwork and "Cathedral knobs," weighing 175 pounds, could be had for $24.

Advertisement in the *Crimson*, June 22, 1900:

> Do Not Forget to have your razor sharpened before you go home. *La Flammes* is the best place. Dunster Street.

The most popular American family dogs were the shaggy, gentle Newfoundland, and the puffing, wheezing pug. Sporty college men kept dogs; the bull terrier—black and tan, or white,[5]—was popular with the speedy set. Also the English bulldog, especially in New Haven where he is the official mascot of the Northeast School of Taxidermy.

Everybody was howling over the big best-seller of 1900, *David Harum*. ("Do unto the other feller the way he'd like to do unto you, and do it fust.")

The Cunard Line was running the *Saxonia* and the *Invernia* between Boston and Liverpool and their advertisement in the *Crimson* states "No cattle carried."

The *Crimson* said that

McDONALD'S
is the only place in Boston where the
GENUINE TINGALINGS
are sold
16 Winter St. and 132 Tremont St.

Out in the rural districts genuine hayseeds still abounded, chewing on straws.

Nobody had heard of "Caesar salad."

Franklin D. Roosevelt wrote home: "One of the Brooks suits is just right, double-breasted waist-coat . . . the $31.00 one. . . ." For the student from Horners Corners who could not aspire to the magnificence of Brooks Brothers, Montgomery Ward offered by mail a VERY HEAVY ALL WOOL BLACK CHEVIOT SUIT for a five dollar bill ($5.00).

John F. Kennedy's grandfather, John F. Fitzgerald, was Mayor of Boston. He was the first of Boston's native-born Irish Catholic mayors to sing high tenor and play the banjo simultaneously.

Adjoining Cambridge, in Allston, a small boy named John Florence Sullivan was living with his father, a $1000-a-year bookbinder, and his Aunt Lizzie. Every Sunday his father would walk the lad and his brother Bob three miles to Cambridge to visit Grandmother and Grandfather Sullivan who lived on Emmons Place. His father's

---

[5] See "The Bar Sinister," by Richard Harding Davis. Most popular dog story of the age. A great story in any age.

four brothers also paid this weekly visit. His father and each of the four brothers always brought a Sunday present to the old folks—and always the same: each brought a pint of whiskey. The young man later changed his name to Fred Allen. Walking through the Harvard Yard on Sundays, he said, was "the closest I ever came to going to Harvard." [6]

Harvard itself was far different from the small New England college that President Eliot had taken over in 1869. It was on its way with a rush to becoming (here we go again) a Great University; and its faculty was loaded with such a prodigious cargo of famous brains and beards that the Yard actually sank three inches a year under their weight. Two historians and three philosophers were so famous that they had to be shored up with pilings and reinforced concrete. Dormitories had been built, with their rates and accommodations carefully planned for the rich, the well-to-do, the comfortably well-off, the uncomfortably pinched, the poor but honest, and the destitute slobs. Then there was Boston Society. If you had Connections you were In, and if you did not, you were Out. It was not much to worry about. Often students who were Out managed to crawl, scratch and worm their way In, at least on a One-Night-Stand basis. Once inside the pearly gates they sometimes stood behind a potted palm wondering why they had bothered. If you came from Omaha, talking to a Boston girl was likely to be a pretty slow trip. Once you had told her you only knew Freddie Coolidge slightly, things petered out pretty fast. And the mothers were worse than church. Even in my time, and I daresay today, few proper Bostonian mothers were very clear about "Iowa." It was all so confusing—there was a place called "Idaho," too, and then there was "Ohio." I

---

[6] In the process of becoming one of the best-loved comedians of his time, young John Florence Sullivan was successively a runner in the Boston Public Library, a student at the Boston High School of Commerce founded by Mayor Fitzgerald, and a window-washer and bad-debt collector for the Colonial Piano Company of Boston.

am not knocking Boston society, you understand. If you work at it you can even learn to like it. Of course some of its members appear to be embalmed, but others are quite lively and have really been all over, to places like—well—Kittery, Maine and even Fabyans, N.H. Personally I always have found Bostonians gracious and charming, if a little quaint. As a matter of fact they are very friendly. Abbott Lawrence Lowell is dead.[7]

There was one thing about the social set-up at Harvard, though, and that was, that You Never Could Tell. That was one thing about it and you never knew where you stood or where anybody else stood and unless you belonged to the patent-leather-pumps group you ended up not caring.

If you cared it could be pretty terrible. I knew boys who cared, and they suffered. And if things didn't go right they suffered all their lives, especially the Boston boys.[8] FDR lived in style on the Gold Coast with lovely plumbing, Persian rugs, and a piano ($40 a year), and ate at the "Groton table" in his freshman year, slit open all the proper invitations from all the proper Bostonians with a solid gold paper knife, juggled Back Bay and Beacon Hill teacups with casual aplomb—but he never made Porcellian. So you just Never Could Tell. That bumptious Cousin Teddy, now Governor of New York, had made it! Zounds! Thirty-two years later, to get back at the Porcel-

[7] Some students got up a subscription once upon a time to put up a plaque in the Yard commemorating the spot where President Lowell "once spoke to a Freshman."

[8] It always bothered Robert Benchley, apparently, that he didn't make a final club. Someone once asked him if he was going back to the class reunion. "Why should I?" he said. "No one paid any attention to me when I was there." This was a strange reply considering that he had been in Hasty Pudding, President of the *Lampoon*, Vice-President of the Dramatic Society, on the Union Library Committee, a member of the Mandolin Club, the Memorial Society, the Exeter Club, Delta Upsilon, Stylus Club, OK Society, Student Council, and was the Ivy Orator and President of the Signet Society. What he meant was, "The hell with them. I never made a final club." That's what happens, if you come from Worcester, Mass. No use to get sore about it.

lian Club, Franklin founded a club of his own called The New Deal.

The Boston girls called him "The Feather-duster," which in late Victorian Boston meant a lightweight and a prig. A lot of the fellows down there at the Harvard school thought him cocky, pompous, conceited, in short an ass. No doubt he betrayed many of the distressing symptoms of a bright only child with plenty of money. On the other hand, his enthusiasm, energy, optimism, and buoyant spirits attracted many friends. In other words, them as liked him thought he was a great old sport and them as didn't waited a few years and then, grinding their teeth and rolling their eyeballs like Lionel Barrymore, rushed to the polls and voted feverishly and fruitlessly for Herbert Hoover (Stanford, '95), Alfred Mossman Landon (U. of Kansas, '08), Wendell Willkie (U. of Indiana B.A., '13, L.L.D. '16), and Thomas Edmund Dewey (U. of Michigan, '23)—all in more or less rapid succession. The object of their affections continued to show his dental work. One man's "infectious smile" was another's "cocky grin."

He certainly hopped around like a Hudson River jumping bean. From a letter home in freshman year:

On Thursday morning I went out to Franklin Park and umpired a football game, went to lunch at the Sturgises, and to dine at the Lords, so I was pretty well filled (with food I mean) and had a most pleasant day . . . on Saturday went to lunch with Mrs. Brown at the Touraine and went to the theatre in the evening. On Sunday I met Sidney Lord in Harvard Square at 9:30, and we went to Oakley and had a very good game of golf . . . I hustled back at 12:30 and went to a stag lunch with Willy Burnham. After lunch, at 3:30 I went to Dr. Parks Church (in Boston) for afternoon service. After service I paid several calls, one to the Forbes but they were out. I hustled back here and in (to Boston) again to dinner at Gerry Chadwick's . . . Tonight I go in to the Boys Club again.

At this same time he was playing as captain of one of

the scrub football teams, trying out for the *Crimson*, shooting pool pretty regularly at Sanborn's on Massachusetts Avenue, and carrying six courses. His energy was exhausting to contemplate. He was extremely active on the *Crimson*, becoming Editor in his fourth year. He stroked one of the crews for two years. He was President of the Political Club. He served on committees of the Harvard Union, the Memorial Society, and Hasty Pudding. He attended club banquets with their inevitable blue points, mock turtle *aux quenelles*, broiled Savannah shad, and roast sirloin of beef *aux* olives. He skipped nimbly in and out of Boston and paid frequent visits to Groton. He went to Newburyport to shoot ducks (but didn't get any). He went to the Somerset to "the Warren's dance" and didn't get back to Cambridge until 6 A.M. He met the Crown Prince of Siam at the Fly Club. He entertained ten freshmen in his rooms. He attended a dinner of the Massachusetts Republican Club. He interviewed captains at Lawleys Ship-Yard in South Boston for the family schooner *Half Moon*, and on the advice of "Mr. Robert Saltonstall and Mr. Rantoul" hired Chris Michelson.[9] He had his teeth fixed and he played golf. He wheeled "Marjorie and Dorothy Peabody down to the John Lawrences in a baby carriage." He worked with poor boys at the Boys Club. He was the Librarian of Hasty Pudding and added to its collection. He attended christenings, weddings, balls, parties, teas, and picnics. He "was one of the three cheer leaders in the Brown game and felt like a D — — — F — — — It's a dirty job, one gets chiefly ridicule—but some poor devil has to suffer and one can't refuse." He went to the

[9] Note to Yachtsmen: The *Half Moon* was a sixty-foot, eighteen-ton auxiliary schooner, originally named *Brynlys*. FDR's father, James Roosevelt, bought it three years after its launching from Nathan and Henry Clifford through A. Cary Smith and Barbey, ship brokers. In a letter from Groton at the time of purchase (April 1900), FDR says "I wonder where the engine will go and why have you changed from Daimler to Globe?" The English Daimler engine was being distributed from or manufactured in Steinway, N.Y., but I have no data on Globe.

Automobile Show of 1903. He saw *The Prince of Pilsen* and *Show Girl.* He went to church and supped at the Touraine. In one week he dined at "The Quincy's, the Amory's, and the Thayers, three as high-life places as are to be found in blue-blooded, blue-stockinged, bean-eating Boston!" In his junior year he became engaged to his distant cousin Eleanor Roosevelt and he wrote, "It is dreadfully hard to be a student, a society whirler, a 'prominent and democratic fellow' and a fiance all at the same time but it is worthwhile. . . ."

"Dreadfully hard" indeed—just thinking about it makes me feel like lying down for a while in the spare bedroom. Recalling Harvard years it seems to me that it used to take me the better part of a day just to take my shirts to the Chinaman and buy a new squash ball.

The astonishing thing about this virtual caricature of frenzied collegiate activity was that on top of it all, he took his A.B. degree at the end of his junior year—having polished off fifteen courses in three years with creditable grades, and spent his senior year in the Graduate School in which he knocked off five more courses while running the *Crimson.*

His success on the *Crimson* was the real feather in his Harvard cap—or derby (from Collins & Fairbanks). To be Editor of the *Crimson* took more doing than playing football or singing in the Glee Club.[10] This was real accomplishment and real work. And it showed Endicott Peabody and the Groton bunch a thing or two. Or at least he hoped it would. There is nothing quite so satisfying in life as showing your prep school or high school teachers and classmates that you are not the completely feeble character they took you for. Not that you could impress the Reverend Peabody. In 1932, after the slender, nonathletic member of Groton '00 had been elected President

---

[10] "But swell clubs and exclusive societies were of small account to the youth beside the honor of being elected an editor of the *Crimson.*"

—The Story of Young Franklin Roosevelt

of the United States, Rector Peabody wrote another old Grotonian:

There has been a good deal written about Franklin Roosevelt when he was a boy at Groton, more than I should have thought justified by the impression that he left at the school.

Getting out a daily paper was something he never forgot, and he always in later life felt a kinship with reporters and newspapermen. It may be that they felt something less than kinship with him, although he was popular with them, but that wouldn't bother Franklin any. If he sensed it he ignored it. One of his greatest self-renewing talents, and one he shared with Scarlett O'Hara, was the ability to forcibly thrust out of his mind unpleasant facts. Schlesinger, Jr., calls this his "jovial obliviousness" which he used to deal with "tense human relationships." It is a rather unpleasant trait for others to live with and he had developed it in later years to a meticulous science.

He was a good *Crimson* editor. He was earnest and he viewed with alarm a number of standard subjects, among them the football team. (Ho hum.)

[The undergraduates] have grown somewhat weary of the slow, listless play of certain men in the line, who seem to think that their weight is a sufficient certificate of admission to membership on a University team . . . all that is needed is a spirit in the team of aggressive, vigorous determination. . . . [The University] is waiting to see the team resolve actually to make itself, by fierce and vigorous playing, as formidable as it ought to be.

How much longer must the University wait?

Where have we heard all this before? Like last week? But in addition to this typical fare he also insisted on broadening the scope of the paper. He went further than cataloguing meetings, scores, and lost mandolins, and dug up news. He got mad about the Boxer Rebellion in print, and also the Boer War. There is no doubt that he had not only a feeling for "the news as it develops" (Urp!) but a professional attitude toward "the power of the press" (Ugh! groan!) in influencing "men and events" (awk!). The novel institution of the presidential press conference (an innovation which our poor long-suffering Chief Executives seem to be permanently stuck with) was a direct result of FDR's early newspaper work and interest in getting the news to the people effectively, while at the same time making a public spectacle of the Big Guy.

Then there was The Voice. The Voice that brought tears of hope and gratitude to the millions under its spell, and tears of rage from other, but lesser, millions, to whom it was the voice of the Devil on earth, come to plague them and raise their taxes. This famous, or infamous, voice and elocutionary manner which seemed so careless and unstudied, was the result of careful, meticulous training in English 18 at Harvard: "The Forms of Public Address," under the famed George Pierce Baker. The extraordinary Baker, some of whose other students (in his drama workshop) were Eugene O'Neill, John Mason Brown, Thomas Wolfe, S. N. Behrman, Sidney Howard, Donald Oenslager, George Abbott, Philip Barry, etc. etc. (but not including Jed Harris or Gallagher and Shean) had a way of instilling confidence in his students and giving them a feeling of their importance. He also wore pince-nez glasses and told O'Neill that *Bound East for Cardiff* (which subsequently became *The Long Voyage Home*) was not a play at all. O'Neill laughed that one off.[11] Whether or not George Pierce Baker taught Franklin Roosevelt to throw his head back and grin while wagging his head back and forth, in a way that was particularly annoying to

[11] When George Pierce Baker died in 1935, Eugene O'Neill's glowing tribute appeared in a letter to *The New York Times:* ". . . the most vital thing for us, as possible future artists and creators, to learn at that time (Good God! For any one to learn anywhere at any time) was to believe in our work and to keep on believing. And to hope. He helped us to hope—and for that we owe him all the finest we have in memory of gratitude and friendship." (January 13, 1935)

registered Republicans, is not on record. If he did, all the said Republicans who went to Harvard can stop weeping in their grog because of the fact that Baker eventually slipped through President Lowell's not unwilling fingers and joined up with Yale.

In spite of his elocution lessons with Baker, FDR was at first but an indifferent speaker given to long and painful pauses. But during his first campaign, for State Senator from Dutchess County, New York, which he conducted from a two-cylinder red Maxwell, he gained confidence and oratorical momentum, and The Voice was born. "Whenever a Roosevelt rides," Elihu Root said, "he wants to ride in front." In addition to The Voice, FDR possessed all the excellent qualities of showmanship that make a star. Like Shirley MacLaine, he had enthusiasm, charm, high spirits, good looks, more enthusiasm,—all of which he was able to *project*. So he kept on talking until he was riding in front. And it was a good long ride, on which there was always somebody else along to fix the blowouts; the foliage was magnificent, and every night the best suite was waiting at the Mountain View House, the Pemige-wasset House, the Ocean View House, the Flume House, and other elegant and well-appointed hostelries. Yes, it was a nice long ride, and if you mix a few bottles of Hub Punch (C. H. Graves & Company, 35 Hawkins St., Boston, since 1879) properly iced, with lemonade, some small bits of Pineapple and a few Strawberries, you'll have a convivial cup satisfying to the most discriminating. Why not try a few bottles today?

Why did FDR go into politics? Well, my guess is that for one thing he was bored with the law, and in the second place he was bored with the sappy conventions of upper-class New York life. He was bored with talking about yachts and Herreshoff. He was bored with sitting on country-club porches. He was bored with talking to Percy, bored with parties and wealthy noses tilted slightly toward the ceiling. And he was bored with talking about Money. Gentle reader, if you think the members of the

Harvard Club of New York stand around the bar talking about Baudelaire and Ivy Compton-Burnett, disguise yourself as a martini olive and listen in and you will soon discover that this august company is talking about Dough. During my last visit to this handsome saloon a bird on my right in a 55 per cent dacron polyester and 45 per cent wool worsted olive-tone sharkskin said to his companion while I studied the ceiling, "Just let me formulate our concept of this expansion program," and on my left, a hearty type in 65 per cent wool, 35 per cent orlon acrylic gray simulated Irish tweeds stated frankly, in a booming voice that carried all the way out to the backgammon tournament in the lounge: "Charlie, all we happen to need at the moment is twelve million dollars." Brother, the closest these fellows get to culture is when their wives drag them to an entertainment by Mr. Tennessee Williams and that don't add up to much culture, especially after a big dinner. The John Jay ski movies don't count.

After all that excitement on the *Crimson* at Harvard, large and uninterrupted doses of the High Sassiety stuff gave Mr. Roosevelt a big pain. And besides, everybody called him "Franklin." How would you like it if people came right up to you and called you "Franklin"? He couldn't go back to Harvard as they have a rule up there which states that graduates who have been out for more than five years are not allowed to be editors of the *Crimson* or lean against the buildings. So he went into politics.

Franklin D. Roosevelt graduated from Harvard on June 24, 1904. Part of the Class Day Exercises consisted of a joke session around the Class Tree behind Hollis Hall closed to all but seniors although, according to the Boston *Globe*, "a number of inquisitive people made things a bit unpleasant for the men by occupying the back windows of Hollis Hall."

"At this meeting," says the paper, "grinds were passed out on various men of the class. Harold Otis and John Densmore had charge of the program, and it was full of wit and humor."

From the hard-boiled eye of 1962 the jokes look about as witty as those perpetrated on Hazel at the wedding shower given her by the other girls in the office. For example President Burgess of the Class was given "a pair of suspenders as a symbol of the dependance [*sic*] of the class on him." (*Zowie!* What a grind on old Burgess!)

Here's another hot one:

"Charlie Shea, the leading actor of the class, was given a little colored girl to act as his leading lady. The girl came packed in a big dry goods case, which was opened at the tree."

Don't sweat it, N.A.A.C.P., it was fifty-eight years ago. Pretty funny sketch on Shea, if you ask me.

But the biggest howl followed the unwrapping of the real live diminutive colored girl:

"Captain Carr of the baseball nine was arrested on a warrant for stealing bases" (Stop it, I can't stand it! I'm gettin' hysterics!) "served by F. D. Roosevelt, who was given a New York policeman's helmet to start him on his political career as the successor of his uncle, Theodore Roosevelt."

Guess who had the last laugh on that one?

Just for fun, and for the benefit of the genealogists, local historians, and the morbidly curious, here is a list of the Class Day Officers of FDR's class, 1904:

First Marshal	James A. Burgess	Boston
Second Marshal	Carl B. Marshall	Brookline, Mass.
Third Marshal	Edgar C. Rust	Boston

(Greater Boston had that pretty well sewed up.)

Secretary	Roy S. Wallace	Freeport, N.Y.
Orator	Arthur A. Ballantine	Springfield, Mass.
Ivy Orator	Walter R. Bowie	Richmond, Va.
Poet	Arthur D. Ficke	Davenport, Iowa
Odist	Samuel A. Welldon	Brooklyn, N.Y.
Chorister	John H. Densmore	Somerville, Mass.
Class Committee Chairman	Franklin D. Roosevelt	Hyde Park, N.Y.
Class Committee	Rob Roy Alexander	Minerva, Ohio
Class Committee	Albert Goodhue	Salem, Mass.

Class Day Committee   Edward B. Krumbhaar   Philadelphia, Pa.
Class Day Committee   Payson Dana   Brookline, Mass.
Class Day Committee   Louis Grilk   Davenport, Iowa
Senior Spread Committee Harold G. Dillingham Honolulu, H.I.

(NOTE: Dillingham unable to attend Class Day as he was Captain of Varsity Crew working out at Red Top for Yale race.)

Senior Spread Committee   William G. Clothier   Wynnewood, Pa.
Senior Spread Committee   Chester H. Robinson   Dedham, Mass.
Photograph Committee   John Daniels   Grafton, Vt.
Photograph Committee   Reginald Foster   Baltimore, Md.
Photograph Committee   Ralph Sanger   Dedham, Mass.

That's ten New England men out of twenty-one. And seventeen Easterners out of twenty-one. It is nice to see those two good boys from Davenport, Iowa—way out in the Indian country—making the palefaces sit up and take notice. Ficke and Grilk. It sounds like a vaudeville team in snappy duds ready to get off all the late ones.

And one of them a poet, at that! You'd thing that here in the seething Atheneum of Bostonian culture they could have shaken a New England poet out of some tree along Brattle Street, or out Concord way, or along the Ipswich River, without going clear to the banks of the Mississippi and the shores of the Rock Island rapids. It's a surprising choice—bardwise, that is—and a tribute to the Hawkeye State.

(Time Out, while everybody rises and sings the Iowa Corn Song in honor of Ficke and Grilk.

> Oh we're from Ioway! Ioway!
> It's the best state in the land,
> And we'll have you understand . . .
>   Etc., etc.)

After FDR's death there was a battle royal in the Harvard Club of New York as to where his portrait should be hung. Some were for having it hung in the crew's toilet of a Dalzell harbor tugboat, while others favored locating it near the exhaust fan in Lester's All-Nite Lunch in Weehawken. After a prolonged sweat, sometimes known as a heated controversy, the portrait was taken out of the main hall and placed in the dining room, behind the buffet table, from which location the eminent member of the Class of '04 looks benignly upon the cold boiled lobsters and potato salad.

Franklin D. Roosevelt's contribution to the world of art has long been underestimated. He was a boon to struggling artists, hundreds of whom broke into the big time by drawing pictures of apoplectic anti-Roosevelt clubmen and selling them to the funny magazines.

RAINY DAY FUN DEPARTMENT

First ask Mummy for a pencil and a nice clean piece of white paper. Now put on your Thinking Caps! (If you don't have a Thinking Cap get Mums to order you one from Gimbels or Jordan Marsh.)

Here's what you do:

Listed below are all the nice Roosevelts whose names are in the 1948 edition of the Harvard Alumni Directory. The object of the game is as follows (Pay attention, Roger dear, it is still raining like hell outside):

1. Put the names in chronological order of birth.
2. Describe each nice man's favorite dessert (junket, nesselrode pudding, gin and tonic, etc.)
3. Tell which ones are afraid of New Jersey.
4. Tell which ones belong to the Fruit-of-the-Month Club.
5. Tell which ones
   (a) don't like John Crosby
   (b) don't like novelty cuff links
   (c) don't like President Pusey *or* Sammy Davis, Jr.
   (d) don't like little-neck clams.

Ready? Get Set! *Go!*

Archibald Bullock Roosevelt
Archibald Bullock Roosevelt, Jr.

Cornelius Van Schaak Roosevelt
Franklin Delano Roosevelt
Franklin Delano Roosevelt, Jr.
George Emlen Roosevelt
Gracie Hall Roosevelt
Henry Parish Roosevelt
J. Willard Roosevelt
James Roosevelt
James Roosevelt Roosevelt
James West Roosevelt
John Aspinwall Roosevelt
Kermit the First Roosevelt
Kermit the Second Roosevelt
Nicholas Roosevelt
Oliver Wolcott Roosevelt
Oliver Wolcott Roosevelt, Jr.
Philip James Roosevelt
Quentin Roosevelt
Theodore Roosevelt
Theodore Roosevelt, IIIrd

THE PENNY ARCADE

Poesie Annex: Radcliffe Section

Cassandra, or Virtue Rewarded

Cassandra tied her ribbon bow
And shined her sharptoed, spike-heeled shoe,
Daintey rouged her delicate lips
And thought "Shall I stay until one or two?"
She donned an earring, thought "Perhaps
I'll stay until I see the sun
Come up; Perhaps I'll stay all night—
But no! I'll just sign out till one."

Scarce had she set her pen to sign
"Cassandra Smith, c/o Badman, phone

UNiversity 4-8584"
When she heard her date in anxious tone:
"Cassandra, won't you stay till dawn?"

"Ah, no," said she, "For, once begun,
A moment's wicked carelessness
Will never stop unless stopped at one."

"A rather small party," he told her, as
They entered his utterly barren place,
Barren of noise and people too,
And a lustful smile suffused his face.
"Have some madeira, m'dear," he said,
"The evening has only half begun."
She cried, "We must not dally here!
" 'Tis seven, and I must be back at one."

The evening pressed on, and so did he,
But his argument weakened at rapid rate,
For the later it got, the more she was right
In saying "It's liable to keep me too late."
So at half-past twelve she rose to go,
And he said, "But, Cassandra, you may think it's fun!"
She repulsed him, secure in her purity and
The thought that she had to be in by one.

So she went to her virginal pillow in peace,
And awoke the next morning to find by her side
A note, to a bunch of white roses attached,
Saying "Cassie, my dear, will you please be my bride?
For a man must take pleasure wherever he can,
But in choosing the mother of his son,
He wants a woman faithful and strong
And bound and determined to be in by one."

Envoi:

And so, whatever may be the rules,
From all those things you might have done,
You can save yourself (and get married too!)
If you always remember to sign out till one.

—Marian Henriquez
Radcliffe, '63

CHAPTER XIII

Bricks

vs.

Cinder Blocks

SOME NEOREALIST or neocranium-strainer said the other day and got it in print while nobody was looking due to a big dance at the Brookline Country Club, that Sever Hall is really, after all, let's look the thing directly in the face, Harvard's "most American building." Since Sever Hall was built in 1880 and is one of Henry Hobson Richardson's (Class of 1859) fairly gloomy Romanesque creations it seems an odd description. Especially when a good centerfielder could stand on the roof of Sever Hall and heave a baseball through a window of University Hall in one direction and turn around and make the Dana-Palmer house on the first bounce, or better, in the other.[1]

The Dana-Palmer House, for example, was built in 1820 and was the home of Richard Henry Dana (A.B.

---

[1] It is roughly 350 feet from Sever Hall to University Hall, and 450 feet from Sever to the Dana-Palmer House. Outfielder Don Grate of the Minneapolis Millers [American Association] on August 27, 1956, threw a baseball 445 feet 1 inch at Metropolitan Stadium, Minneapolis. He retired his arm from business at the end of the 1957 season.

1808), poet and essayist and father of the author of *Two Years Before the Mast.* Subsequently it was the first Harvard astronomical observatory, and the home of Professor Cornelius C. Felton (A.B. 1827), who was later President, Professor Andrew Preston Peabody (A.B. 1826), twice acting President, Professor George Herbert Palmer (A.B. 1864), renowned philosopher and translator of Homer, Dr. Richard M. Gummere (A.M. 1904), and President James Bryant Conant (A.B. 1914). This pleasant clapboard house is slightly more American than apple pie, ice water, and Will Rogers.

University Hall, of white Chelmsford granite, built in 1815 in the middle of the Yard, and surely one of Harvard's few "most beautiful" buildings, is American of course only in the sense that it was planned by Charles Bulfinch (A.B. 1781), who was also the architect of the Massachusetts State House on Beacon Hill. On a purely Stars-and-Stripes basis I would have almost thought that University Hall captures the pennant, as for years it was the seat of public dinners and orgies of oratory, exhibitions, commencement exercises and other fancy functions, and has in its time welcomed Presidents Monroe, Jackson, and Van Buren, as well as the grand and glorious Marquis de Lafayette. In former and funnier times, the Governor of Massachusetts was annually welcomed here, escorted by a troop of horses and preceded by trumpeters. Nowadays the Governor arrives in a Yellow Cab with a Faulty clutch.

Charles Bulfinch, no relation to the Eastern Purple Finch (*Carpodacus purpureus purpureus*) or the Rosy Finch (*Leucosticte tephrocotis*), was born in Boston, attended Boston Latin School and graduated from Harvard in 1781, after which he bounced around Europe for several years studying, sampling the vintages, and murdering several languages in cold blood. In 1787 he became the first professional architect to hang up his shingle and begin making excuses to the clients that Boston had ever seen. In 1793 he was responsible for the design of the old

Federal Street Theatre, the first playhouse in all New England. (Seeing that the Devil had in fact at last arrived in Boston in the person of actors, actresses, stage managers, and the Stage Hands' Union, there was a mass exodus of Puritans to Milwaukee and St. Paul and that's how the Northwest Territory was opened.) His next important work was the State House on Beacon Street at Park, across from Trefry and Partridge, up the street from the Boston Athenaeum and a few blocks from that other and more important Athenaeum dedicated to the art of Ann Corio, now in ashes (the building, not Miss Corio), known as the Howard Athenaeum. The splendid wooden dome of the State House, the pride of the Bay State, which can be seen even on a foggy day all the way from the post office in West Dover, Vermont, was covered with copper in 1802, first gilded in 1861, and covered with gold leaf in 1874. More Irish politicians have congregated under this dome in the last sixty years than any other place except Jack Sharkey's bar.[2]

Bulfinch then provided the still-Elizabethan city of Boston with new drainage and street lighting, reorganized the police and fire departments, providing each fireman with a free red shirt, and "straightened and widened the streets." Which streets he straightened and widened remains a mystery. Going from the South Station to the Parker House for some tripe the other day I got so tangled up in narrow streets and streets bent double that I eventually began to feel like Stan Laurel lost in the famous maze scene [3] and was forced to ask help from an improper Bostonian emerging from a place of entertainment and wiping his mouth with the back of his hand.

Bulfinch was also one of the promoters of the first voyage to carry the Stars and Stripes around the world,

[2] BOSTON POLICE CHIEF FIRED BY MASSACHUSETTS GOVERNOR—Boston (UP), Gov. John A. Volpe yesterday formally fired Boston Police Commissioner Leo J. Sullivan . . .—*Herald Tribune*, March 8, 1962.
[3] *A Chump at Oxford*, Hal Roach Studio, 1940. Originally conceived as a four-reeler, this screen classic was given added footage and released as a feature.

that of the *Columbia,* under Captain Robert Gray. Hooray for him.

Finally, he succeeded B. H. Latrobe as architect of the national capitol in Washington. Mrs. Kennedy may or may not know it, but Bulfinch constructed the rotunda and designed the new western approach and portico. She probably does know it and also has a cute cuddlesome voice.[4]

Charles W. Eliot may not have been an authority on architecture, but he was wondrous wise and of Bulfinch's University Hall he told the students of the School of Architecture: "Here is the great architectural effort of the College in the early part of the nineteenth century." And John Hays Gardiner declares the Faculty Room in University, "with its round top windows on each side, . . . the handsomest room in the University." Eliot also said Wadsworth House (1726) is in "my eyes one of the best of the college buildings," and, Hollis, "the most agreeable from the architects' point of view." He doesn't mention whether either is most "American" or not. But neither of the buildings in question is very gothic.

Eliot, of course, registers as a Square with his comment, and further shows that he is completely out of touch with things as he does not even mention Richardson, Sever Hall, or Austin Hall in his architectural tour of the yard, much less Louis Sullivan, Frank Lloyd Wright, Orville Wright, or Martha Wright, and completely ignores Le Corbusier, Felix Candela, R. Buckminster Fuller's space

---

[4] BIGGEST HOOT OF EVENING DEPARTMENT: The Kennedys came in for some razzing at the ultra chic mid-season dinner dance the other night which featured a miniature musical by Scottie Fitzgerald Lanahan, entitled, "How to Succeed in Washington by Really Trying."

Biggest hoot came when beauteous socialite Mrs. Neil Carothers, playing Jacqueline Kennedy and mimicking her soft, youthful voice perfectly, was taking Lord Possumbrook (played by Sir Kenelm Guinness of the World Bank) on a White House tour and said, "Here is the Green Room. Today it's green, yesterday off-white, tomorrow it's going to be the Peppermint Room, if you know what I mean." Betty Beale, *New York World Telegram,* March 17, 1962.

frame pavilion made of 1800 wooden dowels, and Antoni Gaudí. One of the reasons he lived to be ninety-two was because he did not get excited about Frank Lloyd Wright and have to take ¼ tsp. bicarbonate of soda in ½ glass warm water several times a day. He believed in the past as part of the present, including its architectural remains, however plain they might be.

He was mightily peeved, for one thing, about the disappearance from the Harvard scene, of buildings which he considered to be traditional and romantic. Gore Hall, for example, the college library built in 1839–42 and a wildly entertaining Walter Scott-type edifice in the fourteenth-century gothic style (in the form of a Latin cross, with towers, pinnacles, buttresses, and a gilt cross above the entrance, a trophy of the siege of Louisburg in 1745) in 1909 was ruthlessly sacked, decimated, leveled to the base earth and the historic shards and holy fragments hauled away to provide foundation fill for an elastic-tape factory. "Despite the fact," says Mr. Eliot, "that it bore the name of Christopher Gore, eminent citizen, governor, and the largest benefactor the College had ever had ($95,000) in 1831." Gore Hall was the college library, and when Widener Library came into the picture Gore was doomed. Nobody could think of anything else to do with it so they knocked it down and stomped on it.

You readers who are located in the plumbing game may be interested in President Emeritus Eliot's remarks on the Gore Hall heating system. Personally I am not and have never been in the close-nipple and reducing-valve trade myself, but still find this type of factual information of equal interest with purely esthetic reports. Eliot is telling us:

"The original heating apparatus was invented by Daniel Treadwell, Rumford Professor of the Application of Science to the Useful Arts (1824–45) and was a memorable piece of pioneer work. . . . It was a low pressure steam-heat system, the radiators for which were very tall and large, and built of large copper tubes soldered together. These tubes, however, were apt to leak steam, in consequence of which the atmosphere of the library became charged with aqueous vapor, and this vapor condensed, not only on the windows in the colder seasons of the year, but also on the books themselves. This defect ultimately led to the complete reconstruction of the heating apparatus of Gore Hall."

Mr. Eliot was also put out by the fact that the President's house he had lived in for forty years, a gift to the College in 1846 from Peter C. Brooks, father-in-law of Edward Everett, had been demolished by his successor, Abbott Lawrence Lowell. This was a rather unlovely but quaint house with a mansard roof and two tall chimneys looking a bit like a seaside home at Little Boar's Head or some such place. The curved, slated roof absorbed heat on a summer's day which, according to Eliot, made the second- and third-story rooms "intolerable." Still, he believed that this "monument to a considerable giver" should have been preserved. His feeling was that if anybody thought enough of Harvard to dip into his holdings in Amoskeag and Calumet and Hecla and build a building for Harvard, that building should stand through ten thousand New England winters and summers to the perpetual glory of its donor's memory.

Not so Lowell, who was not only on speaking terms with God but offered Him suggestions on how to improve His management, His hiring-and-firing policy, and His public-relations department. Lowell decided at once on becoming President that the old Brooks homestead was totally inadequate for one on such intimate terms with the Deity.

"Mr. Brooks' gift disappeared twelve years ago," said Mr. Eliot. "It has gone forever. President Lowell wished to give the University a larger and better President's house, but essentially on the same site. He did so."

Don't say another word, Charles, we've got the picture.

Lowell's new President's House, designed by Guy Lowell and built in 1912, is a very lovely colonial house on quite a grand scale. It cost $155,000 in 1912, which will give you some idea. But Lowell was no cheapskate. *He personally footed the bill.* It was his gift to the University. How many college Presidents can toss around $150,000 from their own bank account? [5]

So after all the downtalk we must in all fairness give three cheers and a long Harvard for Lowell, even if his sister did smoke cigars, preferring the Ben Hervey pana-tella. The house was altered in 1929-34 at a cost of $37,000. During the latest war it served as headquarters for Navy units stationed at Harvard and when they departed it was found necessary to spend $55,000 to sweep out the ciga-rette butts and eliminate the poetry from the bathroom walls.

And speaking of bathrooms, the first bathtubs to appear in Harvard dormitories were installed in the basement of Matthews Hall in the 1870s. Up until the sixties there was no water supply of any kind in the Yard. Neither was there any sewer. For bathing purposes the students car-ried water to their rooms in pails from one of the two pumps in the Yard. Perhaps they heated some water on their own fire—otherwise they had nice, cold water. Con-sequently "the amount of bathing done in the college was very limited."

There has recently been a grand remodeling program going on in the old Yard dormitories with the view in mind of bringing them up to date. This is in line with the twentieth-century ideal of systematically eliminating all color from the American scene. (*Cf.* decline and fall of the steam locomotive, and the disappearance of the Cincinnati Incline, Kranz's candy store in Chicago, the coin-operated mechanical piano, double-breasted vests for men, the interurban, Tiffany glass, burl ̲ ̲, derby hats,

[5] "[Mr. Lowell] fulfills the most rigid conditions which the most august member of the Harvard corporation could require. He is of the Brahmin caste; he is distinguished in letters; he has had ex-perience in financial affairs and administrative boards; he is an inheritor of reasonable wealth . . ." The New York *Sun,* October 6, 1909.

the seven-passenger touring car, the beer garden, the chemise, fancy garters for ladies, etc. etc.). A picture story on the remodeling in the Harvard *Alumni Bulletin* resulted in the following letter from one testy graduate.

Mud Slough,
East Dubuque, Illinois
November 6, 1961

Mr. Norman A. Hall, Editor
The "Harvard Alumni Bulletin"
Wadsworth House
Cambridge, 38, Mass.

To the Editor of the "Bulletin":

One can't help but deplore the change in college quarters when inspecting your interesting art gallery in the issue of 14 October. Hollis 28, in 1905, appears as a comfortable, homey room fitted out for comfortable living, sleeping, and study, with the added cheery note of a glowing open fire in the grate. In the lower picture, of the new and up-to-date Hollis 28, we see two students at home in what appears to be an abandoned storage warehouse or the office of an unsuccessful tannery in Peabody, Mass. The contrasts between the old and new versions of Weld 14, Holworthy 7, and Mathews 31 are even more grisly and give a sad picture of the decline of warmth, good cheer, and good living enjoyed by our fuddy-duddy predecessors not only at Harvard but every place else.

Sincerely
Old Sorehead,
Class of '36

Just to prove that I am not completely alone in the deploring business, I quote from another old grad, William G. Morse, '99.

There was no heat in any of the buildings, except that supplied by the open fireplaces in each study. Students bought their own coal, kept in a locked closet in the cellar, except in Gray's Hall where the closets were outside the door of each room, and during the winter fires were kept going day and night in the little coal grates. This kind of heat had its advantages over present methods, for not only was it a pleasant, healthy heat, as the chimney kept taking the bad air out of the room, removing all need of modern air-conditioning gadgets, but the fire was a delightful place for the midnight saucepan of hot chocolate, made with condensed milk; nor is there any modern way of making toast as delicious as the eleven o'clock Sunday morning toast, made after the fire had been raked, fresh coal put on, the window closed, and two roommates had crawled under the covers until the room warmed up and the fire was right. For toast made this way the bread must be fresh, slices cut thick, a hole poked in the slice so it can be hung on the poker (it will not be right if toasted on a gridiron); the butter should be sweet butter, kept on the window ledge inside the double window, so that it cannot be "fished" up by the thieves living in the room overhead, though it will taste better if it has been secured by that method from the room below; the fire should be very hot and the toast crisp on both sides, soft in the middle, buttered hot, and eaten instantly. If funds are in, a few lamb chops cooked the same way, but impaled on a stolen fork lashed to the poker, will taste as no other chops ever tasted; they too must be eaten as hot as fingers can hold them and should be torn limb from limb without benefit of knife and fork. Now Harvard heats these buildings, fireplaces are dark, and toast cannot be made on a radiator.[6]

When Eliot was an undergraduate in 1849-53, there were no lights in the Yard. "No lights at all." Eliot wanted gas lights in his room, Holworthy 11, and went to President Walker and asked him if he might be allowed to talk to the Cambridge Gas Company about installing gas pipes in Holworthy. President Walker threw up his hands and registered horror just like Henry B. Walthall throwing up his hands and registering horror. He said the students would "play all sorts of pranks with the gas . . . leave gas cocks open, and blow up the building." After a second visit to the President, however, the alert youth and Presi-

[6] *Pardon My Harvard Accent*, by William G. Morse (Farrar and Rinehart, New York, 1941).

dent-to-be succeeded in gaining permission to approach the Gas Company and before long Holworthy was ablaze with light to the envy of the other lads in surrounding barracks. No catastrophes resulted from the experiment, and within a few years gas had been installed in all the dormitories, making it possible for the students to play stud poker and black jack continuously without the annoyance of trimming wicks, cutting the cards to see who would go out for more coal oil, and other interruptions to the game.

It is hard for anyone wanting to landscape Harvard to do anything much about it. It was not laid out on a drawing board like the University of Mexico or Duke University, and with the exception of the Yard, the buildings are jammed together pretty much like the downtown section of Bridgeport.[7] Even the Yard, with its wild conglomeration of architectural styles, can only be kept filled with elm trees, supplemented by sporadic foundation cover of bushes here and there. There is no chance here among these New England bricks for knots, mazes, terraces, temples, pergolas, dovecotes, fountains, serpentine walks, topiary works or banked floral effects. Flowers, in fact, are not considered necessary or to blend harmoniously with Government 205a—"Systematic Political Theory and Analysis"—or even with *La Guerre de Crimée et l'attitude des Puissances européenes.*[8] There are no buses arriving in spring loaded with pilgrims come to see the Harvard cherry trees in bloom, or even the Harvard lilac bush. Stylish matrons from the Hingham Garden Club do not destroy the calm of these cloisters by descending in ecstatic groups to follow the Peony Trail from Eliot House up past La Flammes barber shop and through the Square and the Yard to the Cambridge Fire House. In short, it's never Tulip Time at Harvard. The romantic

---

[7] Van Wyck Brooks ('08) describes the grounds of Charles Eliot Norton's "Shady Hill" as "an elegant park, unrivalled in *homely Cambridge.*" It's true, but then, New Haven is no Versailles.
[8] Vicomte de Guichen (Paris, 1936).

student who wants to walk hand in hand with his Radcliffe darling and her spook haircut through a bower of floral delight can only propel her up two flights of cast-iron stairs at the Botanical Museum and squeeze her through the turnstile into the Glass Flowers. It will cost him fifty cents, and there is always the chance that after one look at the insect-eating Venus Fly Trap plant she will run screaming from the building.

Harvard is a regular hodge-pudding architecturally. There are the old colonial buildings, and there are several unusually dreary nineteenth-century dormitories, one of them being Matthews, which at the time it was built (1872), was considered "the finest college dormitory in America," its majestic gothic style being widely admired for its "ornamental" qualities. Across from it is Weld Hall, also of 1872, in "the Elizabethan style," with two towering skylights, which was a wonder of elegance in its time. The trouble with both these buildings is not that they are Victorian but that they are really not Victorian enough. If we are going to go in that direction, friends, let us go all the way in the matter of turrets and spectacular fenestration—let us have a taste of the Philadelphia City Hall, a Fulton Ferry House, a Banvard's Castle, a Tampa Bay Hotel. Neither of these buildings has a very heady flavor and either one would be completely in character as a Methodist theological seminary. Most disappointing of all, however, is Thayer Hall, the first of the larger dormitories in the Yard, built in 1870, the gift of Nathaniel Thayer, a well-heeled Boston merchant who supplied $100,000 for its construction. Even at the time hardly anybody could think of anything nice to say about Thayer except that it was a big and it was built of brick. It is totally lacking in character or style of any kind and could easily pass for one of the more uninteresting nineteenth-century textile mills in Lawrence or Lowell. Here is a building that could be removed, for example to Pawtucket, without causing any tears or lumps in throat, but

I am not plugging for it, because if they knocked it down and hauled it away we would no doubt soon see rising on its site a structure in the new mode, made of aluminum rods, ceramic discs, and copper filings, rich in *Einfühlung*, identity between object and emotion, spatial relationships and relational spaceships, and with toothbrush holders of stark simplicity which reject all sentimentality.

For we live in an age when we are asked to stand in art galleries and museums staring at an oil painting composed of a totally flat and unrelieved expanse of lampblack. We are afraid to say anything for fear of losing caste and our only recourse is to borrow a dime and write something naughty on the wall of the men's room. Like "The hell with Mark Rothko!"; "William Baziotes Go Home!"; "Grace Hartigan sucks eggs"; or "We want Rosa Bonheur!"

Sad to relate, Harvard has decided to go along with the New Architecture and we are now confronted with the hair-raising effect of the new Leverett House Towers, a glass skyscraper-dormitory quite handsome in itself, but flanked on two sides by the Georgian buildings of the House Plan, and on the back by one of the finest displays of cockeyed frame tenement buildings in all of greater Boston (which incidentally has more frame tenement buildings than Peru has unemployed Indians).

How this came about one scarcely knows. Last summer I stood in the courtyard of the New Quincy House, which has split-level or double-decker or duplex student suites and enough glass to make any director of Libby, Owens-Ford call for drinks all around, and David Rockefeller was explaining to me how great it all was. Mr. Rockefeller doesn't scare me a bit even if he does have a Braque and two Picassos in the men's room down at his iron foundry—I can remember him when he was just a poor boy washing dishes at Hayes-Bickfords and selling laundry contracts to get through college. He is a good guy and it says in his Class Report that he goes to Seal Harbor, Maine, in the summer but in spite of this I was forced to disagree with him and not because I go to Indiana Harbor.[9] These modern buildings jammed in among the architectural catch-as-catch-can of Cambridge only aggravate the conditions esthetically; they don't alleviate nothing. The new Medical Center up there on Mt. Auburn Street, a Way-Out modern skyscraper which looks like its architect wears sandals, is about as out of place in its setting (Mike's Club, Elsie's, Harvard Provision Co., Joe's Place, Nifty Cleaners, etc.) as Chartres would be plunked down in the middle of the Caterpillar Tractor plant in Peoria, Illinois.

Somebody must have got to the Overseers and issued some humiliating comment to the effect that Harvard was taking a back seat to Brasilia and Conrad Hilton and had better pull up its socks and get with it. Blushing furiously and digging their toes into the gravel, they issued but feeble protest. Torn between esthetic and pragmatic demands—between reason and faith—works and leisure—French, roquefort or thousand-island dressing, they succumbed.

"The Georgian buildings are a fake, more imitations. Le Corbusier is real," they faltered. "At least Harvard shall be, as always, true to its time, and to contemporary values."

So is Elvis Presley.

Oh, I know what you're saying. "He's an old sourball, dreaming of Chestnut Street in Salem." "Probably carries his change in a coin purse." Listen, I just wear these Congress gaiters because they're comfortable, see. I really like modern art. Honest. Like those Renoir flesh tones, and those covers on *Time* by Henry Koerner. And I've been thrown out of the Guggenheim not once but twice. Take that Grandma Moses, for example . . .

All right all right, so the new buildings are great, they're the neatest things since the post and lintel, and they have nice sanitary cement corridors. So all right already. "Nothing is so dangerous as being too modern. One is apt to

[9] The truth is, seals make me nervous and self-conscious.

grow old-fashioned quite suddenly." Who said it? Not me, I didn't say it. Oscar Wilde said it. Probably a Communist.

I am always discovering something new about our advanced civilization. Like recently I found out that they have invented a type of gum that you can blow bubbles with, and another thing I learned is that nowadays all Harvard students have to have a refrigerator—what we call an "ice box" around Specht's Ferry—in their rooms at the College.

Everything is very modern up there, including the bed-making. The students take the same attitude toward a bed as Jack Kerouac's followers, which is that the natural state of a bed is a mass of tangled sheets and blankets half on the bed and half on the floor. There are over 11,000 students in Harvard University and a recent survey made by the Percale Sheet & Pillowcase Institute indicated that on any given day in Cambridge 38, Mass., after 1 P.M. there are an estimated 10,900 unmade beds.[10] The decor may be Motel Modern, and the architecture by McKim, Mead and White—Coolidge, Shepley, Bulfinch and Bud Abbott—Corbusier—or Alvar Aalto—but the bedrooms are strictly from a section-gang bunk car on the Milwaukee Railroad.

These students' refrigerators, though, they are a great institution and a big advance and a talking point in persuading bright prospects to come to Harvard instead of St. Olaf's. For one thing, they prepare students for the Status Symbol which they will soon meet in adult life, as they seem to serve no other function. I mean there is never anything in them. There is no beer in them, for example, as it is consumed instantly on arrival on the premises before somebody else drinks it. A can of beer in a Harvard refrigerator has the same life expectancy as a cigarette butt on the sidewalk in front of a flophouse on West Madison Street, Chicago, Illinois (The Land of Lincoln). A

[10] Before 1 P.M. there are an estimated 6000 unmade beds and 5000 beds with students in them sleeping through classes.

recent investigation of a Harvard refrigerator in a four-student suite on the third floor of Leverett House disclosed the following:

1. ½ can of sardines dating from the James B. Conant regime.
2. An olive bottle with 2 olives adrift.
3. ¼ cream cheese-and-caviar sandwich, emeritus, from Elsie's.
4. A can of smoked oysters waiting for the D.A. to dig up new evidence.
5. A bottle of Moxie.
6. A lemon.
7. A tennis ball.

It's terrible, though, how much it costs to build a dormitory these days. Every time they put up a new building somebody gets nicked for a few million. And just back in 1911 you could buy a whole school for $650. Not an old used school but a brand-new one. You don't believe me? I quote:

SCHOOLHOUSE NO. 63B200
    $320.00
We will furnish all the materials required to build this one-room Schoolhouse for $320.00. This includes all mill work, flooring, siding, ceiling, finishing lumber, building paper, eaves, trough, sash weights, hardware, painting material, lumber, lath and shingles. By allowing a fair price for labor, brick, and plaster, which we do not furnish, this schoolhouse can be built for about $645.00, including all materials and labor.

This public-spirited institution, none of whose directors had read up on Charles Richardson, was located in Chicago, Illinois. Its president was the former railroad-telegraph operator at North Branch, Minnesota, Richard Warren Sears. The firm was Sears, Roebuck and they could also supply a twenty-inch schoolhouse bell for $6.08, freight extra on 165 pounds. You were supposed to

FOR $1.00 WE WILL FURNISH A COMPLETE SET OF PLANS (BLUE PRINTS), BILL OF MATERIALS AND SPECIFICATIONS FOR THIS SCHOOLHOUSE.

Schoolhouse No. 63B200.

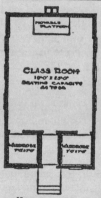

MOVABLE PLATFORM

CLASS ROOM
18'0" x 24'0"
SEATING CAPACITY
44 TO 50

WARDROBE
7'0"x7'0" WARDROBE
7'0"x7'0"

$320.00

We will furnish all the materials required to build this One-Room Schoolhouse for $320.00. This includes all mill work, flooring, siding, ceiling, finishing lumber, building paper, eaves trough, sash weights, hardware, painting material, lumber, lath and shingles. By allowing a fair price for labor, brick and plaster, which we do not furnish, this schoolhouse can be built for about $645.00, including all materials and labor. The amount of money you will be able to save on this schoolhouse by purchasing the building materials from us will go a long way toward paying for all school furniture and a complete line of best grade equipment for the class room.

This or any other plan may be changed slightly without additional cost for the building plans. However, any change which is made requiring more lumber and materials than called for in the original specifications will be charged for at the regular rate. If none of the plans shown are satisfactory we will quote prices on special plans drawn according to your own ideas upon receipt of a rough sketch showing the kind of a building you want to put up, also a letter telling us how much money your school board is authorized to spend for the building.

No. 63B200 Complete Plans, Bill of Materials and Specifications. Price......$1.00

Note These Savings Out in Utah.

137 North 8th West St., Salt Lake City, Utah.

Sears, Roebuck and Co., Chicago, Ill.

Gentlemen:—I received all mill work in first class condition and will say that I was very much pleased with the entire shipment. I saved on casings 220 per cent; flooring, 35 per cent; sash and doors, 50 per cent, and it was superior to material that I could buy at these figures here.

Yours very truly,
MARTIN FOSTER.

dig up your own schoolmarm, but if a market had developed Richard Sears would have added a few models to the catalogue, F.O.B. Chicago, DO NOT FORGET TO STATE COLOR AND SIZE.[11]

The thing about Harvard that we like to think is different from many colleges is that everybody can have his say without getting ridden out of town on a rail. So I have had my say about the new buildings, which summed up is that to me they are about as attractive and inspiring in their setting as Elsa Maxwell doing the Twist. If any Harvard man don't like it he can cheerfully lump it.

"Harvard," as Santayana says, "has freedom, both from external trammels, and from the pleasant torpor of too fixed a tradition. She has freedom and a single eye for the truth, and these are enough to secure for her, if the world goes well, an incomparable future."

The world is not going well at all, but Harvard is still heading for an incomparable future, and we love her every damn brick, cinder block, and soil pipe, from the dawnage foundations of the Indian College under Matthews Hall, to the most minute fragment of concrete in the new Le Corbusier 5-Level Visual Arts Center in "open flexible space" with knobs on it.

[11] Mr. Roebuck sold out his third-interest in the company in 1895 for $20,000. It was shortly worth $15,000,000. Mr. Roebuck's comment in late years was: "Sears made $25,000,000—he's dead. Skinner made $1,500,000—he's dead. Rosenwald made $100,000,000—he's dead. Me, I never felt better."

Words & Music

My great virtue is that I have no vanity. People criticize me, but when they meet me nobody can help liking me.

—WLADZIU VALENTINO LIBERACE

FOR SOME REASON never explained by the psychology department, large numbers of college students feel impelled to congregate publicly and sing songs. Since this entertains nobody and never has entertained anybody including Mother and Aunt Mabel who are sitting in the fifth row with fixed smiles and waiting for the number to end so they can continue discussing Roger and Sally's divorce, you would think this practice would die out, but no such luck. Group strumming and plucking on mandolins, which created a rather soothing sound inducing slumber except during the novelty numbers, has gone by the board except in Philadelphia Street parades, but the so called Harvard-Radcliffe Glee Club is going like a lard factory on fire and has more members than the U.N. They make recordings, yodel with the Boston Symphony, go on concert tours to Europe, and startle the Yard squirrels by bursting lustily into song on the steps of Widener in the springtime as well as everyplace else. Just stand in the middle of the Yard and blow on a pitch pipe and within minutes a crowd of at least two hundred extremely gleeful choristers will be bending the elm trees double with a mirth-provoking rendition of Bach's funeral ode for the Duchess Eberhardine. Since merriment is the watchword of the Glee Club (*cf*. Anglo-Saxon: *gleo;* Icelandic; *gly*) its members can easily be spotted as they are chock-full of high spirits and constantly wreathed in smiles.

A Radcliffe graduate, Miss Nora Sayre, confesses in *Holiday* magazine that she "sang myself to near collapse in my first year—in Bach's *St. Mathew Passion* with the Boston Symphony, his *Magnificat* at Sanders Theatre, two madrigal groups, and the chorus of a baroque opera." (If she was nearly collapsed, imagine the condition of the fathers in the audiences.) But Miss Sayre may not be entirely representative of Radcliffe. If she is, things have gotten pretty well out of hand up there since my time. For example, she seems to have had a peacock-blue velvet raincoat and also tells us that one of her "cleverest Harvard acquaintances spent hours on the floor with a Tinker Toy set. With huge concentration he built a model of a pea-cock rampant. It was, he has since confessed, a mother substitute." (Wait a minute, while I put on my hip boots.) Now what the hell chance have us old grads got with this kind of information about Harvard appearing in the pub-lic prints? OK, so I *did* have a Meccano set at Harvard, but I just played with it once in a while, late at night, and in the closet. And I didn't know anybody who was pea-cock-happy, either. Miss Sayre had some dandy girl friends up there at Radcliffe, which, if you have got any budding daughters, might make you think twice before writing the Director of Admissions for an application blank, such as "a cynical madrigal singer, who mastered the music, but loathed all Elizabethan lyrics; a girl who went to Dylan Thomas's funeral in tight black silk, veils, and jet earrings, weeping because she'd never met him; a Renaissance scholar who grew small trees in her room; and a six foot visionary who was sometimes depressed by Mozart's precocity. . . ."

Has anybody got a Tums or a Rollaid? Sometimes I get this heartburn——

It is true that the Harvard Glee Club pioneered among college glee clubs in the singing of good music. For example they have not sung "Glow Worm" or "The Rosary" for over forty years, and a new member was voted out recently for remarking, at the conclusion of a medley of sixteenth-century madrigals: "Hey fellas, what say we wind up with 'The Road to Mandalay?'" I'm telling you, you could have heard a pin drop.

And this brings to mind a hilarious story about Ralph Waldo Emerson and the Harvard Glee Club. He went to try out for the Glee Club when he was a freshman, and presented himself to the singing-master who, "when his turn came, said to him 'Chord!' 'What?' said Emerson. 'Chord! Chord! I tell you,' repeated the master. 'I don't know what you mean,' said Emerson. 'Why sing! Sing a note!' So he made some kind of a noise, and the singing-master said, 'That will do, sir. You need not come again!'"

This howl is from the pages of *R. W. Emerson* by Oliver Wendell Holmes, a volume literally jammed with similar side-splitting anecdotes. Some years after publication it was made into a movie with Joe E. Brown playing the part of the beloved philosopher to perfection.

Some of us were hoping that maybe President Kennedy's program for a better world would place some legislation on the priority list to make choral singing a federal offense, instead of wasting time on that abortive attempt to reopen the Shanghai Theatre and Sloppy Joe's in Havana, but no dice. You notice when the President wants some entertainment at the White House he doesn't bring in the Rutgers Glee Club, but Pablo ("Cat") Casals for his swinging strings rendition of "Rock Island Line."

The Harvard orchestra, which goes by the name of the Pierian Sodality of 1808, is the oldest college orchestra in the country and also has the funniest name. "Pierian" has nothing to do with pastry goods but refers, of course, to the fabled home of the Muses in Pieria (Jimmy Hatlo,

I make you a present of that name for one of your heroines), a district in ancient Thessaly. Never mind about Thessaly, if you're so curious go look it up. Can't you see Daddy is busy making some money to pay for your new stereo set, Lambretta, and spring trip to Fort Lauderdale? "Sodality" signifies a fellowship, or association, as, "There were military *sodalities* of musketeers, cross-bowmen, archers, swordsmen in every town." [1] The original Pierian sodalities of Harvard were armed with nothing more lethal than flutes. In fact the records show that at various times the orchestra consisted of nothing else *but* flutes. In 1832 the orchestra shrank almost out of sight, the entire instrumentation consisting of Henry Gassett, '34, and his solitary flute. Better times were ahead, however, and by 1893 the orchestra planned a concert in Sanders Theatre for which Paderewski, during his first American tour, was to be the soloist. President Eliot refused to allow this because admission would be charged. From the Pierian Spring sprang the Harvard Musical Association of Boston which performed the earliest chamber music heard in Boston, organized the first Boston Symphony concert in 1865, insisted on expansion of the Music Department at Harvard, and in other ways promoted melody and song among the beanpots. This bursting forth of the violin sections, the groaning horns, and the rumbling tympani in Boston and Cambridge rather amazed Professor Walter R. Spalding (1862–1962) of the music department, for as he said: "This development has taken place in a locality where for generations any secular expression of emotion was looked at askance, and among a people who, since The Reformation, have generally regarded music as 'effemi-

---

[1] *The Rise of the Dutch Republic,* John Lothroy Motley, Harvard Class of 1831. Motley's interest in swordsmen began early in life, when he used to enact impromptu melodramas in cloak and doublet in the old garret on Walnut Street, Beacon Hill (by the Chestnut Street opening), with his chums Thomas Gold Appleton and Wendell Phillips (both also Harvard 1831). Motley's "efforts at novel writing, the results of which were depressing" converted him into a famous historian.

nate.'" And President Eliot, whose ideas about charging admission to hear Paderewski keep haunting me, remarked that music was "not especially congenial to the evolved or opened-out Puritans who for a hundred years have had the management of Harvard College." [2]

The Pierian Sodality is now known as the HRO, or Harvard Radcliffe Orchestra, and they do not fool around with "The Whistler and His Dog" or "In a Clock Shop," or even "Country Gardens" (there's a nice little tune). Look at their Christmas Concert this past December. "Michael Senturia, the principal conductor of the evening," says Anthony Hiss in the *Crimson*, "chose a formidable program, demanding Stravinsky (his *Symphony of Psalms*) and sprightly Beethoven (The *Second Symphony*). It takes great temerity on the part of any college conductor to think of scheduling even the Beethoven . . . let alone the Stravinsky."

My experience has been that all college orchestra conductors as well as those of all high school and junior high school orchestras have the great temerity to tackle anything. I have heard Mozart played by a high school orchestra with a violin section which should have been arrested, and I imagine the kindergarten rhythm bands are now doing Sibelius. But never mind that, the HRO is really good if we are to believe Mr. Hiss, who has got the musical lingo down better than the *Times*. Like where he says: "The first desk winds handled the fugal introduction to the psalm with ease, a particularly delicate passage full of grace and restraint, and in the more monolithic third psalm the brasses showed strength and carefully controlled enthusiasm."

I happen to like my psalms monolithic just as well as the

---

[2] Even in non-Puritanical literature we find the carefree playing of a solo instrument as a constantly recurring symbol for idleness: the improvident artist fluting in his garret; the grasshopper fiddling while the ant works; the shiftless hillbilly strumming the banjo while his wife does the plowing. And Nero, who is supposedly even more irresponsible than Tommy Manville, fiddles while the Shopping Center and the Drive-in Bank burn up right in front of him.

next guy and I'm sorry I missed the program, which naturally also included Bach, in this case his *Motet V.* It is too bad that Frescobaldi, Buxtehude, and Pachelbel are not more popular as these names have so much more genuine pazazz than old Bach.[3]

As late as 1929, Professor Spalding was saying of a certain more frivolous musical group that they "are entitled to enjoy playing such instruments as the banjo, mandolin, and guitar, the tone of which is produced by plucking with the finger." Well sir, Professor, these innocent amusements have now taken on all the holy aura of an art form and the guitar madness has hit Harvard like a spanking nor'easter.

John Jacob Niles, balladeer and folklorist, appears in a concert at Eliot House.

Carlos Montoya appears at Jordan Hall on the following night.

The Cantabrigia Book Shop offers a *folk song special:* 12" L.P. Records by A. L. Lloyd, Peggy Seeger, Ewan MacColl, Jean Ritchie, and many others.

CRIMSON AD:

"SALE: magnificent rosewood and ebony classical guitar with hard case. Long neck 5 string banjo. Vega "White Lady" body maple and walnut neck. Scruggs pegs if desired.[4] UN 4-5578. Thayer 45."

Caption under picture of guys with guitars and banjo on front page of *Crimson:* "The harmony of many voices, two guitars, and one banjo echoed through Leverett House last night during the swinging Hootenanny."

Fred, at KI 7-2766, has an electric guitar for sale with a Jack cadet speaker, $115.

Two Cliffies and one Wellesley girl faint from emotion listening to Joan Baez. Miss Baez is a Cambridge product and made her singing and playing debut at the Club

---

[3] Joe Bach used to cut our grass and his brother Sam Bach was a caulker at the Boat and Boiler Works.

[4] NOTE: The ban on "Scruggs pegs," outlawed since the seventeenth century by the Cambridge police, has been lifted.

Mount Auburn. *Hi Fidelity* describes her soprano voice as "achingly pure." *Saturday Review* says she is "a major new folk singing talent," and *The N.Y. Times* grabbed its hat and left the office, "scurrying for superlatives," to describe her talent.

Canada's Favorite Folk Singer, *Alan Mills*, is on at Jordan Hall with The Great Canadian Fiddler, Jean Carigan. (This show couldn't have drawn flies twenty years ago.)

At M.I.T. you can slide right in and hear William Clauson, balladeer, for $3, unless you would rather hear the original Lilly Brothers Country Band at Eliot House for $1.50.

This kind of stuff used to be poor folks' music and it shows if you wait around long enough anything can get fashionable. I'll bet Gene Autry's records will become collectors' items almost any minute now. I'm starting up the Tex Ritter Club, myself; he's a "balladeer" and doesn't know it. When is somebody going to bring back Freddie Fernsprecher and his Musical Saw? Now there's an art form that's been badly neglected by the folks down Folkways way. But what I'm really waiting for is a concert in Jordan Hall by Uncle Si and His Jug Band. While waiting I'll just sit here with the pipe and slippers and play over some old Fletcher Henderson and Hudson-Delange disks and if I get that craving for folk music I'll dig out Don Redman's *Shakin' the African*.

But it's not all folk music, Handel, Bach, and Palestrina at Harvard. You can Rock with Ricky Coyne, Relax with the Nassoons, Jump with Art Blakey and the Jazz Messengers, Lurch to Don Quinn and his Jazz Playboys, or Twist to Herbie's Hot Shots, the Molten Marvels of Music. And then there is the Harvard Band.

Over the years the Harvard Band has managed, in spite of increasing difficulties in recruiting members (because it is so time-consuming) to maintain its reputation as the "best in the business," a quote from a *New Yorker* critic who had seen the band perform its intricate marching and musical marvels at the 1946 Princeton game. Regardless of the fate of the team on the field, "Harvard never loses at half time." Its repertoire includes medleys written for it by such famous composers as Leroy Anderson, '29, and Jack Finnegan, '47. These Harvard classics, which the N.Y. *Herald Tribune* calls "Harvard's Three-minute Symphonies," provide a sprightly bit of entertainment, especially for those wives and sweethearts who, after being dragged to a hundred football games, are still vague as to why that Dartmouth boy is throwing the ball to that other Dartmouth boy. The Harvard Band has the world's Largest Tuba and the biggest playable Bass Drum in the world. As boys will be boys the opposition band often attempts hilarious pranks such as tipping over the drum, putting dead mackerel in the tuba, etc. In a recent fracas of this kind tempers flared, several pates were cracked, and two lads failed to see the second half of the game because they were arrested and marched off to the Cambridge pokey.

The Harvard Band sells album recordings, goes on concert tours, sometimes plays on Opening Day of the Boston Red Sox at Fenway Park, practices like mad, and dissolves the old grads into sodden lumps of teary sentiment when it plays its arrangement of the traditional "Wintergreen for President." What this number has to do with Harvard may puzzle the non-Cantabrigian. To refresh our memories—way back in 1931 (which seems like the week before last), Morris Ryskind and George Kaufman wrote the book for a musical called *Of Thee I Sing*. George Gershwin and Ira Gershwin supplied the music and lyrics. The cast was headed by Victor Moore as Alexander Throttlebottom (as though we could forget *that*), William Gaxton, George Murphy, Lois Moran, and June O'Dea. It was the first musical play to be awarded the Pulitzer Prize. "Wintergreen for President" was the opening number. It was sprung on an unsuspecting football crowd as part of the half-time ceremonies by the Harvard Band and caused a sensation. Since then it has been a perennial favorite. And sitting in the stands, groggy old characters from the class of '36 with silver threads among the gray, hearing the familiar strains, exchange sappy smiles with the same old girl they were with when they first heard the grand old tune. The only difference being that back then, since he was a student, they sat on the fifty-yard line, whereas now, being merely an old grad and one of that number who recently presented Alma Mater with 85 million dollars, they are in row ZZ in the end zone. And the song still has nothing to do with Harvard.

There is something musical going on all the time either in Cambridge or Boston and the din is terrific. Aside from the longhair stuff there's Mahalia Jackson, Al Hirt, The Dukes of Dixieland, Satchmo, and such thin soup as Johnny Mathis and his brethren of the Black-suit-and-abundant-hair school of singing. She's bedlam around Massachusetts Bay these days and the faculty is forced to stuff their ears with cotton in order to get any work done.

Thus the Harvard musical pendulum has swung away from where it was stuck for over two hundred years in the Bay Psalm Book and its equally dull successors, to the opposite extreme of its arc and is being temporarily detained by a howling mob of guitarists, harpsichordists, twisters, bassoon bugs, boppers, Bach swooners, paradiddlers, students of the triangle and washboard, folk singers, folk listeners, folk fainters, Stravinsky shouters, jellybeans of the stereo set, authorities on James P. Johnston, hot and cold clarinetists, banjo bums, titillating tympanists, Out oboists, platter plugs, Symphony sharks, and one guy who plays Berlioz on the comb.

"Harvard," as Professor Spalding says, "the oldest of American colleges, may fairly claim to have done the most for music." And look what music has done for Harvard! Formerly a third-rate agricultural college devoted largely to soybean research, the Department of Music almost single-handedly has raised it to its present position of world renown. In a recent poll conducted by *Down Beat* magazine under the heading "College of My Choice I Would Most Rather Matriculate At," Harvard won hands down, being unequivocally endorsed by such greats of the music world as Oistrakh, Ornette Coleman, Spike Jones, and Paul Anka, to mention but a few.

Close on the heels of the Do Re Mi set at Harvard, and breathing heavily, is the dramatic group. Second only in the entertainment field to the Music Mania (which has been compared to the mass witchcraft delusions of the Middle Ages and the Mah-Jongg hysteria of the Twenties) there has arrived with a thunderous roar on this rockbound coast a tidal wave of passionate theatrical involvement. And like everything having to do with the theatre, it is complex. It is hard to understand its motives. It is harder still to describe its ambitions or unravel its plot. And to add the professional touch, it is In Trouble.

We all know that Broadway is In Trouble, that Off Broadway is In Trouble—that the new show in New Haven is In Trouble and likewise two new ones in Philadelphia and one in Boston, one in Detroit and one in Wilmington—we know the Star has walked out on the Big Director and he is In Trouble—the songwriter and the playwright who can't repeat after their Big Smash Hit are In Trouble. Even at The Lambs they know that the costs are eating the Producers alive and that those lovable darlings are In Trouble. The volume on chocolate-covered peppermints is down and the concessionaire is In Trouble. And Vincent Sardi, Jr., even told me the other day that business was slow. The only people in well-known Show B. who are not In Trouble are Jean and Walter Kerr, James Durante, and Liberace—they are always booked solid. Even the Wallenda Brothers laid an egg.

So it is perfectly natural if they are having Troubles on the boards at the Big H. and they all should feel real happy and professional about it. Even if their troubles are slightly special.

As I get it, where these drama boys at Harvard are behind the hedge is that somebody gave them a brand new million-dollar theatre and it is so fancy that everybody is afraid of getting fingerprints on it. Add to this the facts that (1) Harvard has no department of the Drama *per se* in the college, (2) the Harvard Dramatic Club has not developed a New Policy [5] in regard to its new pleasure dome, and that (3) thus far efforts to develop the magnificent new Loeb Theatre into a real Drama Center have not succeeded—and you'll have a faint notion of some of their problems. See, Morty, it's not so bad sitting on the edge of the bed here in the Taft Hotel trying to fix that Second Act. Think of the trouble they got up there at Harvard. So how about you write a fast little novelty number for Gwen there in that lousy night-club scene, huh? Wait a minute—I'll call Room Service and have them send up a couple nice sirloins with the sliced tomadas on the sides OK?. . . . Yes hello hello . . . room service? . . . Gee, Morty . . . I forgot . . . no room service after 9 P.M.

Due to exhaustion, it is time to quote the Harvard newspaper again:

"Tonight is Saturday night. There will be a queue around the block of the University Theatre. The Brattle will have standing room only.[6] But the Loeb Drama Center will be deserted as usual, except for a few technicians and the faithful band of HDC members who come regularly to gossip and just hang around." (Sounds like the corner pool hall on a rainy night.)

"One year after its opening, the Loeb suffers from malaise.[7] And the inbred criticism of Harvard drama circles helps little to diagnose the illness. . . .

"Amidst all the arguments over faculty judgment and student competence it is important to remember that the Loeb was not built merely to furnish Cambridge with a fancy esoteric theatre. It was intended as a center for Harvard dramatic activity . . . And Harvard can be educated in the Theatre in many ways. . . .

[5] "The New Policy for the Year Nineteen Hundred and Forty will be: _____ Everybody! _____ 'em All!"—An East Moline bartender.
[6] Two local nickelodeons.
[7] Fainting spells and double vision.

"The Loeb or the HDC could sponsor informal dramatic readings . . . amateur readings . . . a playwriting contest . . . short runs of original plays . . . might try producing one play that was frankly popular. . . ."

(I'll go along with that. How about "The Cat and Canary" or "Potash and Perlmutter"? I'll even get out and sell tickets, that's how tired I am of Mr. Ibsen.)

"But if the Loeb is to be used it can no longer be worshipped. Harvard drama must lose its awe of the Loeb's physical facilities and its accompanying fear of using them to produce anything amateurish. It costs several hundred dollars a day just to keep the Loeb open. It is about time that Harvard got its money's worth."

Wind definitely from the east.

It's true that the Loeb Theatre is very fancy and very shiny and new, and needs a bit of bunging up. Everything backstage is done with electric winches controlled from a master switchboard that can do everything except write a good one-set comedy for the road calling for five actors. The stages rise, fall, slide, and do the Twist and Mashed Potatoes. The carptenter's shop is big and airy and nobody spits on the floor. The wardrobe department is better than a suite at the Ritz. The dressing rooms are lavish but nobody has written on the wall in lipstick: "The Stage Manager is a Dirty Little Creep" and there is no calendar saying Shanghai Palace Restaurant Chow Mein Our Specialty and there is no card stuck in the mirror with an invitation from the New Paris Hotel rates $1.50 Up, Members of The Profession Welcome. In other words it is not very homey. There are sanitized bathrooms for the actors like in the best motels on the Newburyport Turnpike. The stage lighting is all controlled via a magic push-button and switch panel from a projection booth behind the audience. The seats are beautifully upholstered. The architecture is stunning and the whole layout won the Rogers and Hammerstein Prize for Theatrical Design. No wonder everybody is a bit self-conscious.

All this place needs is to be lived in for a while and it's

going to be all right. Now I suggest that the management set up cots in the dressing rooms and the shop, and the next time some out-of-town baseball team is visiting Fenway Park (say the Chicago White Sox) they be quartered here at the Loeb for four or five days. When they don't have a night game the players will be supplied with free tickets to *Hedda Gabler*, and they can carve their initials on the armrests, park their gum under the seats, hurl fruit at the actors, and get the place broken in.

"If only the audience would throw things or get up and leave at the end of the first act of a really bad performance," said Loeb director Professor Robert Chapman recently. He was bemoaning the "pious placidity" of the audience. The reason for this is that in these cases the audience is sitting there in a nervous sweat and all tensed up worrying about whether Charlie is going to blow his lines and whether Jennifer (Radcliffe '64 and doing a swell job as the Second Prostitute) is going to fall over that chair behind her that they are scarcely in a fit condition to hear the lines at all, much less react to them.

There is a big difference between amateur theatricals and the professional stage. From the entertainment point of view the situation is just reversed. In the professional theatre the actors are up there working and suffering while the audience sits around out front rattling their programs, coughing, dropping marbles on the floor and enjoying themselves and having a gay old time. In amateur theatricals nobody has a good time except the performers. They cavort around up there missing cues and having a ball while the audience sits in damp underwear, twitching, wondering if they left the keys in the car, and struggling to understand what the actors are saying, since they each have a different accent and one seems not to be speaking English at all.

Since this is all perfectly well understood to be the rules of the game by both parties to the festivities, I suggest that all persons involved in dramatics at the Loeb quit worrying about "raising the standard," cast out fears of putting on too "amateurish" performances and just dive in. This theatre was not built to entertain guys with dates looking for a cheap place to take their girls (tickets are $1.50), or to furnish high-caliber Shaw, Ibsen, Ionesco, Williams, or whoever to graduate students and their wives who can't afford to go to New York; it was, I presume, created as a practice area for enthusiastic amateur actors, set designers, directors, costume designers, etc. etc. So write, act, pound, paint! Get with it.

There is a big legend about George Pierce Baker and his famous theatre workshop at Harvard, but hear what John Mason Brown, '23, says about his courses:

"Most of the plays his students wrote for him were bad; very bad, I am afraid . . . As a rule, the good plays that Baker's more famous pupils wrote were written long after they had ceased to work for him."

What he did teach them, according to Sidney Howard, was that "plays are important and hard to write; that few subjects are worthy of dramatization;[8] that characters must be imagined beneath their words; that art is an obligation, not a Sunday suit."

So just relax, boys, and remember that no matter how lousy you are, you are probably better than some of the choice items that have appeared both On and Off Broadway, during the 1961-62 season, which witnessed horrors never before imagined and which sent hardened critics into rest homes.

In addition to the Loeb Theatre and the Harvard Dramatic Club, the Houses also put on plays, usually, but not always, costume pieces. *Volpone* has had more performances at Harvard than *Abie's Irish Rose* did in New York. In early December 1961 there were seven Harvard Theatrical productions running simultaneously, among them *Tamburlaine the Great, Rosmersholm, Murder in the*

---

[8] Well that's all been changed. Now *any* subject is deemed worthy of dramatization, including the decline and fall of filling-station attendants and the lives of the mentally sluggish. Some plays have no subject at all.

Cathedral, Iolanthe, The Rain Never Falls, and *The Country Wife.* This made it difficult to concentrate on the books, especially since in the same week the Poets Theatre presented "An Evening with Mary McCarthy" (live), T. S. Eliot gave a reading in Boston (also live), "The World of Apu" was at the Brattle, "Girl with a Suitcase" was at the Fenway, Mary I. Bunting, Pres. of Radcliffe, was holding forth on "The Problems of an Educated Woman in American Society," the Bach Society Orchestra presented a program, Wellesley College offered *Orpheus Descending,* Piet Kee gave an organ recital at M.I.T., Celedonio Romero and his Sons ("The Royal Family of the Guitar") appeared at Jordan Hall, "The Brothers Four" were at Tufts, Sylvia Marlowe and her tin-pan harpischord was at Jordan Hall again, the Venus Beauty Center at 1615 Cambridge Street was offering Complete Perm @ $5.95, and the Center For Research in Personality presented Thomas S. Szasz on "Bootlegging Humanistic Values Through Psychiatry." Wow, what a week!

There is one theatrical group at Harvard which is certainly not overly concerned with raising its amateur ranking, and that is the Hasty Pudding Club. It's another aggravated case, almost without exception, of the cast having all the fun, while the audience, after an initial chuckle at the "hairy-leg heroine" and "hairy-leg chorus," sinks slowly into a state of complete paralysis. It's all a grand lark though (I have had about enough of this condescending bastard, who does he think he is, anyway?), and the greatest show on earth for kid sisters, kid brothers, mothers and fathers and uncles and aunts, and if you see it at the Harvard Club of New York, remember the bar remains open during the performance and can be reached by a very slight tour from an aisle seat in the back row. The *Alumni Bulletin* recently stated that "this annual event, now so acclaimed," is "polished to nearly professional standards." That just goes to demonstrate how many professional shows *they* have seen lately, and I hope

Equity doesn't hear about it, which would almost certainly result in picketing the Bulletin Office in Wadsworth House, stink bombs in *Bulletin* wastebaskets, threatening letters, and other shocking incidents.

The Pudding's first show was in 1844, but its biggest success was Owen Wister's *Dido and Aeneas* in 1882, which went on tour and "took the country by storm." It was either an "opera bouffe" or "the first musical comedy ever performed in the United States" depending on which paper you subscribe to. The Pudding has had a number of graduates who went on to become famous in show business, which has been mentioned far too often, as Harvard has had an even greater number of hot shots in and around show business who don't even know where the Pudding clubhouse is located at.

Among the Pudding's current celebrities in the profession are Alan Jay Lerner, '40, whose *My Fair Lady* has been running for fifty years and is still packing them in, and Jack Lemmon, '47, who was the President of Hasty Pudding, and who played a typical "hairy-leg heroine" Pudding part in *Some Like It Hot* with every red-blooded American boy's dream girl, Norma Jean Baker. Robert Benchley, '12, undoubtedly one of this country's most comical Massachusetts products, played the part of *"Dardanelles Bixby*, ward of *James Higdig* and office man in *Chalkstone's* office" in a romp called *Below Zero*, the Pudding Show of 1911. Reading old playbills is a bad habit.

But to give the Pudding its deserts, they do sometimes entertain the audience as well as themselves. Their 114th production, 1962, demonstrated this. It was called *Peace Decorum* (a rib on the Peace Corps, get it?). Let's leave off talking about "near-professional standards" and just say this noisy spectacle kept audiences both awake and happy. The music, by Walter H. Moses, Jr., was more tuneful, hummable, and varied than a good many Broadway shows, and the lyrics, by Alan H. Lutkus, were reasonable and witty and who can ask for more? G. Carter

Wilson's book is not going to drive Abe Burrows into hiding but as they say in *Variety*, it was serviceable. The leads, David Rawle and Peter Gesell, hopped around up there like a couple of demented dervishes and could even sing. Sing better than Rex Harrison, anyway, and look at the contracts he gets. The audience was in stitches, which is where we like to see them.

Here are a few of the Show Biz celebs the Ivy League has donated to the world's nuttiest business.

Princeton:	Josh Logan
	Bosley Crowther
	Franchot Tone
	Jimmy Stewart
Williams:	Elia Kazan
	Stephen Sondheim
Amherst:	Burgess Meredith
Cornell:	Arthur Laurents
Penn:	Harold S. Prince
	Harry Kurnitz
	Sidney Kingsley
Dartmouth:	Budd Schulberg
	Robert Ryan
Yale:	Vincent Price
	Harold Rome
	Rudy Vallee
Yale and Harvard both:	Monty Woolley
	Cole Porter
	Archibald MacLeish
Harvard:	Leonard Bernstein
	Virgil Thomson
	Lawrence Spivak
	Robert Sarnoff
	Gilbert Seldes
	Leroy Anderson
	David Susskind
	Donald Oenslager
	Robert Anderson

	Brooks Atkinson
	John Mason Brown
Columbia:	Richard Rodgers
	Oscar Hammerstein
	Arthur Schwartz

Yes, I know that list is very incomplete. Take the elevator, the Complaint Department is on the third floor.

And as George Arliss said to me at Delmonico's one evening over a stuffed crab with Otis Skinner, Henrietta Crosman, and Frank X. Silk, "Don't rush your speeches as though there was a fire backstage. And don't mumble, boy. Let the audience in on it."

In addition to all these perplexing entertainments, Cambridge also has all the latest film fare, both domestic and foreign, and film clubs which present classics of the silver screen from bygone days. Stern decisions are called for almost daily by the solid film fan (*Potemkin* or Tony Curtis? *Animal Crackers* or Yvette Mimieux?) and movies are hashed over and dissected with enormous relish. And the *Crimson*'s movie reviews read like theses for Honors on the Elizabethan poets.

I never know where I stand (or where *to* stand) after reading the *Crimson* editorials. I am trying to be a Right Thinker and take the Correct Attitudes, but just when they have set me straight on Argentina something else comes up—the Peace Corps, Vivisection, Police Brutality in Jamaica Plain, and I am all at sea again. (I have the same trouble figuring out Who I Am For with the *Saturday Review* and the *Stamp and Coin Journal*). So just about when I feel I am matching up to their requirements in the broad field of modern living and thinking, I read one of their movie reviews that says this German flick, *Rosemary*, is "a stilted manikin act" (Fellows, I must have had too much chow mein before the show, I thought this girl was a living doll), but that nonetheless we should all hurry over there because the short feature is a "classic Donald

Duck cartoon that shouldn't be missed." There they go again. Shouldn't be missed by who? (OK, "whom." But it's an ugly word.) The slow section in the Fourth Grade at Big Sandy, Tennessee? The girls' basketball team out in Strawberry Point, Iowa? When I get into such a condition that I am rushing my dinner to see a feature picture which I am told is no good in order to see six forgettable minutes of Donald Duck I am going to ask for a complete physical checkup. And Doc, listen, you can tell me the truth. I can take it, and all my kids have these trust funds, see, and the oldest one, he's a cute little shaver, he does an imitation of Donald Duck that will kill you. It's killing me, too.

THE PENNY ARCADE

"Pardon me for butting out," remarked Waldo; "I'm going to study antiquities."

"Where? At the Germanic Museum?" was asked with languid curiosity.

"No. At Radcliffe. I have a lady couisn there."

"Skirts are all right in their place," said Motley, "but when a man's at college he must be careful where he feeds. No feminizing influence for mine."

"Right," agreed a pal. "It is better to be rough. Why?"

"Because," said Waldo, "they *will* call us Cultured."

All groaned at the fearful word.

"But look at Teddy Roosevelt," cried one.

"We point with pride," said the others in unison as they drifted away arm-in-arm.

And in the distance I could hear the strains of the grand old college anthem of which I give the following impressionistic version:

When a fellow goes to college
It is not so much for knowledge

As for contact with his equals by selection.
If, perchance, he may deserve a
Smile from matronly Minerva
  It's because of his good family connection.
Wisdom's flame is not convulsive—
We should never be impulsive.
  Helter-skelter in our choice of friends erratic
In the State of Massachusetts
There are very, very few sets
  Whose companionship would make us democratic.

    So it's drink, drink, drink
      At the jolly Pipe and Bowl!
    And it's three times three for Harvard
      With a skoal, skoal, skoal!

If our looks grow rather frigid
And our stately spines stand rigid
  At the thought of what the Outlanders begrudge us,
Treat them gently, friends—remember
That of Truth we are the Ember
  And the Shrine—so who are they that they should judge us?
For our learning is the surest
And our accent is the purest,
  And the man who can't admire us is an odd fish.
One who never knew the mission
Of our classical tradition
  Or the wisdom of the Contemplative Codfish.

    So it's sing, sing, sing
      At the jolly Cap and Gown!
    With a three times three for Harvard,
      Drink it down, down, down!

We have passed the puerile season
And have reached the Age of Reason,
  Though it's futile to explain how we arrive here.
Still, a certain pride is owing
To our quality of rowing,
  For victorious water-babies sometimes thrive here.
But our Great Men all remind us

We have ancestors behind us
   Are our logic-ally to the manner born, sir;
So the man who gets his knowledge
From another brand of college
   Should be looked on more in pity than in scorn, sir.

    So it's cheer, cheer, cheer
      At the jolly Book and Bell,
    And it's three times three for Harvard
      With a yell, yell, yell!

—Wallace Irwin

CHAPTER XV

What a Century!

*"Should you like very much to go to college?" said
Mr. Morton.*
"Better than anything else in the world."
*"Then you shall go. I will defray your expenses
through college."*
Frank could hardly believe his ears.
*"How good you are to me," said Frank, impulsively
seizing his friend's hand. "What have I done to de-
serve so much kindness?"*
"You have done your duty, Frank. . . ."
— *Frank's Campaign,* HORATIO ALGER, JR.

WHERE TO BEGIN on the nineteenth century? There was so much of it. In January 1800,
U.S. citizens were still using stone implements and living
in caves, but by January 1900 the Chicago River was full
of garbage and old shoes and seven thousand building construction workmen were on strike in the same city; Standard Oil Company declared first quarterly dividends on
April fifteenth amounting to $20,000,000, and Edison had
invented the talking machine, which would soon make
it possible for even the humblest cottager to hear "Cohen
on the Telephone."

In 1807, Charles Francis Adams was born in a homestead
on the corner of Boylston and Tremont streets; by 1900

his grandchildren were gourmandizing in European style on the same site in the grand dining room of the Hotel Touraine. ("Magnificently furnished throughout and attracts the most fastidious customers. Its restaurant is one of the handsomest in the city and in the basement are several grillrooms and cafes, fitted up in the German style . . ." The rates, for Boston's finest hotel, started at $2 per day.)[1] Other advances of civilization never dreamed of by the Adams family of Boston in 1800 which became accomplished facts due to American genius were cream-style corn, streetcar transfers, men's sleeve garters, and shoes. (Grover Cleveland invented "shoes" after experiencing constant trouble with splinters in his feet from the White House floors.) And there was the Civil War, that grim struggle which pitted brother against brother and has sold over 300 million copies as well as keeping Raymond Massey almost continually employed.

While these great events were taking shape and the course of Empire and Monongahela rye whiskey pressed ever westward toward the setting sun, La Cienega, Rodeo Drive, and I. Magnin—what snows were falling in Beacon Hill areaways, what transcendental fragrances drifted through Cambridge under the soft spring rain, and who threw the random crust of bread that put out Prescott's eye?

By the year 1800 Harvard had the beginnings of a Medical School.[2] She had also recovered from the estate of John Hancock the monies (minus the compound interest) which he had mislaid during his long and confusing tenure as Treasurer of Harvard, an office which he held from Philadelphia and in the course of which he scrambled the account books so badly that an even dozen Philadelphia lawyers could make neither head, tail, or feathers of them. In the college the courses of instruction remained limited.

[1] The Plaza Hotel in New York, built in the same period, has maintained its magnificence and advertises "moderately priced" rooms at "from fifteen to twenty-five dollars per day for one guest."
[2] "My uncle was a Harvard man, and he's still there—in a bottle."

Freshmen and sophomores were expected to grind away at Hebrew, but amazingly were now allowed the option of substituting French, a daring breakthrough. The Greek department had gone modern with a vengeance, was doing the Charleston and permitting students to read Homer and Xenophon. Not to be outdone, the Latin department donned plus fours and for the first time took notice of Horace and Sallust (which up until now students had been sniggering over in closets by the beams of smuggled flashlights, together with *Pep* magazine and *The Plastic Age*). Some attempts, then, were being made to break loose from the rigid academic discipline of the founding fathers, but there was little choice of subjects outside the classics.

Building continued with Stoughton Hall (1805) and Holworthy Hall (1812), both financed by lotteries and neither of which embodied any cinder block, plexiglass, duralite, formica, vinyl-tile, tinyl-vin, texticote, cellofab, aluminole, galvaslab, spunroc, fabristone, or lumatubes in their construction. They were built of brick.

All sorts of things could happen and they did. The Med. Fac., a group of jolly lads devoted to practical and impractical jokes, sent a phony honorary degree to the Czar of Russia. Highly flattered, this Slavic potentate responded with the gift of an elaborate set of surgical instruments. The Class of 1823 was composed almost entirely of hoodlums who passed their time in lighting fires, exploding homemade bombs in the yard, rolling cannonballs down staircases, arranging trick Hans and Fritz water buckets that drenched tutors with ink or worse, releasing rats in classrooms, breaking windows and each other's heads, battling in dining halls, staging dogfights and entertaining naughty ladies in their rooms. The college split into two factions, the aristocrats and the bums—a full-scale rebellious riot then took place, followed by the expulsion, shortly before Commencement, of forty-three students out of a class of seventy. One of the fun-loving lads who was expelled was the son of the Secretary of State in President Monroe's cabinet, John Quincy Adams. Father issued a strong protest from Washington, but although he had been successful in playing a leading part in the annexation of Florida and in the promulgation of the Monroe Doctrine, he was not successful in reversing the verdict on his playful heir, who remained bounced. The President and Fellows of the college, as well as chambermaids, publicans, and the local fire department, had had enough.

New England almost split its seams when Harvard, by the election of the Reverend Henry Ware to the Hollis Professorship of Divinity and of the Reverend Samuel Webber as President, in 1806, openly threw its weight on the side of the Unitarian movement and against the Calvinism which had founded the college. Attended by "as much intrigue as was ever practiced in the Vatican," as the Reverend John Eliot wrote, this election ranks in Harvard history as of equal importance with the election of Charles W. Eliot to the Presidency in 1869, the hotfoot given Increase Mather in 1701, the Harkness Plan, and the appointment of Percy D. Haughton as football coach in 1908. This was the first large double-page advertisement to the public that Harvard was definitely on the liberal side and would henceforth in no way be hampered by inherited dogma. Clearly this academy now and forevermore would be definitely opposed to ideological spite fences and barbed wire. It was a daring statement and it had explosive effects. For if Boston was largely Unitarian (and many of its oldest families still are[3]), most of New England and the rest of the country was not. Shocked and horrified Harvard fathers in New Hampshire and more remote provinces withheld donations and shunted their sons to other colleges.

The rise of the Unitarian faith at this time in New England is a historical curiosity whose origins and large meanings can best be explored today in the sand dunes of Wide-

[3] "For the last twenty years of his life, George Apley was a pewholder in Kings Chapel, where he attended services regularly each winter."

—*The Late George Apley*

ner Library. Even in mid-eighteenth century, Harvard College was showing the most advanced thought of its time in this country. Already at that time a number of New England clergymen were openly expounding what was in effect Unitarianism. And, believe me, when you got expounded in the vicinity of Salem or Hampton Falls in those days it was the full treatment. Especially in the Unitarian sense.

All very well, but what *is* it?

It is a faith based on two principles: the demand for personal religious freedom, and the demand for clear, distinct, and coherent religious thought and teaching. It rejects inherited guilt, eternal punishment, and vicarious atonement. From this one could think that its religious services might resemble a reading of the profit-and-loss statement and the minutes of the last stockholders' meeting, but on the contrary, they follow, in form at least, other Protestant services such as the Methodist—up to and including the Offertory Anthem and preachers with rich and vibrant voices.

Its membership isn't and wasn't a collection of nuts. Thomas Jefferson, Daniel Webster, Susan B. Anthony, Horace Mann, Oliver Wendell Holmes, scads of other celebrities, and great blocks of rich, conservative, thoughtful, and very proper Bostonians were and are Unitarians. But I mention it only in connection with Harvard, for there its nineteenth-century influence was far-reaching. Six Harvard Presidents were inaugurated in the First Parish Meeting House (Unitarian) on the Cambridge Common, and Commencements were held here until 1873.

Ever-available Samuel Morison gives the picture of what it meant:

. . . Harvard had become a fortress of the liberal outlook and faith. In that sense, but in no other, Unitarianism sealed Harvard with its spirit. We can never measure the relief, the stimulus, the exuberant joy, felt in the last century by thousands of young men who, after a stern upbringing in expectation of a hard struggle to escape eternal damnation, entered a college where hot-gospelling was poor form, hell was not mentioned, and venerable preachers treated the students, not as limbs of Satan, but as younger brothers of their Lord and Saviour.

The surge of the Unitarian movement was on the wane by the end of the century, and Harvard has for many years been a completely nonsectarian college. Yes, there are religious services, and the Divinity School as well, but there is also what Santayana calls "a vaguer but deeper religion—the faith in enlightenment, the aspiration to be just, the sympathy with the multiform thoughts and labors of humanity."

As the nineteenth century progressed and the citizens of the Great Republic threw themselves wholeheartedly into the program for mass extinction of our two minority groups, the American Indian and the American bison, "culture" flourished in New England at an alarming rate. Perhaps never in history have so many ladies and gentlemen written so much bad poetry, admired so many questionable paintings, or swooned in such battalions over the memory of Greece and Rome. Never have so many little papers been written and read aloud: reminiscences, local history, biographies of famous men and famous mill owners, philosophy, phrenology, the habits of the codfish, "A Visit to Pompeii," "Thoughts on First Viewing the Parthenon." George Apley's biographer, the amiable Mr. Willing, says, "the activities of intelligent discussion and the necessity for taking a part in them, have led many of the author's acquaintance, toward the end of a Boston winter, into periods of great nervous weariness, sometimes ending in actual nervous breakdown." Harvard, of course, was partly to blame. Harvard was experiencing a cultural explosion whose effects were bound to influence the Back Bay and the leafy countryside.

There was George Ticknor, a Dartmouth M.A. who came in 1819 to teach at Harvard after studying at Göttingen and after celebrity-hopping all over Europe, in the course of which junket he became friends with such divergent characters as Goethe, Lord Byron, and Robert Wilhelm von Bunsen—who gave him a free autographed burner. Six months he spent traveling in Spain meeting everybody who was anybody and even some who weren't quite. Arriving in Cambridge to take over the new professorship of The French and Spanish Languages and of Belles Lettres, he heaved a heavy sigh and in fact shed tears as he observed the crudities of Harvard teaching methods compared with the high scholasticism of the German universities. The German universities? What German universities? Boston was not concerned with Germany. In 1814, while intellectual Bostonians were busy admiring themselves in the mirror, Ticknor was unable to find a German dictionary in the city of Boston. "I sent to New Hampshire, where I knew there was a German Dictionary, and procured it." Under Ticknor's influence, possibly with an assist from Edward Everett, then Professor of Greek Literature and later to become Harvard's President as well as America's leading windbag,[4] a few reforms were attempted in the college organization. Students were put into sections based on proficiency, instead of alphabetically; special students were admitted; more frequent and stiffer examinations were begun; the faculty was separated into departments; there were advances in the modern languages; and at least the beginnings of the elective system came into being.

If these attempts at reform did not stick, it was not Ticknor's fault. They flourished in his department at least. And he even imported peculiar foreign scholars, not only French, but Italians and Germans, with strange eyeglasses, rings on their fingers and bells in their heads. And meanwhile he reigned as the central figure of a cultivated group in Boston of such exalted reputation that the city was soon being referred to as "the Athens of America" (*Never on*

---

[4] "The perfection and model of all that is bad in American oratory."
—George B. Hill

Sunday, the Greek movie hit starring Melina Mercouri, recently broke all box-office records in Boston). And at Harvard Ticknor had broken through the stone wall, tumbling the granite boulders every which way, and was giving modern lectures organized in sequence, on the literature of France and Spain. Prodigious!

When Ticknor resigned he was succeeded by Longfellow. When Longfellow resigned he was succeeded by James Russell Lowell. That's the kind of a century it was at Harvard.

There is no building named for Ticknor, but there should be. There is none named for Edward Everett either, even though he was President.[5] He was President for three years, in which brief span his pomposity and ludicrous deportment won him the title of Most Unpopular President Since Nathaniel Eaton (1637–39).

Here is a sample of Everett [The scene is the President's study.]:

President Everett: Young man, I wish to know why, when I passed you on the street today, you did not take off your hat to me.

Student Goodwin: I don't think that I saw you, Sir.

President Everett: If I saw you, you must have seen me.

The principal of this skit is the same man who bent the crowd's ears down at Gettysburg, Pennsylvania, one afternoon in November, 1863 and put several thousand people to sleep, and who was followed on the program by the father of a Harvard undergraduate, who talked for two minutes and got his speech into all the anthologies and onto bronze tablets.

About the only sensible thing Everett did during his presidency was to appoint Louis Agassiz as Professor of Zoology and Geology. Agassiz (born in Switzerland 1807, died in Cambridge 1873), one of the "ablest, wisest, and best informed of the biologists of his day," was the founder of Harvard's great Museum of Comparative Zoology.

[5] NOTE: To avoid embarrassment no House has been named in honor of President Hoar.

He completely revolutionized the study of natural history in America and in the last half of the nineteenth century, every important teacher in this field had been at one time or another one of his students. He cared little for fame and fortune [6]—what he liked was a dead fish to take apart. When he came to Harvard in 1847 the Crimson's bones and fossil remains were in a deplorable state. Some of them were in the furnace room at the Lawrence Scientific School, some were in cigar boxes out in the garage, others in the coat closet over at the Grange Hall, and a dismantled saber-tooth tiger was in the left bottom drawer of President Everett's desk under a pile of soiled celluloid collars. The rock-and-bone Lending Library was completely disorganized and fourteen-day bones were sometimes not returned for six months or more. Agassiz himself was an avid collector of specimens and when he had filled every nook and cranny of the Lawrence school he began to tuck the overflow into an abandoned boathouse on the Charles River under the Brighton bridge. Visiting this "chicken coop" one day, Harvard treasurer Samuel Eliot remarked, "I never thought Harvard would work itself down to a shack!"

But in addition to his vast erudition (*Recherches sur les Poissons Fossiles* [1833], *Etudes Critiques sur les Mollusques Fossiles* [1839], *Nomenclator Zoologicus, Etudes sur les Glaciers* [1840], *Lake Superior* [1850], etc. etc.), Agassiz was gifted with a warm and lovable disposition and the persuasive powers of an Egyptian rug merchant. He wanted a museum and he was going to get it. Not just any old museum, but one on a grand and glorious scale, the best that money could buy. First there was a private subscription list which netted $12,000. This helped, and the shanty museum was abandoned and the curios moved to a building on Holmes Field. In 1858 Agassiz began to work his mystic charms on the Massachusetts state legislature. This group had developed a cold heart toward the

---

[6] He once turned down a very lucrative lecture tour with the comment, "I can't afford to waste time making money."

college in Cambridge and had been in the habit of turning up its coat collar and walking rapidly in the other direction when the subject of financial handouts to the old school was mentioned. Amazing Agassiz, however, mesmerized the bunch on the Hill and pried them loose from $100,000, a feat not unlike securing a very dry martini (Dixie Belle, please) from squeezing a turnip. Other donations began to roll in ($50,000 from Mr. Francis C. Gray, may he R.I.P.), more aid from the state followed, and lo!, a great museum for the American people was born. As the museum grew, one of its greatest benefactors as well as its director was Louis Agassiz' son Alexander.

Let us digress and examine Alexander. (When are we going to get to Emerson and Thoreau? Probably never.) Alexander Agassiz was in his teens when his father dusted Europe off his coattails forever and settled in Cambridge. He was Harvard '55. He moved in the best of social circles. Hawthorne, Emerson, Holmes, and Longfellow frequently left their rubbers in the Agassiz front hall while they had tea, toast, and talk. But father was constantly buying stuffed ocelots and dried toads with the carfare and grocery money. Although his salary as Professor was but $1500 a year, he could never resist picking up a good used rib cage or a secondhand shark fin; his home on Quincy Street was so full of rock specimens it was like living in a quarry fitted up with gas lights and a base burner. There was an outcrop of gabbro on the mantelpiece and a pyroxenite porphyry dike ran right through the dining room. In order to maintain credit with the butcher Mrs. Agassiz conducted the Agassiz School for Young Ladies on the second floor. It looked as though young Alex would have to get out and hustle.

His sister had married a Bostonian named Quincy Adams Shaw who, in addition to his name, owned some mines. Mr. Shaw was a Boston Brahmin whose ancestors, spurning the cramped accommodations on the *Mayflower*, had made the trip over in their own steam yacht, the *Blushing Pilgrim II*. He was having a few perplexities with some copper properties he owned out on the wild and rambunctious Keweenaw Peninsula in Michigan and decided to send brother-in-law Alex out to amygdaloid land to look the situation over and find out who was stealing the money. Dan Jackling, Bill Greene, Marcus Daly, and the other copper-coated roughnecks who hung around the bar of the Douglas House in Houghton had a good haw-haw when they heard that one of them high-tone Bostonians was coming out to nose around, and a Hah-vud man at that.

On the way to the railroad station when leaving Boston, Alexander ran into a Hah-vud classmate who was later to become president of the college, Charles Eliot.

"Charlie," said Alex, "I'm going to Michigan to make money. Then I'll be a naturalist and help my father at the Museum. It is impossible to be a productive naturalist in this country without money."

Now as is well known, people who take that kind of an attitude toward the holy rites of capitalism as merely a sordid means to an intellectual end are doomed to falling on their faces and wearing frayed shirt cuffs all the rest of their lives. But Alexander was a Harvard man and feared not. Arriving in the wilderness, this son of a biologist took one look at the mine and came to the conclusion that the superintendent, jolly old Ed Hulbert—who incidentally had discovered the deposit—was doing literally everything wrong: he was mining it wrong and milling it wrong and furthermore was hauling the conglomerate thirteen miles by wagons up to the hub in mud. Agassiz reported back to Boston. Quincy Shaw returned him at once to the mine as treasurer of the company. Ed Hulbert was given the squeeze and ended up broke. Alex stayed for two years, working sixteen, eighteen, and sometimes twenty-four hours a day putting the mine on its feet. Checking over his bank stubs a few years later he discovered that he was a Millionaire. His famous father died in 1873 and Alexander, true to his word, took over the management of the Museum. In the next twenty years, while acting as Curator of the Harvard Museum and writing learned papers on the nervous system of the coelenterata, he ruled over the mine and led the Corporation to "an Eden of dividends." Thus we see a professional zoologist running the affairs of the richest metal mine in the world, the Calumet and Hecla, as a sideline. Curious place, Harvard.

Yes indeed, a curious place, Harvard. A Cambridge lady, Maria Fay, who lived in Radcliffe College's original home, Fay House, said to her niece:

"If you had only come an hour ago! I let my women go over to the Yard, and was shelling peas on the porch, when Mr. Longfellow came to call and asked if he might stay. I said yes, if he would shell peas. Then James Lowell appeared and Mr. Longfellow told him he too must shell peas. Finally, Mr. William James came and those men were never in a more brilliant mood than over that bowl of peas. If you could only have heard them . . . !"

Out in Concord, Harvard graduate Henry Thoreau was not only shelling peas, he was growing his own peas at Walden Pond and I hope nobody writes me and says he was growing beans out there by the railroad and not peas, because he distinctly says his expenses for food over the two year period were $.74 "not counting potatoes, a little green corn, and some *peas*, which I had raised. . . ." He is a slippery fellow when it comes to figures though, because although he lists one watermelon on the balance sheet at .02 cents he admits to catching "a mess of fish" but enters no cost for one fishhook. He did have a crop of beans in his plot but he traded them in the village for rice, partly as another one of his protests *a outrance*, this one directed at bean-eating Boston which insisted, despite his remonstrances, on going to work every day, and partly because he was a "quasi-Pythagorean." [7] The firm stand Pythagoras took on Boston baked beans is too well known to require comment.

[7] "As a quasi-Pythagorean, Thoreau seldom indulged in Beans."— Van Wyck Brooks (Harvard '08)

Although he afterwards always sneered at the "vapidity" of Harvard, he did complete the course there and graduated in the Class of 1837. He helped to found the Natural History Club, and the literary pieces which he wrote for Channing and others are still in existence. He was a completely typical and "modern" student in that he neglected courses which he didn't enjoy to pursue on his own highly unorthodox investigations into such mysterious fields as modern Persian literature. Henry apparently thought that the top men of his class were second-raters. He was right. None of the top ten except Richard Henry Dana made any lasting impression after graduation. It seems clear that President Josiah Quincy considered Thoreau a rebel and a social outcast bordering on the freakish. What could practical, ex-Boston Mayor Quincy do but shudder over Thoreau's Commencement discourse which contained such hair-raising suggestions as:

"The order of things should be somewhere reversed; the seventh should be man's day of toil, wherein to earn his living by the sweat of his brow; and the other six his Sabbath of the affections and the soul, in which to range this widespread garden and drink in the soft influences and sublime revelations of Nature."

Every town in New England has its local characters which the townfolk are as proud of as the new blacktop road to the Corners. "Who is that?" the stranger says, as he watches a middle-aged man in hip boots and ski cap trundling a hoop past the First National store. ("Why that's old Tob Smucker," replies the native with a chuckle. "Quite a character. The old fool." Another chuckle. "He hasn't paid his taxes in forty years so when old Gabe Tunkett said to him 'Tob, when are you going to pay up your taxes?' you know what he said, oh he's a character, he said 'Never give it much thought!'" Laughter from narrator and bystanders, who crowd in to fill up the stranger on more Tob Smucker witticisms.

Henry Thoreau, Harvard 1837, was the town character in Concord, Massachusetts, but not cherished so you would notice it by the townfolk. He furnished some amusement, it's true, by trudging through the fields all alone in the rain and snow. Tongues clacked with relish over his refusal to get a steady job. He didn't have the time of day for women, even the little women up the road at the Alcott cottage, and that was odd. He had a big nose and dressed like an educated bum. That helped. And he went off and built that shack and lived in it all alone. So far so good.

But Henry was not lovable like old Tob Smucker. Henry had a tongue as sharp as Bronson Alcott's axe, which he borrowed one day near the end of March 1845, to cut down some "tall arrowy white pines" for that shack at Walden Pond. He liked to take people down a peg and his manner of execution was far from comical. Worst of all, he was not agreeably stupid. His mind was like the arrow of God, a terrifying instrument of reason and destruction, a flame-thrower amid the dry brush piles of New England tradition.

His social graces were a fright. "He wanted a fallacy to oppose, a blunder to pillory," says Emerson. "It seemed as if his first instinct on hearing a proposition was to contravert it,[8] so impatient was he of the limitations of our daily thought. This habit, of course, is a little chilling to the social affections . . . it mars conversation. . . . 'I love Henry,' said one of his friends, 'but I cannot like him; and as for taking his arm, I should as soon think of taking the arm of an elm tree.' "[9]

You see, a totally unsatisfactory town "character." And Emerson ought to know, for Henry lived at Emerson's house as a combination handyman and intellectual sparring partner. Thoreau was a terror. Everything he saw in society irked him. Yet he got on with Emerson, and even permitted Emerson to go walking with him. ("I have no walks to spare on company.") He needed an editor. And

[8] Reader, have you got any relatives like that?
[9] "Biographical Sketch of Thoreau," by Ralph Waldo Emerson, the *Atlantic Monthly*, August 1862. Read it.

his method of composition was appallingly time-consuming. Yet he remains one of the most extraordinary thinkers and writers in our brief history. I could almost say, with the usual fear of contradiction from today's crop of iconoclastic Thoreaus, *the* most extraordinary.

He was without distinction at Harvard. What did they know about the true nature of things? He said his Harvard diploma was not worth the five dollars he had to pay for it. But though he scorned the place more scorningly than even Henry Adams, he had acquired somewhere the fashion of learned classical allusions. Where else than at Harvard? Wherefrom his

> *Ipse semipaganus*
> *Ad sacra Vatum carmen affero nostrum?*

Emerson was once bragging that Harvard revealed all the branches of learning.

"Yes, indeed," replied Henry, "all the branches and none of the roots," and he went for another walk to his favorite swamp to see if the Menyanthes was yet in flower.

This year, 1962, marks the hundredth anniversary of Thoreau's death at the age of forty-four. The Thoreau Society held ceremonies at the Pierpont Morgan Library; the Rev. Donald S. Harrington preached a Thoreau sermon at the Community Church of New York, and a ceremonial unveiling of Thoreau's bust (done from memory no doubt, like the statue of John Harvard in front of University Hall) was held at New York University's Hall of Fame. At a luncheon of the Thoreau Society the philosopher's "favorite foods" were consumed: brook trout, wild rice, green beans, cornbread, apple pan dowdy, and fresh cider. The cost of this ceremony was estimated in advance at $10,774, including $125 for elegant academic robe rental and $200 for lilies and other floral displays. Brooks Atkinson says of these doings: "Respectability entails accouterments and rituals that are likely to make Walden Pond boil."

How do you like that, Henry? Listen, Henry, hold still a moment, we want to crown you with this laurel wreath and pin this genuine imported medal on you. Hey, wait a minute, where are you going? For a walk? But Henry . . .

Thoreau ignored Harvard and Harvard ignored Emerson, until long after he had become famous. Emerson worked his way through Harvard from 1821 to 1827. In 1829 he became associate pastor of the Second Church in Boston, the old Mather Church, which had now become Unitarian. But he, too, was as strong-minded as the Mathers and resigned over doctrinal differences. He was in favor of a seven-day religious week and opposed to the closed shop in the praying business. In 1846 he referred to the "corpse-cold Unitarianism and Immortality of Brattle Street," in a description of President Everett's inauguration. In 1833 he settled in Concord, where he remained for the rest of his life as leader of the Transcendentalist movement. He scared the wits out of many in Boston and Cambridge, who thought him "an atheist or worse." I don't know what could have been worse in these times and these places. Maybe he failed to mail his proxies in to State Street on time. Finally at the age of sixty-four he was elected to the Board of Overseers, and in 1870 he was called to Harvard at the age of sixty-seven to give a course of lectures later published as *Natural History of Intellect*. He was a rare bird, who said of the caterpillar, "How dost thou, brother? Please God, you shall yet be a philosopher!" He saw eye-to-eye with Thoreau on many aspects of life and they shared a mutual dislike for reform societies and culture colonies. "I had rather keep bachelor's hall in hell," quoth irascible Henry, "than go to board in heaven." Emerson seconded the motion.

Harvard claims them both now. "At least we still have Emerson, Thoreau, and Roosevelt!" cried a dejected alumnus after a particularly disastrous football season. One bystander was heard to murmur that he didn't know which Roosevelt was up for honors but that it seemed a fine example of anti-climax. The usual fight ensued and the affair ended with the arrival of the pie wagon from the local police station. The fracas made the afternoon papers in Boston but that night a manhole cover blew off in Dorchester which squeezed the incident off the front pages on the following A.M.

From the sublime to the almost unbelievable: Question: What Harvard author of the nineteenth century alone sold more copies of his works than the combined total output of Thoreau, Emerson, Hawthorne,[10] Prescott, Parkman, Motley, Dana, Lowell, Longfellow, Henry James, and Owen Wister? What did this writer do, as an undergraduate, when the landlady of his rooming house appeared in his room one night completely naked, wearing only an inviting smile? You give up? Well, he was not a transcendentalist, but he was a Unitarian. I'll give you a clue: at Harvard his nickname was "Holy Horatio." Got it? Yes, it was Horatio Alger, Jr., and that was his real name,[11] and you, sir, have won a kewpie doll.

At Harvard he was called "Holy Horatio" because of his announced intention to follow in his father's footsteps in the ministry. When the amorous landlady invaded his room he fled in horror to another boarding house. After graduating from Divinity School he made the scene in Europe and decided after a trip or two to the sample room in Paris that his former aversion to undressed ladies had been pure folly. "I was a fool to have waited so long," he reported to Dear Diary. "It is not nearly so vile as I had thought." Horatio wrote *Ragged Dick, Adrift in New York, Ben, The Luggage Boy, Bound to Rise*, and 115 other books, all with the same identical plot. It is estimated that he sold perhaps 250,000,000 copies—more than any American writer before or since. His literary works proved conclusively that the only sure way to become

[10] Longfellow and Hawthorne were Bowdoin College, Class of 1825.
[11] "Burt L. Standish," the prolific author of the "Frank Merriwell At Yale" series, was really William Gilbert Patten.

President of the First Third Union Bank and Trust Company was to start with holes in your shoes and a widowed mother with a mortgage. He proved it 119 times.

When Charles William Eliot was elected President of Harvard in 1869 most of Ticknor's attempted academic reforms had faded away. Eliot found himself master of an aging New England seminary (Everett's painful word for the college), very backward in Medicine, Law, and Science, and evidencing many of the signs of senility. Yale, Johns Hopkins, Michigan, Wisconsin, California, Columbia, Cornell, Princeton, were forging ahead, but Harvard had pulled over to the side of the road with a flat tire and a boiling radiator. Eliot, only thirty-five years old, set to work. He stayed for forty years, the longest presidency in Harvard's history.

Under Eliot, the elective system flourished. It was now possible to get a Harvard degree without almost choking to death on mammoth doses of Greek and Latin. Heretofore the student presenting himself at Harvard with his carpet bag was told that he must take both Greek and Latin during all of his freshman, sophomore, and junior years. Although there had been no course in English literature, each and every student, regardless of his interest or ability, had been required to take a year of Anglo-Saxon.[12] Professor G. H. Palmer (A.B. 1864), twice chairman of the Division of Philosophy, said of his college studies that "a prescribed course in advanced chemical physics . . . stirred so intense an aversion to physical study (in me) that subsequent years were troubled to overcome it," and he adds: "One meagre meal of philosophy was perhaps as much as most of us Seniors could digest, but I went away hungry for more." The historian William

[12] " 'I have come here to study Anglo-Saxon,' said a very superior young Harvard graduate to the Master of Balliol in the early seventies. 'Then,' said Jowett, 'you have come to the wrong place. Professor Child at Harvard knows more on that subject than anyone in Oxford.' 'What? "Stubby" Child! I didn't know *he* knew anything!' "—*Three Centuries of Harvard*, S. E. Morison.

Prescott [13] (A.B. 1783) had a blank spot for mathematics. To get through the requirement he committed every mathematical demonstration to memory "so as to be able to recite every syllable and letter of it as they stood in the book, without comprehending the demonstration at all, or attaching any meaning to the words and signs of which it was composed."

I have attempted in my time to do the same, but with indifferent success. In the year 1929 I startled the College Board examiners by gaining a mark of 6 (six) out of a possible 100 in Elementary Algebra. For details of my subsequent career in mathematics write, phone, wire, or send flowers to Mr. Ezra Pike Rounds, formerly Mathematics Instructor at Phillips Exeter Academy, now Dean of Admissions. And a classmate of mine, who is rather addicted to flamboyant exaggeration (he not only wears a gray flannel suit but also a gray flannel necktie) in a recent discussion of the required courses in Latin of our youth (we were sharing a delicious dish of salted peanuts at the Biltmore bar) said to me: "Flash, the precious golden hours of youth I wasted dissecting the required corpse of Latin would have been much more profitably employed in counting the number of rats on the town dump." But Ferdie was always an extremist. I myself was an outstanding child authority on Cornelius Nepos.

Eliot changed all that, but it took him seventeen years to put the new system into effect. And by the end of his glorious reign students were free to follow their bent in all the Arts and Sciences, be it Indic Philosophy or Egyptology. Charles Eliot Norton's lectures in Fine Arts were so popular that no lecture hall large enough could be found. The same applied to the vivacious lectures of personality-packed, scholarly Nathaniel Southgate Shaler in

[13] *Conquest of Mexico, Conquest of Peru, Ferdinand and Isabella,* etc. etc. Prescott never visited Spain, Mexico, or Peru. He lived in one of those elegant Beacon Street houses, number 55, near the foot of the slope.

Geology.[14] Albert Bushnell Hart's abundant and untidy face hair was on view daily in the History Department, which also boasted Edward Channing; between the two of them Harvard was virtually in charge of all the slopes leading into American History at all levels. The department also proudly displayed our country's foremost medievalist, Charles H. Haskins, as well as Roger Bigelow Merriman, who was giving the first lectures in Latin American History. Leo Wiener, J. D. M. Ford, C. H. C. Wright, Copeland, George Baker, Barrett Wendell, Kittredge, William James, Josiah Royce, Hugo Munsterberg, E. K. Rand, Gulick, Bliss Perry, Grandgent, George F. Moore, A. Lawrence Lowell, William B. Munro, Julian Coolidge, T. W. Richards, Alex Agassiz, Le Baron, Russell Briggs the Delightful Dean, Lanman and his "Sanskrit Reader," Robinson, Francke, the Economics team of Carver, Ripley, Gay and Bullock—all these and many more, even Frederick Caesar de Sumichrast (winner of the "Funny Name" poll for 1902) were at Harvard, handpicked from scholarly depots of the wide world by President Eliot. The faculty of the Law School had quadrupled. The faculty of the Medical School had quintupled. The faculty of the college had increased from 27 to 332. And the student body had grown from 1060 in 1869 to 3692 in 1909. Eliot had made the small-town college into a great University completely filled with students looking worried about their Midyear Exams.

Let us close these impressive ceremonial rites with a quote from William Allan Neilson, formerly President of Smith College, as he described "the unique place in American public life" held by President Eliot of Harvard.

"For 40 years the head of a great university, he exercised on all classes of his countrymen an influence far beyond that of the usual academic dignitary. During the latter

[14] Famous quote by Professor Shaler to Theodore Roosevelt as an undergraduate in his class: "See here, Roosevelt, let me talk, I'm running this course."

part of his presidency, and still more after he became emeritus, he was looked up to by hundreds of thousands of his fellow-citizens as a guide not merely in education matters but in all the great questions that have agitated the public mind, political, industrial, social, and moral. Other leaders of opinion have come and gone, and some for a time have been more conspicuous; but it is impossible to name a figure who so continuously dominated our intellectual horizon for so long a period."

This is a fairly steamy endorsement from brother Neilson, and it's mostly correct. Up until Eliot's time, when a Great Educator rose to speak everybody went out for a smoke. Eliot developed the role of college president into something bigger than that of referee between the students and the faculty and now these academic dignitaries enjoy all the prestige of pop vocalists, prizefighters, and other national heroes.

Harvard meanwhile had become so big that the coastline of Massachusetts Bay sank eleven inches. Space was at such a premium that classes in Icelandic Language and Literature were held in the waiting room of the Revere Beach roller coaster. Today the college covers the entire state of Massachusetts, part of New Hampshire, and has branch plants all over the world including Cuba (temporarily closed down). Students with a nine o'clock class in Framingham and a ten o'clock class in Newburyport keep writing letters of complaint to the *Crimson*. That's the way students are. Always grousing about something.

CHAPTER XVI

One Minute to Play

or

Jack at Harvard

This is the Augustan age of power and poetry.
—ROBERT FROST

IT IS CUSTOMARY for the management of the American League baseball team in Washington, D.C., to present the President of the United States with an annual pass, and the First Lady with a suitable gift on Opening Day. An alligator handbag has usually struck the diamond magnates as what the President's wife is most in need of and the newspaper says Mrs. Dwight D. Eisenhower must have received about eight of them. This year, however, Marse Joe Cronin and E. R. (Pete) Quesada went into a deep trance and came out of it with an inspiration worthy of Ty Cobb deciding to steal home. They presented chic, shy, svelte, charming, *Time and Tide*-worthy Jacqueline B. Kennedy with a copy of a rare book entitled *Seventeenth and Eighteenth Century Furniture of France*. When you have one of them Harvard boys up there in the White House you can expect most anything.

From now on when the Senators honor a famed ballplayer who has busted the record for stolen bases, instead of a refrigerator and a Cadillac, he can expect to garner a first edition of Samuel Butler and the works of Marcel Proust bound in full calf. During the season they are going to have Carl Sandburg umpiring at the plate, Gilbert Highet coaching at third base, and Archibald MacLeish at first. The batboy will be Van Cliburn, whereas Kenneth Tynan and Simone de Beauvoir will alternate in the TV booth in reporting the game. Autographed baseballs will be Out. The fans who catch baseballs will trade them in at the boxoffice for rare examples of Venetian glass. At the seventh-inning stretch, selections from the works of Edna St. Vincent Millay and Edwin Arlington Robinson will be read aloud over the p.a. system. And when they raise the American flag the lady soprano will omit "My country 'tis of thee" and sing gems from *Aïda*. Meanwhile I hear there is a motion afoot to persuade Oleg Cassini to redesign the players' uniforms with an emphasis on taffeta and puff sleeves.

It is all part of the administration's startling policy to recognize the Fine Arts as a Living Force in American Life, and all of us various artists were so thrilled we went out and bought typewriter ribbons, tubes of rose madder, greasepaint, and new violin strings. It was pretty obvious that we would immediately find ourselves fawned upon almost as though we were dirt farmers, and soon be receiving large sums by mail for not painting, writing, or performing at concerts or upon the stage. Tax relief for writers,[1] now forty-nine years overdue, would become an accomplished fact. A writer friend of mine got so excited he went up to the company store and bought his

[1] JFK—SHOW BIZ IN LOVE, BUT WHAT ABOUT TAX AND COPYRIGHT? . . . . But copyright extension is not the only problem on which aid is badly needed and not forthcoming. Authors and dramatists are still taxed at maximum rates in the year of a possible jackpot which may have been five or six years in the creation. Few indeed in the Washington whirligig pause to express any sympathy for "intellectual property" as against, say, oil in the ground, beef on the hoof, citrus, or in Virginia, apples.

—*Variety*, May 23, 1962

wife a new washboard and a real pretty hair ribbon. William Saroyan decided to come home to the U.S.

Oh it started out mighty fine. When Robert Frost stood up there at the Inauguration right on an equal footing with all those big ward bosses in their iron suits—I'm telling you all of us artist blokes who were listening to the affair on our crystal sets got all choked up. It was a sacred moment in history, and I, for one, was as overcome as a supermarket manager at a testimonial dinner.

Then what happens? Frost gets the sun in his eyes. He blows the poetry.

"See what I told you happens you make a spot for these here impractical type poets and them?" was the advice rec'd by the highest executive in the land later that evening.

Tax relief? In the words of fellow artist Ira Gershwin: we got plenty o' nuttin capital gains and recognitionwise.

This here Frost.[2] Who needs Him. Him and his "Stopping By Woods on Snowy Evening." He should have stood there.

The next big news we hear for the benefit of artists and poets is that the gov't has given 72 million $ to the Peruvians for a chilblain clinic at Cuzco.

"Children of the night! What music they make!" quoth Count Dracula in describing his trip to the Senate.

But we're not sore. All of us terribly creative chaps are all for President Kennedy. And although I don't care to

[2] Dartmouth 1892; Harvard, 1897–99; M.A. Amherst, 1918; A.M. U. of Michigan, 1922; L.H.D., U. of Vt., 1923; Wesleyan U., 1931; St. Lawrence U., 1936; Litt.D., Yale, 1924; Middlebury Coll., 1924; Bowdoin, 1926; New Hamp. State U., 1930; Columbia U., Williams Coll., 1932; Dartmouth, 1933; Bates Coll., U. of Penn., 1936; Harvard, 1937; U. of Colorado, 1939; Princeton U., 1941; Marlboro Coll., Colgate U., 1950; U. Mass., 1951; Durham Univ., England, 1952; LL.D., Univ. of California, 1946; Duke Univ. and Amherst Coll., 1948.
Charles Eliot Norton prof. of poetry, Harvard, 1936.
Ralph Waldo Emerson fellow, Harvard, 1939–41.
Member Board of Overseers, Harvard, 1938–39.
Phi Beta Kappa poet, Harvard, 1916.
Address: 35 Brewster St., Cambridge, Mass.

say who I voted for, he doesn't come from California and one of his sisters-in-law can detect a pea under the mattress no matter how thick it is. The cultural movement is going forward all right, but the trouble is, hardly any of us are interior decorators, dealers in period furniture, or students of American wallpaper.

As the curtains open on the next romantic scene the audience is treated to moving pictures of a bunch of guys shooting on a beach. One team is clean-shaven and the other has beards. Several poets, an abstract artist, and three oboe players in the audience faint from hunger and have to be carried out. Everybody goes home, the artists walking as they have no fare for the trolley car.

On the following day we hear that a group is trying to raise 5 million $ so as to buy some tractors and model A Fords to exchange for the guys on the beach who got beat and are now swatting flies and cucarachas in a Latin-American jail. Excitement runs very high in artistic circles until it is revealed that the guys in the clink are not only *not* poets, painters, musicians, or ballet dancers, but are not even Americans.

It's been just one thing like that after another so far but we're expecting, as I say, a change most any day now and for some baseball mugs to give Mrs. Kennedy a book is cheering news. And the President sent an author, Kenneth Galbraith, to India as Ambassador. He wrote *The Affluent Society*, and India was picked as the ideal spot for him as it is noted for its social affluence as well as its tasty curries. Schlesinger, Jr., is another author who has made the grade in Washington and is said to be working on a bill which will provide all artists with a free popsicle every afternoon at four o'clock when they are getting tired. This will be paid for by a six-per-cent tax on their royalties, salaries, and the sales of their artistic creations. The surplus will be used to provide paper napkins for the tribes of Borneo who are notoriously sloppy eaters. And if we don't give them free napkins you know who might.

But the biggest news was the appointment of August

Heckscher as Cultural Coordinator. This was in response to many complaints from steel workers in the Pittsburgh and Youngstown areas who marched on Washington and caused a disturbance on the White House lawn demanding a raise in culture coordination. Mr. Heckscher is a Yale man with high ideals and has his work cut out for him as he wants to raise the esthetic standards of his fellow citizens. He is a formidable man in conversation and noted for his ability to "cut your argument to ribbons." I hope this will help in getting everybody's mind off of Elizabeth Taylor and the search for the proper type of bra to give the correct uplift while still providing the wearer with enough freedom of action for her to insert coins in juke boxes, operate slot machines, shove TV dinners in the oven, etc. "A people caring about dignity and excellence in its private lives may be expected to care also about the embodiment of these qualities in the public environment," says Mr. Heckscher, who has a booming voice. (John Gilbert had a squeaky voice, so they say.) "The American scene today is not reassuring in this regard," he says, and he's right. Colorado looks OK but the rest of the country looks terrible except for the parking meters every place which to me, at least, have a certain rugged and authoritative grandeur. And functional, boy!

I like his assumption that the American people have "dignity in their private lives" and at dinner tonight I am going to make the kids put their comic books away while I exchange dignified conversation with the old lady in which we will discuss the artistic aims of Willa Cather and Edith Wharton. After a dignified session in the kitchen washing dishes we will leave the kids with a dignified teen-age baby sitter and her extremely dignified boy friend, glide gracefully to the bowling lanes in full evening dress for a quiet, yet somehow rewarding, session with Vince, Agnes, Leo, Millie, Fats, Bubbles, Chuck, Bumps, and some of our other dignified friends. After the bowling we'll drop in at the Black Pussy Cat Bar and Grill. By midnight the dignity should be at its peak.

I'm really working on the dignity bit ever since I read what Lester Lanin, the leader of the favorite White House dance band, says about the parties he plays for over there at the House.

"They are as cheerful and gay and as dignified a party as you will find from coast to coast. Everybody is having fun but everybody is dignified," is what he says.

The reason I am working on it is that I have never been able to be cheerful and gay, and also dignified at the same time. Like when I am cheerful and gay I usually don a lampshade for a hat, kiss all the girls, do my imitation of Jimmy Stewart, play the trap drums in the band, and tell the story about the French stenographer in the Chinese restaurant. That's not dignified. But I guess I don't have to worry as the only invitation I have had lately was to a P.T.A. meeting to plan bomb-shelter kiddie menus.

Mr. Kennedy understands the problems of the artists because he not only writes books, one of which won a Pulitzer Prize, but he also is a voracious reader. Unlike Adlai Stevenson, he kept the intellectual side of his personality under wraps during the campaign so as to avoid suspicion. But the secret is now out. "I made two mistakes during my first year," he says. "One was Cuba and the other was letting it be known that I read as much as I do." [3] Although he too wrote a book, President Eisenhower did not fall into the bookworm pitfall, realizing full well the bad impression it would create with the electorate, and his library card showed very little wear and tear. President Kennedy undoubtedly acquired this unfortunate habit at Harvard and has been unable to kick it.

Falling in line with the bookish tone of the administration, Vice-President Lyndon Johnson has begun to take steps to dispel any impression that he is just an unlettered country boy by studding his public addresses with literary allusions. In a speech the other day at Pennsylvania State University he quoted Benjamin Franklin, Alexander

[3] "The President and the Press," *The Reporter*, April 12, 1962.

Hamilton, Alexis Henri Charles Maurice Clerel de Tocqueville, and H. G. Wells. A few days before that he spoke to a group of labor editors and hauled out Thomas Jefferson, Franklin D. Roosevelt, Winston Churchill, Justice Tom C. Clark, Edmund Burke, Wendell Phillips, and Mr. Dooley. Not bad. And he didn't get all this dope at Harvard. He went to Southwest State Teachers College at San Marcos, Texas, Class of 1930.

The press has done a good job with their stories, cartoons, and jokes in fostering the idea, first, that Harvard is exclusively Democratic politically and second, that Kennedy has made so many appointments from the Harvard faculty that there is "nothing left at Harvard but Radcliffe." Nothing could be more silly. There are 100 more undergraduate members of the Young Republicans Club at Harvard than there are of Young Democrats. Of the ten Senators in Washington with Harvard affiliations, six are Democrats, four Republicans. In the House of Representatives there are twenty-six Harvard men, of whom thirteen are Democrats and thirteen Republicans. Of the five "Harvard" men in the Cabinet only C. Douglas Dillon, '31, and Robert F. Kennedy, '48, are graduates of Harvard College. The others, from the Harvard graduate schools, went to California (McNamara), Chicago (Day), and Princeton (Stevenson). In a straw vote taken at Harvard during the recent Kennedy-Nixon argument, Kennedy won for the first Democratic victory in the history of the vote. FDR never won it. No Democrat ever won it. It is highly possible that if the Republicans had put up any other candidate but Richard, such as The Three Stooges, Kennedy would not have won. If they had offered Leverett Saltonstall, for example, Kennedy would have polled about six votes, I imagine. Of my friends at college most were Republicans. The viewing with alarm and panic political diatribes in the 25th Class Reports are largely Republican.

There is nothing so strange or special about having Harvard men in Washington. Nobody howled about it at the time but President Eisenhower had four Harvard graduates at one time or another in his Cabinet. Teddy Roosevelt had five. At least forty Harvard men have been in former Presidents' Cabinets, including eight Secretaries of State, ten Secretaries of War, ten Attorneys-General, and six Secretaries of the Navy. So what's all the shouting about? Yes, President Kennedy has taken about fifteen from the Harvard faculty for jobs of greater or lesser importance in Washington. Out of a faculty of 600 full-time members and about 500 part-time Teaching Fellows, that leaves quite a few back in Cambridge to tend the shop.

But counting Harvard noses around Washington has become *chapeau fatigué* by now and the press has turned to other aspects of the young immigrants. Now they're looking at the wives of Kennedy's new collegiate recruits, sometimes known as "Mom," and say, these girls have been having a very tough adjustment to make. In the first place, the *Saturday Evening Post* has to run this article which calls them the "latter-day frontierswomen," which is enough to make any wife go out and sit by the clothes dryer and have a good cry. "Instead of porridge," says the *Post*, "they had to learn how 'to make *soufflé au chocolat, crème Chantilly*.'" Food seems to be one of the main problems, as all the girls who have been accustomed back in Cambridge to clipping new casserole recipes from *Woman's Day* with which to surprise the Professor when he came home from the library are now in Area A, where "everyone else is reported as serving, say, *Pâté truffé de Strasbourg, Truite en gelée* and *Caneton à l'orange*." This means they have to go out and buy not only a cookbook between hard covers but also a French dictionary.

About the only thing that is pulling them through is Mary Bundy's "impish humor," which they chuckle over during "a low-calorie lunch enlivened by some high-level stories." Considering they have recently discovered that gingham won't do in the Nation's Capital and that they need "enough gowns to outfit a TV star," the girls are probably issuing some hollow chuckles no matter how much of a card Mrs. Bundy is.

But it's all turning out OK, according to the *Post*. You can't kill that frontier spirit. The ex-Harvard ladies have learned to weave curtains out of birch bark for their simple log cabins and Marian Schlesinger has begun "painting seriously again." (Evidently during the transition period she was only painting frivolously.) Mary Bundy has "started studying French" (to cope with those competitive menus). Toni Chayes's unfortunate remark about serving spaghetti has been forgotten and she "has her part-time White House job." And most reassuring of all, "many of the wives have joined the P.T.A. again," where they can discuss remedial reading problems and gorge themselves on good old-fashioned Oreo ookies and Hostess cupcakes until the cows come home.

Dedicated as I am to fact-finding and research, I should have interviewed John F. Kennedy's kindly old Harvard janitor and his Chinese laundryman in Cambridge to give the full round picture loaded with unutterably noncommittal quotes. ("As I remember him, he was a real nice young man." "Kennedy? Yeah. His old man was rich.") Instead I saved the carfare and some shoe leather as well as the readers' patience by looking up the Harvard Class Album for the Class of 1940 with the following results:

John Fitzgerald Kennedy
Born May 29, 1917 in Brookline, Massachusetts.
Prepared at The Choate School. Home address:
294 Pondfield Road, Bronxville, New York.
Winthrop House. *Crimson* (2-4); Chairman
Smoker Committee (1); St. Paul's Catholic
Club (1-4); Football (1); Junior Varsity (2);
Swimming (1); Squad (2); Golf (1); House
Hockey (3-4); House Swimming (2); House
Softball (4). Hasty Pudding-Institute of 1770;
Spee Club. Permanent Class Committee.
Field of Concentration: Government. Intended Vocation:
Law

Above Mr. Kennedy in the album is George Clayton Kennedy of Monida, Montana, whose intended vocation was Mining Geologist.

Below him is Bergere Alfred Kennedy of Santa Fe, New Mexico, whose intended vocation was Medicine.

Perhaps some of the results of the Class Questionnaire will be of interest.

How often in the past year have you attended church?

Never	134
Once or twice	274
Monthly	80
Fortnightly	38
Weekly	55
Oftener than Weekly	21
No answer	8
	—
	619

Do you feel the policies of the New Deal should be:

Halted and abandoned	37
Curtailed and modified	301
Maintained as at present	177
Greatly and rapidly expanded	90
No answer	14
	—
	619

Do you anticipate a fairly successful and secure life after college? Or one characterized by possible social and cultural turmoil, crisis, and catastrophe by which you may be affected?

Successful and secure	281
Possible turmoil and catastrophe	309
No answer	29
	—
	619

What is the income of your family?

Under $1250	23
1250-2500	70
2500-3750	72
3750-5000	61
5000-7500	76
7500-10,000	68
10,000-20,000	109
20,000-50,000	74
Over 50,000	20
No answer	46
	———
	619

Among the answers to the above:
"I am completely self supporting."
"It is none of my business—none of yours either."

From what college would you be most likely to select a girl for a date?

Radcliffe	122
Wellesley	166
Smith	59
Bennington	31
Vassar	45
Bryn Mawr	13
Mt. Holyoke	2
Sarah Lawrence	16
Other	92
No answer	73
	———
	619

To the question "Do you believe that Western culture is dying?" one senior answered, "What the hell do you think I am—Spengler?"

During his last three years Kennedy lived in John Winthrop House, which, in case you thought it was a bungalow, cost $1,185,000. Standish and Gore halls were converted and combined in 1931 to form the house, which has its own library, dining rooms, common rooms, and Master's House. The House is on the Charles River. For a good many years Winthrop had the reputation of being the varsity athletes' house, but this obtains no more. Its faculty staff has for years been particularly strong in Economics.

In the four-page story of Winthrop House activities by the Class of 1940 John F. Kennedy's name is not mentioned, although 57 other students were singled out by name for their contributions to House life or other achievements. There were 270 men in Winthrop in 1939-40. The House hockey team, of which Kennedy was a member, was captained by J. A. Rousmaniere of Oyster Bay, Long Island. The team won the inter-House title and played Davenport College of Yale at the Boston Garden for the intercollege title, winning 5-3 over the Yale champions. (Hoo, hah.)

There were three dances during the year, a House Play (*French Without Tears*), which enlisted the services of three Radcliffe girls, parties, lectures, smokers, and Admiral Pratt, former Navy Chief-of-Staff, was the guest at the formal Senior Dinner. "His appearance was most timely, owing to the great naval battles now being waged overseas, a subject on which he was well qualified to speak."

We see that times had not changed entirely when we read that on a warm spring evening a "blitzkrieg of water-filled balloons broke loose on unsuspecting innocents in the courtyard."

Winthrop house men captained three varsity teams: T. H. MacDonald, football, W. C. Coleman, Jr., hockey, and T. V. Healey, baseball.

Winthrop's Thomas V. Healey was also First Marshal of the Class of 1940. He and five other '40 members of the House were Phi Beta Kappa.

In the group picture of the *Crimson* John F. Kennedy

appears in the third row, flanked by Tyng and Hollands, looking earnest and wearing wavy hair and a very broad striped tie.

The House Master was Dr. Ronald Mansfield Ferry, Associate Professor of Biochemistry.

President of Harvard University was James Bryant Conant, A.B., Ph.D., LL.D., S.D., L.H.D., D.C.L.

By the time of the 6th Annual Class Report Kennedy gave his home address as Hotel Bellevue, Boston, Mass., and his vocation as Journalism. The Hotel Bellevue address was for the purpose of establishing a legal residence in Massachusetts and he picked the Bellevue because his famous and colorful grandfather, Honey Fitz, lived there.

"I joined the Navy in 1941, served in P.T. boats in the Pacific and was retired in April 1945, because of injuries. I have had published a book entitled *Why England Slept*. I covered the San Francisco Conference for the Chicago *Herald-American*, and covered the British elections, Ireland, and Europe for the International News Service in the summer of 1945. I was assistant to the Chairman of the Boston Community Fund Drive, and became Chairman of the National Convention of the Veterans of Foreign Wars, for Boston, in September 1946."

And he concludes (get this):

"I am pessimistic about the future of the country."

Must have been one of those long Boston winters. Maybe some naughty girl was being mean to him. Maybe his mother was making him go to dancing school. Maybe he was behind on his board bill.

By the Tenth Report, pessimism shelved, he's changed legal residence to 122 Bowdoin St., a few doors from the Bellevue, and his office address is House of Representatives, Washington, D.C. He says the Junior Chamber of Commerce has selected him as one of ten outstanding young men of 1946. The most notable feature of this report is that he does not say that he has been Chairman of the Community Chest Drive in his home town, nor that he has been all wrapped up in the Little League. No

Class Report is complete without these two statements, and the merit badge from the Junior Chamber of Commerce can scarcely be considered a proper substitute.

The Fifteenth Class Report rolled around and his home address, though not often his home, is still 122 Bowdoin Street but he has a new office address: Office Room 362, Senate Office Building. And he has a wife, Jacqueline Bouvier, whom he married September 12, 1953, at Newport, Rhode Island.

He didn't say much about the wife except that he married her, and little did classmates suspect that within six years they would be unable to pick up a single magazine in the chiropractor's waiting room without seeing this girl's picture on the cover. Although she is not a film star she has been on the cover of *Photoplay* twice, and we expect to see her and the kiddies any day now on the cover of the *Railway Age*.

By the last report, the Twentieth, he has clammed up almost completely and merely states that he has been re-elected to the United States Senate and is father of a daughter, Caroline Bouvier Kennedy, born November 28, 1957.

I wonder what his address will be for the 25th Report, due in 1965, and I'll bet Roger Blough would like to know, too. Will old-grad Kennedy go to the Reunion and march to the Harvard-Yale baseball game in a funny costume? Will he eat lobsters with the gang at some country club and play in the softball game? At the 25th frolic of the Class of '36 at the Essex Country Club eighteen hundred lobsters were disposed of as well as ten barrels of oysters, three barrels of clams, and the alcoholic contents of a one-and-one-half-ton S. S. Pierce truck. Is J. F. Kennedy prepared for this? Can he play tennis with a highball glass in one hand? Is he ready to cope with "You wouldn't remember me I guess but I was in your seismology class. Sally wants to meet you." (Almost all Harvard wives are named Sally.) Will Caroline attend the planned events for the kiddies, sleep on a cot in Thayer Hall, and say she wants to go home at ten-minute intervals like a certain daughter in my family? Will Jacqueline B. K. say "Not another? Don't you think you've had enough?" every half hour like a wife with whom I am intimately acquainted? What will Jack reply to: "Kennedy? Sure, I remember you. What line of work you in? What you been doing since graduation?" These and many other aspects of the 25th Reunion should be carefully reviewed in advance. And clothing for the event should be most carefully considered, too. I recommend an asbestos suit and a crash helmet.

If we rashly attempt to isolate a type and pin a label of Typical Harvard Man on him, John F. Kennedy would almost qualify. Whether those who elected him like it or not he is an "intellectual" (grisly word!). He reads books, both large and fine print. He has a craggy professorial face. His clothes are casual.[4] He doesn't wear a hat. He's on the Harvard Board of Overseers. He was born in Brookline. And he has a funny Boston accent.

On the other hand there is his religion, typical enough in Boston, Cork, and Dubuque, Ia., but *not* typical of Harvard. And his wife. The typical Harvard man should have a Massachusetts wife, or at the very least a Maine, New Hampshire, or Vermont wife (not Connecticut— Connecticut is as far as Oregon from Boston and Cambridge). She should be skilled in the Bostonian art of wearing expensive clothes which always look slightly awful on her. Her name should be Sally and her father has got to be a retired English professor who smokes a pipe, wears shoes from L. L. Bean and does a little sailing in his catboat at Tenants Harbor. Father is quietly humorous and philosophical. And the typical-Harvard-man image does not name his daughter "Caroline." He names her "Sally," after her mother or, in exceptional cases, "Beth."

---

[4] Well, they look casual even if they do come from H. Harris & Co., New York tailors who also supply threads to Averell Harriman, Thomas Finletter, and Nelson Rockefeller. Everything about these togs is casual except the bill for same.

Before the election every place you went you heard these very indignant boys saying, "If that Kennedy gets elected, brother I'm leaving the country. I'm getting out." He did get elected but so far there hasn't been any noticeable mass exodus across the border. Aside from the usual hordes of tourists who keep rushing off to get short-changed in Rome, overcharged in Madrid, and clipped in Paris, about the only large emigration movement is made up of the members of the Peace Corps; and Kennedy's sister, Eunice, is the wife of the director, R. Sargent Shriver. It is too bad in a way because if all the Republicans that said they were going to flee the U.S. if that Harvard dude got elected would actually pack up their matched luggage and go, why a lot of jobs would open up and it would help the unemployment problem. All those unemployed coal miners in West Virginia could be provided with dark blue suits and step into the vacated executive positions and they would not have to cut weeds beside the highway any more @ $1.00 per hour or eat surplus oleomargarine.

So President Kennedy may be a Harvard man but that doesn't mean there won't be another riot at the Harvard Club of New York when the subject comes up where to hang his portrait. Franklin D. Roosevelt was still presiding over the potato salad last Thursday. I understand there is a small faction of Old Frontiersmen working *sub rosa* to have David Lawrence's portrait hung instead and he didn't even go to Harvard. Anyway, according to the Annual Report of the Board of Managers, the bar at the Club took in $295,396.58 in the year ended January 31, 1961, at a profit of $120,815.06. More than likely these figures will go up in the next few years until we get a good solid businessman in the White House who does not drag poets into the inaugural festivities and whose brother-in-law is not a movie actor but an insurance man.

Meanwhile the defeated candidate, Richard Nixon, is going through a Seventh Crisis, namely reading the reviews of his book about his six previous ones.

And out in Chicago they are still hollering for a re-count. They're never satisfied out there. They've got Claudia Cassidy, the Pump Room, and the Drainage Canal; what more do they want? They better hush up or the Kennedys will put their Merchandise Mart on a barge and move it up to Milwaukee. Then Chicago won't think it's so darn smarty.

And after reviewing the Washington scene for the last two years (let's not go into no painful details) there remains only one question unanswered:

Why would any nice young Harvard boy in possession of all his faculties want to be President of the United States when by pulling a few strings he could get a job driving a truck for the County Highway Department where he would get plenty of fresh air and overtime? Then he could not only greet the postman with a smile but also go bareheaded without being lambasted by the National Men's Felt Hat Institute. His wife might have to buy her dresses [5] out of the Fall and Winter catalogue but he could drop into his neighborhood tavern without immediately getting blamed for the TV programming, the quality of the beer and the high tariff on pretzels.

But it takes all kinds to make the world, as everybody knows who has ever been to the Side Show; and whereas some people prefer to make their living sitting on a platform and selling picture postcards of themselves and their extra heads, limbs, etc., still others keep constantly seeking employment as President of the U.S.A. If these aspirants would take time out from sending postage-free

[5] For the first time in recent history, descriptions of the public appearances of the First Lady of the land read like an account of a small-town wedding in the local gazette:

"On arrival Mrs. Kennedy was wearing a two-piece light green silk dress and matching sombrero-type hat. The hat sloped slightly from the brim that framed her head... The double-breasted overblouse had military lapels and three-quarter-length sleeves. She wore elbow-length white gloves ... etc. etc."

New York *Herald Tribune*

(After a wedding trip to the Wisconsin Dells the newlyweds will be at home at 18 Elm Street.)

canning hints to the constituents back home long enough to study the interesting beads of nervous sweat on the Big Chief's brow during the current or any other regime they might get over the notion and go home to Mother.

CHAPTER XVII

Hail to Thee, O Alma Mater! & My Check Is in the Mail

HARVARD UNIVERSITY receives many lovely gifts from people who are stuck on her because she has such nice wavy hair and blue eyes. But instead of silk stockings or souvenir pillow tops from the Mammoth Cave, people usually give Harvard money. Nobody hardly ever sends Harvard a Valentine or a funny Get-Well card. I'm probably the only person that ever sent Harvard a nice box of candy from Fanny Farmer for Easter.

A couple of years ago Harvard wrote the Alumni and said that the crops had been bad and that cousin Roy had been laid off at the box factory and also the house needed painting and some shingles had blown off the roof and the rain was leaking into the front bedroom and please send some money if we had found work. So the Alumni saved on their lunch money for a while by taking peanut-butter sandwiches to the office and sent Harvard $82,500,000. I am glad they did not take up my fund-raising suggestion, which was to hold a turkey raffle.

I figured that 80 million would take care of things in the Alma Mater Department for about fifty years with the price of eggs where it is at but now here I have another letter from President Pusey saying that Roy has been laid off again, the cow died, and there is a new hole in the roof above the summer kitchen and if I am still working on the number four saw at the sawmill how about sending some money? Listen, Mother, I've got these here dentist bills to pay, and my lodge dues coming up. Yes I know it costs $81,000,000 a year to operate the school but gee whiz, you're getting $21,000,000 a year from the government ain't you? Listen, leave us have a look at the old account book, how about it, Mom. I'm getting weary all the time going to the Post Office to send you these money orders. OK? Well that's better. Let's see—you got $717,000,000 worth of common stocks, hey? Uh huh . . . 76,000 shares of Ford Motor Co., 77,000 shares of General Motors, 3,000 shares of Gulf Oil, 6000 shares of Bethlehem, 101,745 shares of Tel and Tel . . . golly, Ma, you got 23 pages of stocks and bonds here and the print is not too big either . . . 18,157 shares of *Time*, Inc. . . . What the heck is the "Itek Corp.?" "Union Bag-Camp?" "Ventures, Ltd?" "Schlumberger?" "Polymer Corp.?" You got me all fussed up here.

HARVARD UNIVERSITY

BALANCE SHEET
Assets
June 30, 1961

Cash in Bank and on hand including for investment		5 970 157
General Investments (pages 21):		
Bond and notes	316 290 905	
Preferred stocks	5 200 652	
Common stocks	178 064 744	
Total bonds, notes and stock*	499 556 302	
Investment real estate**	1 550 392	
Mortgages	2 440 473	503 547 168

* The indicated market values of general investment securities were as follows:

Bonds and notes	311 261 722	
Preferred stocks	4 748 545	
Common stocks	401 267 695	
	717 277 962	

** After depreciation and amortization reserves of   3 751 390

Special Investments (page 37):
  Of endowment funds required
    to be separately invested:

Securities	9 394 967	
Uninvested cash	143 039	
Of other funds:		
Securities	7 976 911	
Real estate	3 456 799	20 971 717
Total investments		524 518 886

Other Assets:

Contract expenditures to be reimbursed by U. S. Government	2 373 538	
Accounts receivable	2 110 745	
Notes receivable for student loans (page 125)	5 891 200	
Departmental inventories to be charged to future operations	1 538 843	
Prepayments and deferred charges	2 407 573	
Construction costs deferred	3 032 210	17 354 112
		547 843 155

HARVARD UNIVERSITY

CONDENSED SUMMARY OF INCOME AND EXPENSES

	Year Ended June 30, 1961	
	Amount	Percent
INCOME:		
Endowment fund income availed of	17 994 219	21.7
Gifts for current use and other receipts for special purposes availed of	13 672 053	16.4
Student income:		
Tuition and other fees	16 892 991	20.3
Board and lodging	6 770 158	8.1
Government contract and grant receipts availed of	21 625 791	26.0

Receipts from other sources including athletic gate receipts and sales of publications, printing and power	6 210 170	7.5
Total income	83 165 383	100.0

EXPENSES:

Salaries of corporation appointees	21 389 630	26.4
Wages	21 184 589	26.1
Equipment and supplies	17 724 403	21.9
Retiring allowances and other employee benefits	4 555 968	5.6
Scholarships and other student awards	5 659 798	7.0
Miscellaneous expenses including travel, telephone and sundry services purchased, and certain expenditures for nondepartmental projects	10 518 169	13.0
Total expenses	81 032 559	100.0
Excess of unrestricted income carried to departmental balances (page 17)	2 132 823	

Well, Ma, you ain't got too much of a margin there and that's a fact. And I see where President Pusey says that "Harvard College cannot simply stand still. In curriculum and research, the process of re-evaluation must constantly go on. A community like Harvard is alive with new ideas." (Mother, I haven't even scratched the surface on the *old* ideas yet, but never mind.) "In such a climate," he says, "there is always fresh opportunity for professor and student alike to share in the adventure of advancing knowledge."

Now here's a part that strikes home with every loyal son:

"The alumni are Harvard's living endowment and her greatest capital asset."

I never thought of myself as an endowment before, I better go change into a clean shirt. Of course everybody on Elm Street knows I am a big capital asset and I stand very big with the landlady since I got my picture in the paper for guessing how many marbles was in that big bottle in the window of the J. C. Penney store during the recent contest (6962).

Listen, Alma, don't think I don't appreciate what you done for me. I am the only one up at the sawmill and that includes Mr. Vollenweider the boss, who reads the *Manchester Guardian* during the noon hour, the rest of them all pitch horseshoes out behind the boiler room. And I don't care if Mr. Vollenweider is sore because you turned his boy down up at Harvard. He had this crazy idea that just because his kid was Valedictorian, Class President, and Captain of the Football, Baseball, and Track Teams up at the High School that he would get into Harvard. I tried to tell him about the hat test but you know how stubborn these Dutchmen are. Do you suppose he would listen to me, oh no! So the boy went up to Cambridge and took the hat test and I'm telling you it was pathetic, the kid flunked it cold with a low size 7⅛. Vollenweider starts climbing on me and I says to him, "Listen Mr. Vollenweider they won't even hire somebody to cut Pusey's grass up there no more unless he wears a minimum size 7¾. So leave me out of it," I says. "Things have changed at Harvard since the times when all you needed was a Latin pony to get through with banners flying, why nowadays a student who is not aiming at the Graduate School is as popular with the faculty as good news at a pessimists' convention."

"Well how and the hell did you get through, might I kindly ask?" says the boss.

"Via my sunny smile and winning personality," I says with a fiendish sneer and returned to my saw.

All right, all right, so it's off to the Post Office again. Every time the new postmistress sees me at the window why she just automatically grabs for the money-order blanks.

"The usual?" she says.

"Yeah, the usual," I say right back.

"Boy I wisht I was as popular as some Universities I could name," she says.

So last time she pulled this one I took her to the dance at the Eagles Hall and it cost me six dollars before I was through.

OK then, but do you mind if I make a personal suggestion? You take that Income and Expense Account. Look at this here item: Board and Lodging, $6,770,158. I love you Mom, but can't you locate some skinny boarders that don't eat so dang much?

I N D E X

ABOUT THE AUTHOR

RICHARD BISSELL was born and raised in Dubuque, Iowa. After his graduation from Harvard in 1936, he shipped out for three months as a seaman with the American Export Lines. When he returned to Dubuque, he entered the family textile plant. After the war he wrote his first novel, *A Stretch on the River*. His next book, *The Monongahela* (written for the Rivers of America Series), was followed by *7½ Cents*, the story of life and love in a pajama factory. After this, Bissell quit the family business to adapt *7½ Cents* into the Broadway and film hit *The Pajama Game*.

Four years later, *Say, Darling*, a novel about Broadway, was converted by Mr. and Mrs. Bissell and Abe Burrows into the musical comedy of the same name. *Good Bye, Ava*, his next novel, was set once again in the Midwest.